Microsoft®
Internet
Explorer™ 4
6 in 1

by Heather Williamson, Joe Habraken, Julia Kelly, and Joe Kraynak

A Division of Macmillan Computer Publishing
201 West 103rd Street, Indianapolis, Indiana 46290 USA

International Standard Book Number: 0-7897-1109-5

Library of Congress Catalog Card Number: 96-72202

99 98 97   8 7 6 5 4 3 2 1

Interpretation of the printing code: the rightmost double-digit number is the year of the book's first printing; the rightmost single-digit number is the number of the book's printing. For example, a printing code of 97-1 shows that this copy of the book was printed during the first printing of the book in 1997.

Screen reproductions in this book were created by means of the program Collage Complete from Inner Media, Inc, Hollis, NH.

Printed in the United States of America

President
Roland Elgey

Senior Vice President/Publishing
Don Fowley

Publisher
Joseph B. Wikert

General Manager
Joe Muldoon

Manager of Publishing Operations
Linda H. Buehler

Publishing Director
Brad R. Koch

Editorial Services Director
Carla Hall

Managing Editor
Thomas F. Hayes

Acquisitions Manager
Cheryl D. Willoughby

Acquisitions Editor
Jill Byus

Product Director
Mark Cierzniak

Production Editor
Audra McFarland

Editor
Howard Jones

Coordinator of Editorial Services
Maureen A. McDaniel

Web Master
Thomas H. Bennett

Product Marketing Manager
Kourtnaye Sturgeon

Assistant Product Marketing Manager
Gretchen Schlesinger

Technical Editors
Christy Gleeson, Sunil Hazari

Software Specialist
David Garratt

Acquisitions Coordinator
Michelle R. Newcomb

Software Relations Coordinator
Susan D. Gallagher

Editorial Assistant
Jennifer L. Chisholm

Book Designers
Kim Scott, Glenn Larsen

Cover Designer
Jay Corpus

Production Team
Erin Danielson
DiMonique Ford
Tim Neville
Lisa Stumpf

Indexer
Chris Wilcox

Acknowledgments

I want to thank the many individuals at Que who helped me complete this project. Stephanie, thanks for signing me on, and Jill, thank you for keeping this book going through all the rough times. Thanks to the excellent technical editors and to Mark, Henly, and Audra for keeping the project running smoothly and on time. To the production team, thank you for making this book look so "smashing." You are a great crew to work with. And for anyone that I may have forgotten...even though I didn't name you, this book could never have been completed without your assistance.

Also, thanks to Ann and Ilan for keeping me entertained when I should have been writing. Jack, thanks for your support and encouragement. I couldn't have done it without any of you. And to Mom and Dad, I'll do the dishes next week.

—Heather Williamson

Trademark Acknowledgments

All terms mentioned in this book that are known to be or are suspected of being trademarks or service marks have been appropriately capitalized. Que Corporation cannot attest to the accuracy of this information. Use of a term in this book should not be regarded as affecting the validity of any trademark or service mark.

We'd Like to Hear from You!

Que Corporation has a long-standing reputation for high-quality books and products. To ensure your continued satisfaction, we also understand the importance of customer service and support.

Tech Support

If you need assistance with the information in this book or with a CD/disk accompanying the book, please access Macmillan Computer Publishing's online Knowledge Base at **http://www.superlibrary.com/general/support**. If you do not find the answers to your questions on our Web site, you may contact Macmillan Technical Support by phone at **317/581-3833** or via e-mail at **support@mcp.com/**.

Also be sure to visit Que's Web resource center for all the latest information, enhancements, errata, downloads, and more. It's located at **http://www.quecorp.com/**.

Orders, Catalogs, and Customer Service

To order other Que or Macmillan Computer Publishing books, catalogs, or products, please contact our Customer Service Department at **800/428-5331** or fax us at **800/835-3202** (International Fax: 317/228-4400). Or visit our online bookstore at **http://www.mcp.com/**.

Comments and Suggestions

We want you to let us know what you like or dislike most about this book or other Que products. Your comments will help us to continue publishing the best books available on computer topics in today's market.

> **Mark Cierzniak**
> Product Director
> Que Corporation
> 201 West 103rd Street, 4B
> Indianapolis, Indiana 46290 USA
> Fax: 317/581-4663 E-mail: **mcierzniak@que.mcp.com**

Please be sure to include the book's title and author as well as your name and phone or fax number. We will carefully review your comments and share them with the author. Please note that due to the high volume of mail we receive, we may not be able to reply to every message.

Thank you for choosing Que!

Contents

Part 2: ActiveX Controls, Plug-Ins, and Add-Ons

Part 3: Outlook Express Mail

Part 4: Outlook Express News

Part 5: FrontPage Express and HTML

Part 6: The Active Desktop

Introduction

Welcome to *Microsoft Internet Explorer 4 6 in 1*! Internet Explorer is a World Wide Web browser that incorporates the latest technology into a feature-rich, easy-to-use desktop interface. It enables you to quickly jump from one location to another with the click of a mouse. Internet Explorer has truly become part of your Windows 95 operating system. It is as easy to use as Windows 95.

You might have received a copy of Internet Explorer when you purchased Windows 95, or you might have downloaded it from the Internet or received a copy in the mail. No matter how you got your hands on Internet Explorer, you can't start using it to explore the Web until you know how to use it. If you have ever tried to learn a software package by reading its included Help system, you may have found that you waste hours of your time searching, and you get five minutes worth of information. That is why *Microsoft Internet Explorer 4 6 in 1* is so useful. Using this book, you can quickly learn to conquer all of Internet Explorer's powerful features in a series of short 10-minute lessons.

Who This Book Is For

No book is perfect for everyone, and this book is no exception. If you know enough about Windows to navigate your way through its interfaces and you know enough about the Internet to get connected, this might be just the book for you. If you have a busy schedule that prevents you from reading through hundreds of pages of technical material, yet you want to learn more about the World Wide Web, newsgroups, electronic mail, FTP, and HTML, this is definitely the book for you.

Internet Explorer 4 6 in 1 was designed to fit into your typical busy schedule, teaching you in a series of short 10-minute lessons how to perform the tasks you need. If this is how you like to learn, take a look at this book.

How This Book Is Organized

Microsoft Internet Explorer 4 6 in 1 is organized into these six parts:

Part 1: Internet Explorer 4.0   In this part, you will learn the basics of working with Internet Explorer and navigating the World Wide Web.

Part 2: ActiveX Controls, Plug-Ins, and Add-Ons   This series of lessons will help you find, download, and install a variety of ActiveX controls, plug-ins, and add-ons that will extend the functionality of Internet Explorer in many ways, including adding the capability to view specialized video and sound files.

Part 3: Outlook Express Mail   The lessons in this part teach you to send, receive, and organize your electronic mail messages using Outlook Express.

Part 4: Outlook Express News   This part helps you use Outlook Express to post and view articles from the thousands of Usenet newsgroups that are available.

Part 5: FrontPage Express and HTML   Everyone wants to have his or her own Web page on the Internet. In this part, you will learn how to use FrontPage Express to create your Web home page from HTML.

Part 6: The Active Desktop   One of the newest and nicest features of Internet Explorer 4.0 is its close integration with your Windows 95 operating system. In this part, you will explore the new desktop features and learn to use them to make finding information a snap.

This book was not meant to be read from front to back. It is a reference book that will help you learn the basics of using Internet Explorer, yet it also allows you to fill in information as you develop as a Web user. If you are new to the Internet and Internet Explorer, you will find this book a good introduction to using Internet Explorer for navigating online information quickly and easily. Each lesson in this book takes roughly ten minutes to complete. Each of the lessons in this book introduces you to a new functionality of Internet Explorer. You will find a series of beginning-level topics (such as moving backward and forward through Web pages) as well as more advanced ideas (such as creating your own Web pages).

Conventions Used in This Book

The following icons are included throughout the text to help you quickly identify particular types of information.

TIP Tip icons mark shortcuts and hints for saving time and using Internet Explorer more efficiently. If you like to take shortcuts, watch for this icon.

 Term icons point out easy-to-follow definitions that you'll need to know in order to understand Internet Explorer and how it fits into the scheme of the Internet. No need to pull out a dictionary when a tough term comes along. Just look for this icon and everything should be explained.

 Caution icons mark information that's intended to help you avoid making mistakes.

CAUTION

In addition to the special icons, you'll find these conventions used throughout the text:

On-screen text	On-screen text appears in bold type.
What you type	Information you need to type also appears in bold.
Items you select	Items you need to select or keys you need to press also appear in bold type.
`Computer output`	Long sections of computer text appear in a monospace font.

Internet
Explorer 4.0

Downloading and Installing Internet Explorer

In this lesson, you learn a bit about Internet Explorer 4.0 and how to download and install it.

Introducing Internet Explorer 4.0

We often hear the terms Internet and World Wide Web used interchangeably, but they aren't the same things. The Internet is a large network of computers that reaches all around the globe. It is made up of almost 50,000 different computer systems, and over 40,000,000 people are connected to it. The World Wide Web is just one part of this large information resource.

Multimedia Web sites are often full of elaborate and interesting content such as videos, brightly colored text, vibrant music, and Java- or ActiveX-enabled applets. When pages use some or all of these components, you end up with an *interactive multimedia* Web site. A multimedia Web site can have any combination of text, audio, and visual components.

In order to explore the World Wide Web, you must have a software package such as Internet Explorer with which you can view HTML or Web documents. *HTML* is a hypertext language that enables you to activate a link to any other document anywhere in the world, as long as it is accessible through the Internet. You might click a link to automatically open a distant document, send a mail message, play a sound file, or view a movie clip. Hotlinks can take you across the globe in a matter of seconds.

TIP   **Versions of Internet Explorer**   This book covers versions of Internet Explorer that run on Windows 95 computers. Other versions of Internet Explorer run in earlier versions of Windows. Even if you don't have Windows 95 or Internet Explorer 4.0, many of the tasks discussed in this book can easily be applied to earlier versions of Internet Explorer.

In order to run Internet Explorer 4.0 successfully, your computer must meet the following requirements:

- You must have a computer capable of running Windows 95. That means you must have a 486 or faster computer with 16M of RAM and at least 24M of hard drive space. (You should have more than the minimum amount of RAM and hard drive space if you want to view a lot of multimedia files; they use quite a bit of memory and can take up huge sections on your hard drive.)

- You need a 14,400 bps modem, but a 28.8 Kbps or faster modem is even better. (At the other end of the scale, you can navigate through text pages adequately with a 9,600 bps modem, but don't expect to load any images quickly.)

- You need a connection to the Internet—either a dial-up Internet service provider (ISP) or a direct network connection. (If you have a network connection to the Internet, you won't need the modem, and you can expect much better performance on multimedia sites.)

All connections to the Internet use a program called *Winsock*. This program creates a connection to the Internet that enables all of your Internet software (including Internet Explorer) to retrieve data from the Internet. Windows 95 and Windows NT users already have Winsock installed on their computers. Other Windows users may need to get a copy of a Winsock client, such as Trumpet Winsock, from their Internet service providers.

Downloading Internet Explorer 4.0 Setup Wizard

By installing Windows 95, Microsoft automatically provided you with Internet Explorer 3.0, which you can use to get version 4.0. The first step to setting up the new version of Internet Explorer is to download it from Microsoft's Web site or a *mirror site*.

Mirror Site   When a Web site is as busy as Microsoft's, the creators sometimes share copies of their software with other computers at various locations
around the Internet. Having more sites means that more people can download
the information. By using a mirror site, people can often download the file from
a location that is geographically closer to them.

Follow these steps to download Internet Explorer 4.0:

1. Open the **Start** menu and select **Programs**, **Accessories**, and **Dial-Up Networking**.

2. To run your Dial-Up Networking connection, double-click the icon you created for your Internet service provider.

3. Click **Connect** to allow the dialer to establish your Internet connection.

TIP   **Can't Connect**   If you don't get connected the first time, just try again. This
is a common occurrence during peak usage hours on the Internet. Simply click
Connect in the failed connection dialog box, verify your username and password in your Dial-Up Networking dialog box, and click **Connect** to try again.

4. When the connection is established, double-click the **Internet Explorer** icon on your desktop, or open the **Start** menu, select **Programs**, and select **Internet Explorer**. In the Address field on your toolbar, enter the URL **http://www.microsoft.com/ie** and press **Enter**. If this field isn't visible, open the **File** menu, select **Open**, enter the URL in the dialog box that appears, and then click **OK**.

5. Click the **Download** link at the top of the page. From the drop-down menu that appears, select the version of Internet Explorer 4.0 you want to download (see Figure 1.1). Select **Internet Explorer 4.0** and then **Windows 95/NT 4.0** unless you are using another operating system.

6. Scroll through this page until you find a link that reads **Download Internet Explorer 4.0**. Click it.

7. Select the exact version of Internet Explorer you want to download, as shown in Figure 1.2. Then click **Next**.

8. Select the language that you need to receive Explorer in, and then click **Next**.

9. Choose a download site from the list (preferably the site that is closest to your physical location) and click its link.

Click this link to
download Internet
Explorer 4

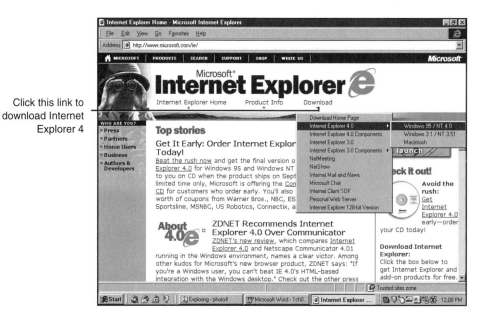

Figure 1.1 The Internet Explorer introduction screen gives you the latest information on Internet Explorer 4.0 and enables you to download it.

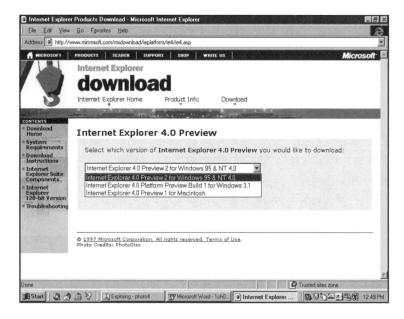

Figure 1.2 Microsoft asks you a series of questions that help make sure that you get exactly the program you need.

10. In the File Download dialog box, select the **Save This Program to Disk** option and click **OK**.

11. Select the directory on your hard drive in which you want to store the Setup Wizard. Then click **Save**. This starts the downloading process, which takes from 2–15 minutes depending on the speed of your modem.

12. When the download is complete, close your existing version of Internet Explorer.

Installing Internet Explorer for Windows 95

Internet Explorer has a unique installation system. When you performed the previous steps, you actually downloaded only a small 400K Setup Wizard. That wizard then directs you to a specific FTP or Web site from which you can get the remainder of the program. The complete downloading process for the remainder of the Internet Explorer installation can take anywhere from 1.5 to 6 hours, depending upon your modem speed and the server to which you have connected.

To download the remainder of the program, follow these steps:

1. Open the **Start** menu, select **Run**, and then click the **Browse** button.

2. Open the temporary directory in which you stored the ie4setup.exe file (this is the directory you chose in step 11 of the previous procedure).

3. Select **ie4setup.exe**, click **Open**, and then click **OK**.

4. In the Internet Explorer 4.0 Active Setup dialog box, click **Next**.

5. Check the **I Accept the Agreement** option button, and then click **Next**.

6. You are asked if you want to download and install or if you just want to download the files. Select **Download and Install** and click **Next**. If you want to copy this program to another computer, select **Download Only** and click **Next**.

 TIP **Download versus Install** If you choose to download and install the product, you won't be able to copy the installation files to another system because the product is automatically installed during downloading. If you choose to download Internet Explorer and install it later, you will have the files to copy onto other systems.

TIP   **Installing from a Download**   When you install Internet Explorer from a download of the program, you need to run the ie4setup.exe file that's located in your c:/Internet Explorer 4.0 Setup directory (*not* the setup program that you previously downloaded into your temporary directory).

7. Choose from the following installation options, which are shown in Figure 1.3. A full description of the installation you select appears below the selection list. Click **Next**.

- **Minimal Installation.** This installation installs only Internet Explorer and its multimedia plug-ins. If you are short of hard drive space, or if you already have an e-mail and news client that you use, this is probably the best option for you.

- **Standard Installation.** This installation installs all of Internet Explorer and its multimedia plug-ins, Outlook Express for reading both e-mail and news, and the Web Publishing Wizard. If you want to use Outlook Express for mail and news, you should choose this option.

- **Full Installation.** This installation installs all of Internet Explorer and its multimedia plug-ins, Outlook Express for reading e-mail and news, the Web Publishing Wizard, NetMeeting, FrontPage Express, and NetShow. This option is best if you want to do all of your Internet exploration through the Microsoft Internet suite.

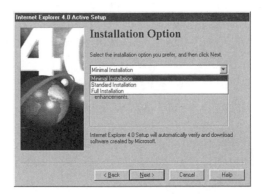

Figure 1.3   Select the installation type you want to use.

8. The Active Channel Selection screen provides you with a series of automatic business and entertainment channels that can be made available on your desktop. Select your country from the list, or choose another country that shares your language.

9. Select the location where you want the files installed. (The default is **c:\program file\internet explorer**.) Click **Next**.

10. Select the FTP site from which you want to download the remainder of the Internet Explorer components (as shown in Figure 1.4) and click **Next**. It can take anywhere from 1.5 to 6 hours at 28.8 Kbps connection to download the program, depending upon the number of individuals currently using the FTP sites.

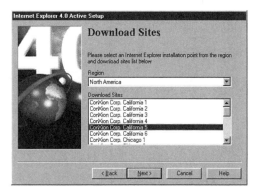

Figure 1.4   You can download the remaining Internet Explorer components from any of several FTP sites.

11. When the download and installation process is complete, disconnect from the Internet (if necessary) and restart your computer.

When your computer restarts, a series of links are automatically updated, and so is your desktop if you chose to install the Active Desktop. When you're done, your screen looks similar to Figure 1.5.

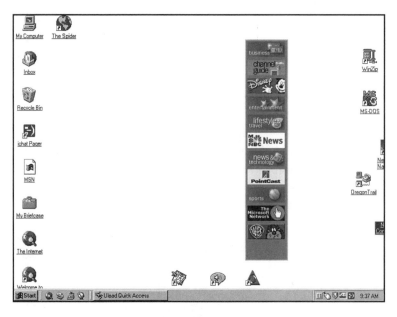

Figure 1.5   After installation, your desktop is updated to show the Active Desktop components included with this browser.

Upgrading Internet Explorer's Options with the Product Updates Site

Microsoft is continually updating its products. By using the Setup Wizard, you can easily keep up with these product updates. Follow these steps:

1. Open the **Start** menu, select **Programs**, select **Internet Explorer**, and then click the **Internet Explorer** icon.

2. Open the **Help** menu and select **Product Updates**. Internet Explorer automatically connects to Microsoft's update site. If there are updates available, you receive a list of them. You can then select the ones you want and have them automatically installed on your system.

3. Select the download site you want to use.

4. Select the components you want to add. The components will automatically be downloaded and installed.

5. Restart your computer to activate the updates.

Additional Notes for Windows NT

If your version of Windows NT isn't already configured to support TCP/IP, you need to do that. First open the **Control Panel** and select the **Network** icon. Click the **Protocols** tab, and then click the **Add** button. Select the **TCP/IP Protocol** and insert your Windows NT CD-ROM when prompted for the files. After the protocol is installed, you enter the network information supplied by your Internet service provider.

In this lesson, you learned how to download, install, and update Internet Explorer 4.0. In the next lesson, you will learn how to start and exit Internet Explorer.

Starting and Exiting Internet Explorer

In this lesson, you learn how to start and exit Internet Explorer. You also learn about the Internet Explorer interface.

Starting Internet Explorer

Now that Internet Explorer is installed, you can run the program. Internet Explorer automatically starts at the end of the installation process, but you need to know how to start it the next time you want to use it. And of course, because you can't be browsing the World Wide Web 24 hours a day, you also need to know how to turn the program off when other things need your attention.

Microsoft freely distributes Internet Explorer. Although they ask that you register the program with them, they don't require you to pay a fee for its use.

To open Internet Explorer, you have three options:

- Open the **Start** menu, select **Programs**, select **Internet Explorer**, and select **Internet Explorer** again (see Figure 2.1).

- Double-click the icon labeled **The Internet** on the left side of your desktop.
- Click the **Open Internet Explorer** icon, located on the taskbar.

When you first start Internet Explorer, it opens to the default Start Page provided by Microsoft (shown in Figure 2.2). When you reach this page the first time, you are asked to register the program. Although this isn't necessary, you can win some cool prizes from Microsoft if you do so.

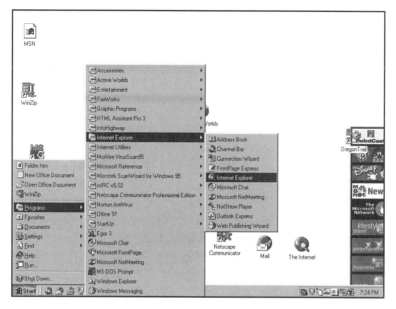

Figure 2.1 Opening IE from the Start menu.

Figure 2.2 Internet Explorer's default Start page.

TIP   **Opening the Start Page**   When you start Internet Explorer, it tries to load
its default Start Page first. If the page doesn't load, generally one of two things
has happened. The first possibility is that the server hosting your Start Page has
quit responding or is busy. The second possibility is that your computer isn't
properly connected to the Internet. In either case, you might be able to fix the
problem by reconnecting, or you can simply wait a few minutes to see if the
server becomes available.

Understanding Internet Explorer's Layout

When you start Internet Explorer, a Channel Guide appears on the desktop, a
series of icons is added to the taskbar, and an additional selection appears in
the Start menu. In addition to these changes, several things appear within the
Internet Explorer window that you might not have seen previously. Figure 2.3
shows the new Internet Explorer interface.

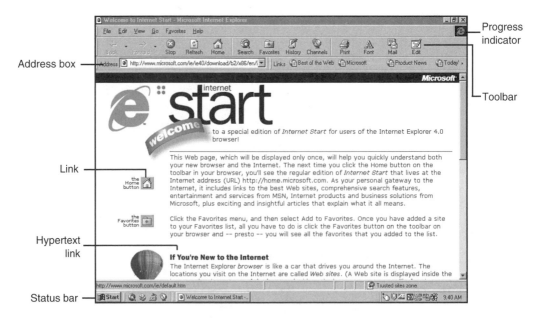

Figure 2.3   The Internet Explorer interface.

The following elements of the Internet Explorer interface might be new to you:

- The *Address box* shows the URL of the page that is currently loaded or being loaded in Internet Explorer. The address itself identifies the computer you are retrieving the Web page from and the file name of the page itself.

- A *hypertext link* is active text. This is text that you can click to travel to another location on the Internet. The new location might be on the same computer, or it might be half a world away. The mouse pointer changes to a hand when it passes over a hypertext link.

- *Links* are buttons or images that enable you to easily navigate between sites on the Internet, newer Internet sites, product information about Internet Explorer, and information about the Microsoft Corporation.

- The *progress indicator* indicates Internet Explorer's current level of activity. If the "E" is spinning, Internet Explorer is in the process of downloading either a Web page or a file to your computer. When the "E" is stationary, there is no online activity.

- The *Status bar* displays the name of the document or file that's being downloaded. Because each graphic on a Web page is an individual file, a loading page that contains a large number of graphics shows quite a bit of activity in the status bar while it's loading.

- The *toolbar* contains buttons that enable easy navigation between Web sites, printing and display options, and a way to stop the current page from loading completely.

Exiting Internet Explorer

When you finish exploring the Internet, you need to close Internet Explorer before you go on to other work. Of course, you can leave the product open all the time, but it will take up processor time that could be used by other programs.

To shut down Internet Explorer, open the **File** menu and select **Close,** or click the **Close** (X) button in the upper-right corner of the Internet Explorer window. Remember to click **Disconnect** in the Dial-Up Networking dialog box to break your phone connection if it wasn't started by Internet Explorer originally.

In this lesson, you learned how to start and exit Internet Explorer. You also took a close look at the Internet Explorer interface. In the next lesson, you will learn how to open your first Web site.

Opening Your First Web Site

In this lesson, you learn how to navigate simple Web sites using tools available in Internet Explorer.

Understanding Internet Addresses

To track the millions of documents available on the Internet, a complex addressing system was created. These addresses, called *Uniform Resource Locators (URLs)*, enable you to go directly to a Web document without having to travel through hundreds of other documents.

URLs have a common format similar to the following:

http://www.mcp.com/que/que.html

A URL can be broken into specific sections, each of which helps the computers on the Internet find the one document you're looking for. The first part, **http://**, lets all the computers know that you are looking for a Web server (as opposed to a News or Mail server). The middle section, **www.mcp.com** in this case, is the name of the computer that contains the document you're looking for. The part that appears after the slash, **que**, specifies the directory in which the document is stored, and the part after the next slash, **que.html**, is the name of the actual document you're looking for. (The .html file extension indicates the type of document.)

  HTML   HyperText Markup Language is the standard language in which all Web documents are written. HTML is a coded programming language that enables you to specify exactly what document text is going to look like and where graphics will be located.

Opening a Web Site

The first time you start Internet Explorer, you're taken to Microsoft's Internet Explorer 4.0 support home page. This is your default Start Page. You aren't limited to using the Start Page Microsoft has created for you. You can change your Start Page to any page on the Internet that you find useful.

Looking at the Microsoft Start Page, you might realize that it doesn't provide links to many pages you will want to visit on the Web. To get to these other pages, you need to know their URLs (Internet addresses).

Be careful when directly entering URLs. Many computers on the Internet are case sensitive, so you need to make sure that every letter that should be capitalized is and that you are using a forward slash (/) instead of the standard back slash (\). Because most computers on the Internet allow long file names, you will also run across characters that aren't allowed in the standard DOS environment.

You can open a Web page for which you know the URL using either of these two methods:

- With Internet Explorer loaded to any page, click your mouse in the **Address** box. Type the address for the page you want see. For example, type **www.mcp.com** to go to Macmillan Publishing's home page. Then press **Enter**.

- You can enter your address into the Open dialog box. Open the **File** menu and select **Open** (Ctrl+O). In the Open dialog box (shown in Figure 3.1), enter the URL in the **Open** text box and click **OK**.

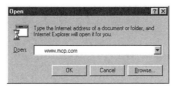

Figure 3.1   Internet Explorer's Open dialog box.

17

TIP **Web Addressing Shortcuts** Although the full address of the Web page is **http://www.mcp.com**, you can leave off the http:// when entering URLs in Internet Explorer. IE automatically assumes that you want to load a Web page unless you specify otherwise. If the address for the site you want to load is in the form of *www.mcp.com*, you can simply type the company name, and the rest of the address will be assumed.

If you typed the address correctly, the specified page appears. Figure 3.2 shows the Web page located at the address used in the example (**http://www.mcp.com**).

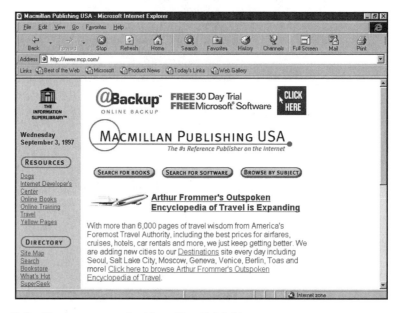

Figure 3.2 The home page for Macmillan Publishing.

The Pages Are Not Loading If the page you requested doesn't load, you need to return to the Address box and double-check what you entered. Remember that spaces and upper- and lowercase letters are important when **CAUTION** you're on the Internet.

Navigating with the Internet Explorer Toolbar

Internet Explorer provides a set of links on the Links toolbar that can help get you going in your exploration of the Internet and the World Wide Web. The Links toolbar (shown in Figure 3.3) comes with connections to a variety of places including the Best of the Web, Microsoft's Home Page, the Web Gallery, Product News, and Today's Links.

Figure 3.3   Internet Explorer's Links toolbar.

Select one of the links on this bar, and Internet Explorer automatically opens to that page. For example, click **Best of the Web**, and Microsoft's Best of the Web page opens. From here, as you can see in Figure 3.4, you can access a variety of pages covering topics as diverse as Travel and Entertainment and Starting Your Own Business. When you select one of the topic areas, you see a series of articles that focus on that topic. Travel through the layers, and you eventually reach an article discussing your particular topic of interest.

Figure 3.4   Internet Explorer's Back button.

Jumping Forward and Backward

Often while navigating the Internet, you need to move back to a page your just visited, and then jump forward to the page you just left. Internet Explorer provides you with ways to easily move among the pages you have recently seen. These steps show you how:

1. Once you've explored some of the available links, if you want to return to a page you just read, click the **Back** button. This takes you to the page you just visited. Click **Back** multiple times to go back through multiple pages one at a time.

CAUTION

Back Is Unavailable You can click the Back button only until you reach the first page you visited during this session with Internet Explorer. Once you reach the first page, your Back button is grayed out, which means it's inaccessible.

2. If you move back through your visited sites too far, click the **Forward** button (shown in Figure 3.5) to go forward through the sites you've already visited. As with Back, you can click Forward multiple times to move through the sites one at a time.

Forward
button with list
of visited sites

Refresh button
reloads the latest
copy of your current
Web page

Home button
returns you to
your Start Page

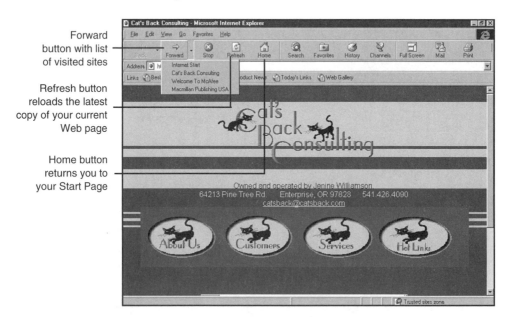

Figure 3.5 Internet Explorer's Forward button.

Forward Is Unavailable   You can use the Forward button only if you have gone back first. When you reach the last new site you have already visited, the Forward button is grayed out. To continue viewing new sites, you have to use the page links.

Starting Over

If you reach a point on the Internet where you can go no further, or if you get hopelessly lost, you'll need to return to your starting point. Internet Explorer makes this easy. Simply click the **Home** button (refer to Figure 3.5), and you are automatically returned to your Start Page (the page from which you first started your exploration of the Internet). To have Internet Explorer download the page again so you'll have the most recent version, click the **Refresh** button.

In this lesson, you learned how to use the Internet Explorer toolbar to navigate pages, open a page using its URL, and move forward and backward through sites you have already visited. In the next lesson, you will learn how to navigate through the Internet using links.

Navigating the Internet

In this lesson, you learn about hypertext links on the Internet and how they're used to direct you to computers all over the Internet.

Understanding Links

The World Wide Web is made up of millions of Web pages that are joined by hypertext links to form a literal web of information. These hypertext links create a true point-and-click environment for surfing the Internet. Each individual Web page can display its links and text using any color, but by default Internet Explorer displays them in blue. Regardless of their color, the links are meant to show that a specific piece of text or a picture provides access to a new location on the Internet when clicked.

Because links can be any color and may or may not be underlined, Internet Explorer uses an additional device to help you identify a hypertext link. When you pass your mouse over a link, the pointer changes to a hand. The hand indicates that if you click the item your mouse is over, you will jump to another page on the Internet. In addition to your mouse pointer changing to a pointing hand, you will see the URL of the link appear in the status bar at the bottom of your screen. If a page appears to have no links, you can use these signs to identify them.

Navigating Links

Every time you activate a link, Internet Explorer loads whatever document or file is attached to that link. In this section, you explore both graphic and text links to other documents. But don't worry, multimedia links are coming up.

If Internet Explorer isn't already running, open it by clicking its taskbar icon. As Internet Explorer starts, you see the Microsoft Home Page being loaded. You can watch the global e logo and the status bar at the bottom of the screen to follow what is happening.

First Internet Explorer attempts to find the computer that's hosting the Web page you want to load. When it finds the computer, it connects to it and starts to load the document. While this entire process is taking place you see the animated e globe spinning at the top of your screen.

Internet Explorer loads the text of your document before it loads the graphics, so you can read the page's text while it finishes loading the graphics. As you can see in Figure 4.1, there will be blank spots on your screen with little image icons to note where the graphics are going to be placed. When the globe stops spinning, the page is completely loaded.

Status bar ——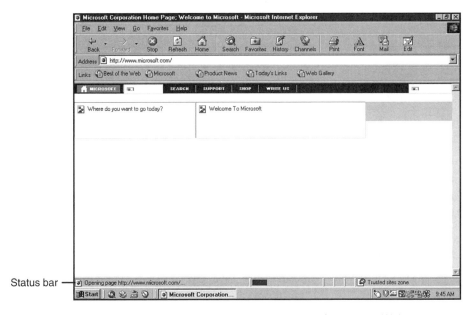

Figure 4.1   Internet Explorer is in the process of loading a Web page.

Problems Loading a Page?   If the globe stops spinning half way through a turn, or if a message similar to "Connecting to Host" appears on the status bar for an extended period of time, you have a problem. The site from which
CAUTION   you were attempting to load is probably busy or not working for some reason. If this happens, click the **Stop** button on the toolbar.

Once you have a page loaded, follow these steps to move through the Internet by way of links:

1. Scroll through the document and look for links in blue underlined text. When you find a link that looks interesting, click it. Your cursor changes to a wait symbol, and your globe begins to turn. In a few seconds, a new document appears.

2. Within this document, place your mouse over a graphic or text link. Your pointer changes from the standard arrow to a hand. Click the link to jump to the corresponding page.

TIP   **Image Maps**   Some graphics have multiple pages attached to them. These graphics, called image maps, are often used in place of a text version of a table of contents. Point to an image map, and a number of Internet addresses appear in your status bar. Each of these addresses represents a document that you can access by clicking that portion of the image map.

3. Keep scrolling through pages and selecting links that look interesting to you. If you want to go back to Microsoft's home page, click the **Your Start Page** link in the upper-left corner of your screen.

Using the Right Mouse Button

Internet Explorer provides a shortcut menu that gives you immediate access to commands for saving images, opening pages, maneuvering through the pages that you have already seen, adding items to your shortcut menu, printing, or viewing a page's properties.

Suppose you come across an image you really like, such as the one shown in Figure 4.2. You might want to save it to your hard drive to add to a collection or even to use it as your desktop wallpaper. You can perform either of these functions by using the shortcut menu. Here's how:

1. Right-click the image, and the shortcut menu shown in Figure 4.2 appears.

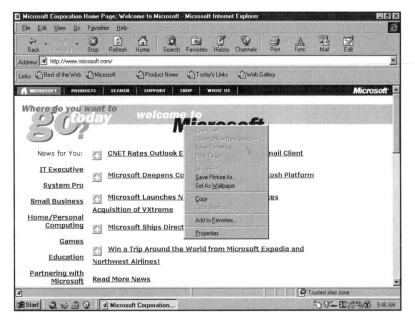

Figure 4.2 Use the shortcut menu to perform common tasks related to the selected object.

2. Choose **Save Picture As** to save the file directly to your hard drive. A dialog box containing your computer's directories appears. Choose where you want to save the file.

3. Choose **Set As Wallpaper** to instantly set the picture as the wallpaper on your desktop. To revert to your normal wallpaper settings, right-click the desktop and choose **Properties** to change the background back.

4. To find out information such as the date the picture was created or the size of the image, choose **Properties** from the shortcut button menu. The Properties screen appears, displaying all of the image's data.

Viewing the History

Internet Explorer provides more ways to view pages than the Back and Forward buttons. It provides a History list from which you can quickly select sites you've recently visited. This list tracks not only the sites that you have visited today, but the sites that you have visited in the recent past.

1. After exploring some sites in one or multiple sessions on the Web, click the **History** button on your toolbar. Internet Explorer displays an additional frame alongside your existing browser window, listing all the sites that you have viewed over the last two weeks.

2. Select an entry from the History list. Then right-click the entry and select **Open**.

 TIP **Time in History**   You can configure your History folder to hold items for more or less than the default two weeks. To configure your History options, open the **View** menu, select **Internet Options**, and select the **General** tab. At the bottom of this dialog box is the History section. Set the **Days to Keep Pages in History** option to the number of days that works for you. (The default is 10 days.) If you browse the Web every day, you might want to lower this number; if you browse the Web once a week, you might want to increase this number.

 TIP **Finding Sites You Have Visited**   If you cannot find a site that you visited a few weeks or even a few days ago, the site is probably still accessible. To find it again, use a search engine as discussed in Lessons 10 and 11.

In this lesson, you learned how hypertext links function on the Internet and how they are used to direct you to various computers all over the Internet. In the next lesson, you will learn how to open, save, and print files using Internet Explorer 4.0.

Opening, Saving, and Printing Files

In this lesson, you learn how to open, save, and print both local HTML files and files off of the Internet.

As you use the Internet, you will find that you might want to open some of the HTML files that are stored on your disk, or you might want to save a page you're looking at. The process used to perform these functions in Internet Explorer is the same as that used in almost any other Windows application.

Opening Local Web Files

There are many reasons why you might need to open up a Web page that has been saved on your computer. It might be one that you have created and are still working on, or it might be a site that you have saved so you can read it later. You also have the opportunity to view any GIF or JPG files through Internet Explorer so you don't have to open another viewing program.

Follow these steps to open a Web page that's stored on your hard drive:

1. In Internet Explorer, open the **File** menu and select **Open** (Ctrl+O). This enables you to open either a local file or a file on the Internet.

2. In the Open dialog box, select the file you want to open.

   To open a local file, click the **Browse** button and search for the file you want. For example, open the **c:\windows\Web** directory and select the **business.html** file. (This is an HTML file that ships with Internet Explorer 4.0.) Click the **Open** button.

3. When you return to the Open dialog box, click **OK**. Internet Explorer displays the selected document. Figure 5.1 shows the business.html document. If you're not currently connected to the Internet, you won't be able to see all the graphics.

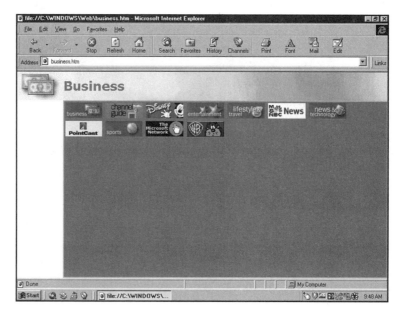

Figure 5.1 The business.html Web page that ships with Internet Explorer.

Saving a Web Page

You have seen many of the features of Internet Explorer, but you haven't yet learned how to save Web pages. Now if you are a Web window shopper, you are probably not interested in saving the information you find. On the other hand, if you are doing research—whether for personal or business reasons—you are going to need to keep track of the information you find. You can do this by printing the information you find or by saving a copy of the page that contains the information. Because Web sites change often, you cannot be assured that an article you find on Wednesday will still be there on Saturday.

Saving files is one of the core functions of computer applications. Having the information visible on your screen does you no good unless you can store it for later use. In addition, saving files can help you keep your online time to a minimum, which is especially important if you're being charged by the hour.

To save a Web page to your hard drive, follow these steps:

1. With any page open, open the **File** menu and select **Save As**.

2. In the Save HTML Document (shown in Figure 5.2), select the directory to which you want to save the HTML document and give the file an appropriate name. Then click **Save**.

Figure 5.2 Internet Explorer enables you to save copies of the Web pages you visit.

3. Open the file you saved. Because all you saved was the HTML code, you are missing the graphics that were on the original site.

Printing a Web Page

After exploring the Internet for a while, you might notice that you are spending large amounts of time reading single pages of information. If you're doing a lot of research and would like to read the information later, you can print a hard copy in order to reduce your online research time. Printing your documents also enables you to file the information for later reference.

1. Go to a page from which you would like to print information. Open the **File** menu and select **Print** (Ctrl+P). The Print dialog box appears.

2. Make sure that your printer is selected and adjust the number of copies to make if necessary (see Figure 5.3). When you're ready, click **OK**.

TIP **Quick Print** You also can start the print process by clicking the **Print** toolbar button. This bypasses the Print dialog box and prints the document immediately using the default print settings.

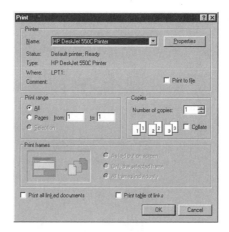

Figure 5.3   Select the destination of the print job and the number of pages you want to print.

Searching for Text

While looking for information on a specific subject, you might find pages that have the answers to your questions, but the facts are hidden in a forest of words. To handle situations like this, Internet Explorer provides a Find utility that searches through the text of the document and shows you every occurrence of the word or phrase you're searching for. If you have ever used the Find feature in other Windows applications, you already know how to use this feature in Internet Explorer.

Once you find text on a page, you might want to do something with it. For this reason Internet Explorer, like all other Windows applications, enables you to copy information from one application to another using the Windows Clipboard. You can copy information that you find in an Internet Explorer window into any other application. But there is one hang-up: You can't copy information from another application into an Internet Explorer window unless you're pasting it into a form field. You can't paste information directly into the text of a Web document because you're looking at a file stored on another computer that you can't change.

The following steps walk you through an example of how to use Internet Explorer's Find feature:

1. Open the Macmillan Publishing home page (**www.mcp.com**) and click the **What's Hot** link in the sidebar.

2. Open the **Edit** menu and select **Find (on this page)** (Ctrl+F).

3. In the Find dialog box, enter the text you want to search for, such as **disney** (see Figure 5.4). Then click **Find Next**.

Figure 5.4   Use the Find dialog box to search for information within Web pages.

4. Internet Explorer searches through the text of the document until it finds the word or phrase and highlights the text to make it easy to find. If you want to repeat the search, click **Find Next** again.

5. When Internet Explorer finishes searching the document, it displays a dialog box letting you know that all instances of the word have been found. Click **OK**. Then click **Cancel** to close the Find dialog box.

In this lesson, you learned how to open, save, and print HTML pages that you find on the Internet. In the next lesson, you will learn how to configure Internet Explorer to make it run in a manner that best fits your style of use.

Setting the Internet Explorer Options

In this lesson, you learn how to configure Internet Explorer's preferences.

Controlling the Cache and History

Internet Explorer, like most other World Wide Web browsers, keeps track of all the sites you visit, storing copies of them on your hard drive for a short period of time. This storage area, or *cache*, keeps a copy of all the pages, graphic, sounds, and movies that you view while on the Web. Because these things are stored in the cache, you can view information while you're not actively on the Web. You can load a page from the cache and read the information without connecting to the Internet.

Even if you are on the connected, it's faster to load a document from your cache than it is from the Internet. The only problem with using a cache is that cached pages don't reflect changes that have been made to the site since the cache was created. In this lesson, you learn how to set Internet Explorer so that you get an updated version of the site the first time you read it each day.

After you use Internet Explorer for a while, your hard drive space will seem to disappear quickly. This is because Internet Explorer caches all of the sites (HTML documents, graphics, sounds, and movies) that you visit on the Web. In order to rescue this space for your own use, you need to clear out your cache periodically or set its space limitations to a level that works better for you. Follow these steps to set such options for Internet Explorer:

1. Open the **View** menu and select **Internet Options**. In the Options dialog box, click the **General** tab.

2. At the bottom of the General tab is the History section. Use the options available to select how many days you want to keep pages in your history folder. (The default setting is one day.) If you use the Internet more frequently than that, you can adjust the settings to meet your own needs. Very frequent users may want to keep pages only a day or two.

3. In the Temporary Internet Files section, click the **Settings** button. The Settings dialog box appears.

4. Your cache stores sites so that you can quickly load them into your browser. You have the option of loading them upon Every Visit to the Page, Every Time You Start Internet Explorer, or Never. Click the option button of your choice.

5. The slider bar enables you to control the amount of disk space used by your cache. The default is 1%. Adjust this value from 0% up to 100% of your disk space (see Figure 6.1).

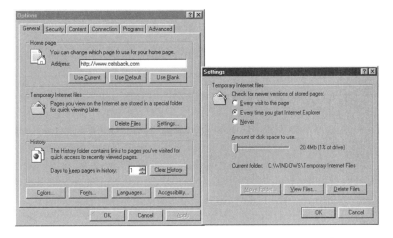

Figure 6.1 Internet Explorer enables you to control how much of your hard drive is used to store temporary files.

6. To empty the Temporary Internet Files directory, click the **Delete Files** button. When asked if you're sure you want to delete all those files, click **Yes**.

7. Click **OK** to close the Settings dialog box.

8. Click **Apply** and then **OK** to save and activate your settings.

Setting Up Security

Security has been a concern since the original development of the Internet. Businesses and governments worry about protecting their secrets; users worry about protecting their privacy and their credit cards; software companies worry about providing that security so everyone can be happy.

Electronic malls are popping up all over the place. The majority of these malls provide secure servers with which to complete your transaction. Other sites don't provide security. Luckily, Internet Explorer makes it easy to tell if you are viewing a secure site. Internet Explorer also provides a number of security features that enable you to carry out your business over the Internet with few worries. Some of those features are described here:

- Proxy servers are programs designed to handle communication between a corporation's secure network and the open Internet. Because proxy servers often track access and authenticate users, they can assist in keeping hackers from invading your system. Without proxies, some corporate Internet Explorer users would not have access to the Internet.

- Firewalls are another security method used by corporations to secure their corporate information. A firewall is like an armed gate that provides the only access into and out of a compound. Some firewalls allow only e-mail traffic, while others allow a full range of activities.

- Cryptography is probably one of the biggest buzzwords that you hear when talking about security on the Internet. Data encryption is used to scramble information so that only an individual with a specific decrypting key can read the it. Combined with the verification and information logging systems that transactions go through, this makes a relatively secure system. Of course, both the Web server and the Web browser must support the encryption key in order for it to work.

Internet Explorer enables you to use all of these systems to protect your information. It also checks each site for you and lets you know when you are sending information over an unsecured link. You also get the chance to stop the transfer of information before it even starts. In the next section, you learn about the various security systems that have been built into Internet Explorer.

Connecting to a Secure Site

When you purchase something over the Internet, you need to know whether the site you are connected to is secure. Internet Explorer helps take some of the guesswork out of this process by warning you each time you send information over an unsecured link, no matter what that information is.

If you know a site is secure, you can tell Internet Explorer not to worry about it in the future. The following steps show you how to mark a site as secure or nonsecure:

1. Open the **View** menu, select **Internet Options**, and click the **Security** tab.

2. In the **Zone** drop-down list, select the zone you want to adjust. For example, select **Trusted Sites Zone**. You must add a series of sites to each zone in order for them to function properly.

3. Click the **Add Sites** button.

4. In the **Add This Web Site to the Zone** text box, type **http://www.microsoft.com/**. Click **Add**, and the URL appears in the Web Sites list at the top of the dialog box (see Figure 6.2). Click **OK**.

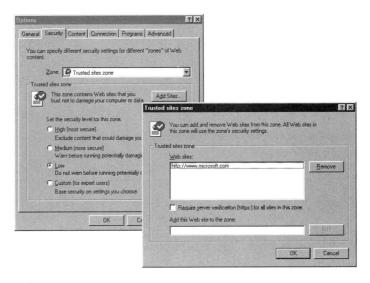

Figure 6.2 You can configure your own security levels.

5. Click **OK** to close the Options dialog box and put your changes into effect.

By default, Internet Explorer warns you of potential danger when you're sending information over the Internet. Follow these steps to see the message you will get if you try to send a lot of information over the Internet.

1. Enter the URL **www.microsoft.com/sitebuilder/** in the **Address** box.

2. If you have never registered for the Site Builder network, read the instructions on how to become eligible for the free software that is available. When you finish reading the instructions, scroll through the form and answer all the questions.

TIP **Purchase Requirements** You have to enter your name, your e-mail address, and your mailing address in order to continue.

3. Click **Send**, and Internet Explorer displays the Security Alert dialog box shown in Figure 6.3. To cancel your form submission, click **No**; to send the form information, click **Yes**; to request more information about Internet security, click **Tell Me About Internet Security**.

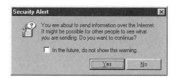

Figure 6.3 Internet Explorer warns you about sending secure information over the Internet.

Using Security Certificates

Security certificates make it easy to tell whether or not you are downloading information from a reputable site. Internet Explorer has a series of built-in security certificates that essentially assure you the information you get from a site will be friendly (not full of viruses). These certificates are just one more way in which Internet Explorer tries to keep you safe while you explore the Internet. To set up security certificates options, follow these steps:

1. Open the **View** menu and select **Internet Options**. The Options dialog box opens.

2. Click the **Content** tab. You can enter a series of sites organized into lists Personal information, Internet sites, and Software companies.

Now every time you visit one of these sites, you are notified that you are receiving secure and trusted data.

No Security If you select **None**, you have no protection against potential security risks. This option is not recommended.

CAUTION

Modifying the Start Page

The first time you start Internet Explorer, you are taken to Microsoft's Internet Explorer 4.0 support home page. The term *home* page is commonly used to refer to two very specific parts of your Web exploration. When you are looking at Internet Explorer's options, a home page is simply the starting page for each day's exploration of the Internet. You aren't limited to using the page that Microsoft has created for you; you can use any page on the Internet that you find useful.

The other definition for *home page* refers to the first page you come to when you visit a site. The home page of a Web site is like a front door. It generally welcomes you to visit the information on the site and gives you an idea of what that site is about. A Web site is simply a series of related documents that have been placed on a computer attached to the Internet. Companies, governments, educational institutions, and individuals generally set up Web sites. Actually, anyone who wants his or her own Web site can have it.

The home page is very important. It is your starting place on the Web. If you pick a page that doesn't have links to any of the sites you normally go to, you might as well start out with a blank page. A useful home page can make your experience with the Web exciting and trouble-free. A poorly designed home page can give you nothing but headaches as you strain to remember the addresses for the pages you want to visit.

To change your home page, follow these steps:

1. To go to your home page, click the **Home** button on your toolbar. This immediately takes you back to the page from which you started.

2. Open the **View** menu and select **Internet Options**. In the Options dialog box, click the **General** tab.

 TIP **Options Shortcut** You also can reach this screen by right-clicking the **Internet Explorer** icon on your desktop and selecting **Properties**.

3. In the **Address** text box, type the address of the site you want to make your Home page. For example, type **www.mcp.com**.

TIP **Starting with a Blank Page** If you don't want any page to open when you start Internet Explorer, just leave the Address text box blank.

Turning Off Image Downloading

If you have trouble getting a site to load, it might be because there are too many graphics or movies attached to the site. One of the easiest ways to keep these types of items from slowing down browsing is to tell Internet Explorer to ignore them. Of course this affects all the sites you visit, but you can load the images that you want to see when you want to see them.

Follow these steps to turn off the image downloading feature:

1. Open the **View** menu and select **Internet Options**.

2. In the Options dialog, click the **Advanced** tab. Then scroll through the list of options until you find the Multimedia settings.

3. Click to remove the check marks from the **Play Videos**, **Play Animations**, and **Play Sounds** check boxes (see Figure 6.4). This tells Internet Explorer not to automatically load those specific elements.

Figure 6.4 Internet Explorer enables you to choose whether to load movies, images, and sounds automatically.

4. Make sure the **Smart Dithering** and **Load Pictures** options are checked so that your pages will maintain some interesting information.

5. Click **Apply** and then **OK**.

Configuring Content Ratings

You obviously have a computer that's connected to the Internet. Do you have any kids? Have you ever thought about what they could be seeing on the Internet? Over 90 percent of the information on the Internet is perfectly safe for children to see. It's that other 10 percent that parents have to watch out for.

Internet Explorer assists parents by using the rating systems already on the Internet to keep children off the sites that wouldn't generally be considered acceptable for children. To set your preferences for what sites your children can see, follow these steps:

1. Open the **View** menu and select **Internet Options**. In the Options dialog, click the **Content** tab.

2. To start configuring the Content Advisor, click the **Enable** button. This starts out asking you for a password. Enter the password you want to use to keep other individuals from accessing confidential information. Verify your password, and then click **OK**.

3. The Content Advisor dialog box appears next. To control what type of ranking is allowed for viewing each type of rating, select the rating type and use the slide bar to set the rate (see Figure 6.5). When you finish adjusting these settings, click the **General** tab.

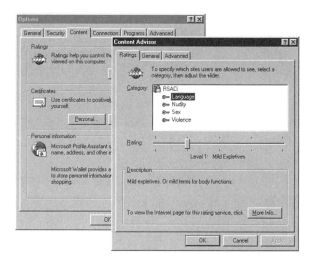

Figure 6.5   You can control the ratings for each type of material you want to monitor.

4. Indicate whether you are going to enable users to see unrated sites, or whether you will allow sites to be accessed after the password is entered.

CAUTION

Sites That Aren't Rated   Quite a few sites on the Internet have not yet been rated, and some of them have questionable content. Of course, if you don't allow users to see unrated sites, you might lock them away from useful educational sites. As the rating services expand, you might change your mind about your selections here.

5. (Optional) If you need to change your password, click the **Change Password** button. This opens the standard change password screen, in which you enter your old password, enter a new password, and then verify the new password. When you finish, click **OK**.

6. Internet Explorer uses rating systems provided by other companies. To expand your rating systems list, click the **Advanced** tab and click the **Rating System** button.

7. To add a new rating system, click the **Add** button and select the new ratings file. When you finish installing the new ratings file, click **OK**. If you've finished adjusting all of the rating settings, continue clicking the **OK** button until you're returned to the main browser page.

8. To test your settings, try to open the Playboy site at **www.playboy.com**. You should see a Content Advisor dialog box explaining that this page is blocked for content (see Figure 6.6).

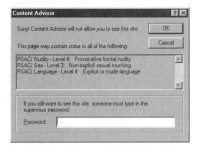

Figure 6.6   Internet Explorer's rating system blocks out adult sites before you or your kids can see any of the material.

Associating Applications

If you attempt to open a file but you do not have an application that's capable of viewing it, you must create a file association. When you install most applications, they automatically configure Windows 95 to use them to open the kinds of files they can view. But not all of them do this. Some configure themselves for their main file types only, leaving off some of the ones you need.

Internet Explorer uses the File Type list stored in Windows 95 to decide which application to open when it encounters a particular file type. You can expand this list whenever you need to. This should not be a common task, however. You should only have to add to the file extensions when you install a new program or if you find new file types on the Web that you want to explore.

Follow these steps to set up a file association:

1. Open the **Start** menu, select **Programs**, and select **Windows Explorer**. This starts Explorer, which gives you access to the file associations that Windows 95 and Internet Explorer use.

2. With Windows Explorer running, open the **View** menu and select **Folder Options**. In the Options dialog, select the **File Types** tab.

3. Scroll through the Registered File Types list shown in Figure 6.7. As you can see, there's an entry for practically every program you have on your computer. Click the **New Type** button to add another entry to this list.

Figure 6.7 The Windows Explorer's list of associated file types.

4. The File Association dialog box that appears requires quite a bit of information before your new file association is usable. You're going to create a file association for a standard log file.

In the **Description of Type** field, type **Internet Log Files**. This is the name that will appear in your Registered File Types list. In the **Associated Extension** field, enter **.log** as the file extension that activates this file association. In the **Content Type** field, select the **text/plain** Mime type, and Explorer automatically fills in the **Default Extension** field.

5. Next you have to tell Internet Explorer what product to open those type of files with. Click **New** to open the New Action dialog. In the **Action** field, type **Open**. The action is simply an order directing what you want to happen with these types of files. Type the path to your Windows Notepad program (for example **c:\windows\notepad.exe**) in the **Application Used** field. When you finish with this dialog box, click **OK**.

CAUTION

Missing Directory   If you don't have a **windows** directory, you might have a **win95** directory; users of Windows NT would have a **winNT** directory. Replace the path and directory in this step with the path and directory to your copy of Notepad.

6. You have entered instructions that tell Internet Explorer what program to use to open files with the .log extension of the standard plain text MIME type. To finish off this file association, click the **Set Default** button. Double-check your settings on this screen (shown in Figure 6.8). When you're satisfied with your entries, click **Close**.

Figure 6.8   The File Types tab shows the details you entered for the new file association.

As you can see, your new log file association has been added to your list of Registered File Types. Next time you run across a log file, Internet Explorer will be prepared to read it.

In this lesson, you learned how to configure Internet Explorer's options. In the next lesson, you will learn to adjust the appearance of Internet Explorer to suit your personal preferences.

Changing the Appearance of Internet Explorer

In this lesson, you learn how to modify the appearance of Internet Explorer so that it can be used the way you want.

Resizing the Toolbar

Everyone who uses software eventually wants to change the way it looks. Items on your toolbars are never in the right place, or they're the wrong size, or the buttons have labels that you don't want. This same phenomenon will occur as you use Internet Explorer. Eventually you may notice that you're unhappy with the layout of the interface. Because this condition is so prevalent, Microsoft has made adjusting your toolbars easy. You can adjust both the size of the toolbar itself and the size of the buttons that you see.

The following steps help you adjust the appearance of your toolbars:

1. Start Internet Explorer. You don't have to connect to the Internet, but being connected won't affect the function of this process.

2. Open the **View** menu and select **Toolbar**.

3. Select the toolbars you want to load, and then check **Text Labels** if you want Internet Explorer to display text labels with your navigational buttons (see Figure 7.1). To remove a toolbar or the text labels from the display, click the corresponding option to remove the check mark from in front of it. When you make your selection, the menu disappears, and your screen is updated.

4. (Optional) To resize the length of a toolbar, place your mouse pointer over the toolbar's handle and drag the mouse.

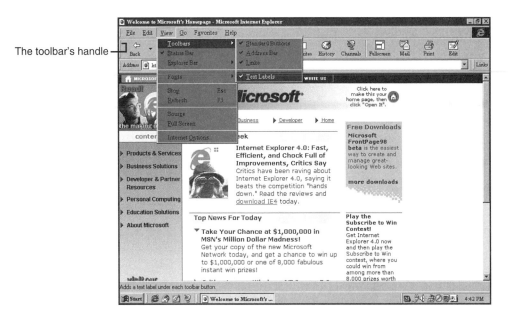

The toolbar's handle

Figure 7.1 Choose which toolbars you want displayed and whether or not labels appear.

Switching Between the Address and the Links Toolbar

Having too many toolbars displayed at the top of the Internet Explorer window can make using Internet Explorer difficult. You can either stack up the toolbars on a single line, or you can place each toolbar on a separate line at the top of your Internet Explorer screen as shown in Figure 7.2.

Figure 7.2 Internet Explorer with all of the toolbars fully visible.

To cut down the amount of space the toolbars take up, you can place multiple toolbars on the same line so they share a line. To do so, select the toolbar's handle and drag the toolbar to another location. In Figure 7.3, for example, the

Internet toolbar, the Address toolbar, and the Links toolbar all appear on the same line.

Figure 7.3 Combine your toolbars so they take up fewer lines and you have a larger browsing area.

Suppose you have placed multiple toolbars on one row to free up space in the browser window. You might run into times when you need to display all of one of those toolbars so you can use its tools. The following steps show you how to accomplish that:

1. Place your mouse pointer over the handle of the toolbar you want to open fully.

2. Double-click the handle, and the selected toolbar opens fully across your Internet Explorer screen.

3. To open another toolbar on that row, double-click its toolbar handle.

Controlling Your Screen Appearance

You can control the items that you see on your screen and the colors that are used for text on the Web documents that you download. Changing some screen appearance options will make it easier to read information on your screen. On the other hand, sometimes you'll want to change screen options simply to open up more room on your screen to see the information in the first place.

Many of the pages you see on the Web have been designed with no thought of readability or color coordination. On these sites, you might have to change the color of the text and links on a page—especially if you can't find your way through a site because you can't read the links. Internet Explorer can control these colors for you. Follow these steps to set it up to do so:

1. Open the **View** menu and select **Status Bar**. This closes the status bar; you will no longer receive messages there.

2. Open the **View** menu and select **Fonts**. The submenu that appears provides options with which you can control the size of your screen font (see Figure 7.4). Choose the option you prefer.

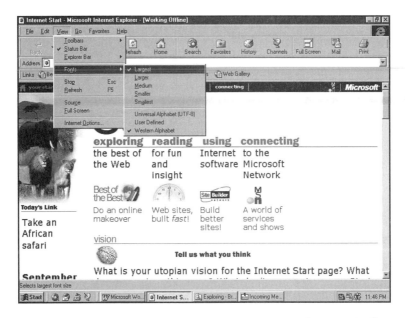

Figure 7.4 In Internet Explorer, you can change your screen fonts on-the-fly.

3. To change the rest of the options you need to access the your Properties dialog box. Open the **View** menu and select **Internet Options**.

4. Click the **Fonts** button at the bottom of the Properties dialog box.

5. In the dialog box that appears (shown in Figure 7.5), you can change the fonts and the alphabet used on your pages. Select the specific font you want to use for your proportional fonts (the default is Times New Roman). You also can choose the font to use for fixed-width fonts, the size of the default font on your pages, and the character set you want to use.

 TERM **Fixed-Width Fonts** In fixed-width fonts, every character takes up the same amount of space. For example, the letters *w* and *i* take up the same amount of space on your page. In a proportional font, the *w* takes up more space that the *i*. Courier is a fixed-width font; Times is a proportional font.

6. When you are satisfied with the options you've chosen, click **OK** to return to the Properties dialog box.

7. To change the text color on your documents, click the **Colors** button. The Colors dialog box appears.

8. You control whether the browser uses the colors designated by the site or by you. If you want to change the color of your text, default background, or links, click the colored square next to **Text**, **Background**, **Visited**, or **Unvisited**.

Figure 7.5   Internet Explorer's Fonts dialog box.

9. When the Color selector opens (see Figure 7.6), select the color in which you want your links to appear. When you're satisfied with your choices, click **OK** to close the selection box.

10. Click **OK** to close the Colors dialog box.

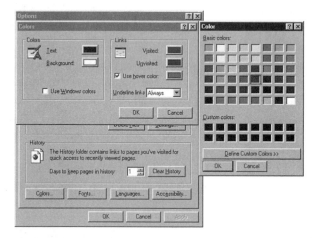

Figure 7.6   You can configure your default colors for all Web pages you visit.

In this lesson, you learned how to modify the appearance of Internet Explorer's toolbars, text, and links. In the next lesson, you will learn how to work with the Favorites menu.

Adding Links to the Favorites Menu

In this lesson, you learn about Microsoft's Favorites Links and how they make using the Internet easier.

What Are Favorites?

When you're cruising the Net, you will find that you return to certain sites frequently. As you may have noticed, Web addresses aren't exactly easy to remember. Remembering and typing something like **www.ncsa.uiuc.edu/SDG/ Software/Mosaic/Docs/whats-new.html** is quite a feat. Fortunately you don't have to type or remember it: You can add it to your list of favorite sites, or *bookmark* it.

Bookmarks on the Internet are just like bookmarks in your books: They mark your place. On the Internet, however, you don't even have to worry about losing your bookmark because Internet Explorer remembers your bookmark and adds it to a list of favorite Web sites. You can mark hundreds of sites on the Internet and call up any one of them whenever you want to visit it, which saves you from the chore of remembering and typing the site's URL.

There is one problem inherent in tracking hundreds of bookmarks. After a while you get so many that you can't read them all. Fortunately, Internet Explorer lets you organize your bookmarks by creating hierarchical folders that you can access from the menu bar. You can create a list of main topics that appear when you first drop down the Favorites menu. Then you can create a practically infinite number of subfolders with which to compartmentalize specific topic areas of Web sites.

Adding Favorites

When viewing a page that you're going to need in the future, you should bookmark it so it will be easy to find later. You don't have to be looking at a page to add it to your list of favorite sites. If you have only the address of the page, you can add it to your list by manually entering the address.

After you add some bookmarks to your list, you can use them to quickly jump from one location on the Internet to another. To bookmark a page, follow these steps:

1. While viewing a page you want to bookmark, open the **Favorites** menu and select **Add to Favorites**. The Add to Favorites dialog box appears (see Figure 8.1).

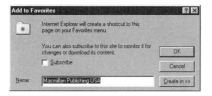

Figure 8.1 Add links to your Favorites menu using the Add to Favorites dialog box.

2. In the **Name** text box, type the name that you want Internet Explorer to display in your list of favorites.

3. Click **OK**, and Internet Explorer adds the site to the list. The next time you open the Favorites menu, you should see the site you just added. Figure 8.2 shows the Favorites menu with several folders and sites added.

 TIP **Adding a Link from a Page** If there's a link on the current page that you would like to add to your list of favorite sites, you can bookmark it. Right-click the link and select **Add to Favorites** from the shortcut menu.

Figure 8.2 Add pages to your Favorites list so you can access them quickly.

Accessing the Favorites Menu

Using bookmarks speeds up your work and provides an easy way to track specific information on the Internet. With a little practice, you can use the Favorites menu to jump around the Internet like a pro.

From any open Web site, open the **Favorites** menu and select the page you want to go to. Internet Explorer displays the specified page, which lets you know that your bookmark works.

CAUTION

No Page Loaded If you're looking at a site that matches the link you select, you won't see any changes to your screen, and you will get the impression that the link is broken. If this happens, change to another page and try the link again. If the link still doesn't work, you can edit it as described in Lesson 9.

Subscriptions

The Add to Favorites dialog box contains a check box with which you can subscribe to a particular site. *Subscriptions* enable you to automatically update your pages whenever a page's contents or address changes. They can cut down on the amount of time you spend trying to find a site or information that has been moved. You can configure Internet Explorer to download subscribed sites automatically based on a schedule that you set. For more information on subscriptions, check out Part 6, Lesson 8, "Managing Subscriptions."

In this lesson, you learned how to add to and use the Favorites list. In the next lesson, you will learn how organize, edit, and remove the links that you already have on the Favorites list.

Editing and Deleting Favorites

In this lesson, you learn how to organize, edit, and delete your existing Favorites links.

Editing the Favorites Menu

After you save twenty or thirty links to the Favorites menu, the list of saved sites can actually grow too large to fit on your Windows desktop. When the list of links becomes unmanageable, it's time for you to organize. Internet Explorer provides an interface for organizing your Favorites. In fact, putting the links in order is just like organizing files on your hard drive through the Windows Explorer. A link saved in Favorites is actually a file just like any other on your computer. Therefore, you can rename a link, move it to another folder, or delete it.

When you add a bookmark, Internet Explorer automatically copies the address and any relative configuration information and stores it in the link. Sometimes site addresses change or the site name changes slightly. When that happens, you need to edit the link information so that Internet Explorer knows where to find the site.

Internet Explorer provides a quick way to update your links. Follow these steps:

1. To edit an existing Favorites link, open the **Favorites** menu and select **Organize Favorites**.

2. In the Favorites folder's list of sites, right-click the link you want to edit and select **Properties** from the shortcut menu. As an example, suppose you've selected the Microsoft Home Page link.

3. When the link's properties sheet appears, click the **Internet Shortcut** tab.

4. Edit the information that has changed. For example, to change the address of the Microsoft Home Page link, you might place your cursor at the end of the information in the **Target URL** text box and add **/ie4/** (see Figure 9.1). This tells Internet Explorer that when you click the Microsoft Home Page link, it should open the Internet Explorer 4 page instead of the main Microsoft page.

5. When you finish changing the link's properties, click **Apply**. Then click **OK**.

Figure 9.1 You can update the necessary properties of links stored in the Favorites menu.

6. To rename the link so that it more closely matches its new destination, right-click the link's desktop shortcut icon and select **Rename** from the shortcut menu.

7. With the entire file name highlighted, type **Microsoft Internet Explorer 4 Information**. When you finish, press **Enter** to permanently rename the link.

Adding Folders to Organize Your Favorites

If you accumulate very many sites in your Favorites list, it might become difficult to keep track of them all. One of the easiest ways to do this is to place the site links in folders organized by topic. By default, Internet Explorer places all bookmarks in alphabetical order, which makes finding the link that you want very difficult after you have been using the product for a while.

Follow these steps to organize the links into folders:

1. From any open page, open the **Favorites** menu and select **Add to Favorites**.

2. Make any necessary changes to the name of the link, and then click the **Create In** button. This opens a small folders list below the Name field.

3. To add a new folder to your list of Favorites, click the **New Folder** button. Type a name for the folder (such as **Computers**) in the **Folder Name** text box, as shown in Figure 9.2. Then click **OK**. When you return to the Add to Favorites dialog box, your new folder appears in the list and is highlighted.

Figure 9.2 You can easily create new folders to store your Favorites links.

4. Click **OK** to place the named link in your Favorites list in the Computers folder. (To see if this worked, open the **Favorites** menu and select **Computers**.)

You might want to create a series of folders to contain all of your saved links. Some useful folders might include:

Search Engines	Kids Stuff	News Wires
Sports	Entertainment	Education
Government		

Nesting Folders in the Favorites Menu

To further organize the links in your Favorites list, you can take the existing links that you have saved in a folder and nest them into more specific categories. You do this by creating subfolders within the Favorites menu. Here's how:

1. Open the **Favorites** menu and double-click the folder in which you want to create subfolders. For example, click the **Computers** folder.

2. Create the appropriate new folders. Under Computers, you might create folders entitled **Software**, **Hardware**, and **Resource Info**.

3. Use drag-and-drop techniques to move the links from the first level folder into the subfolders or to move subfolders from one folder to another. (For example, you could place the Resource Info subfolder in the Software subfolder.)

4. Click **Close**. The next time you open the Favorites menu, you see your new hierarchy of folders and links. Figure 9.3 shows the list created in these examples.

Figure 9.3 You can nest folders to organize links.

Deleting Links in Favorites

The time might come when you find that you never use some of the links in your Favorites list, and they're creating a clutter on your machine. If that happens, it's time to remove them. Cleaning up your list makes finding specific sites easier and makes your list much more useful.

Follow these steps to delete unnecessary links:

1. Open the **Favorites** menu and select **Organize Favorites**.

2. Select the site entry you want to remove and press **Delete**.

3. When you're asked to confirm the deletion, click **Yes**.

Make Sure You Want to Delete When you delete a site link, you cannot retrieve it. Be sure you don't need that link before you remove it.

CAUTION

In this lesson, you learned how to edit, organize, and delete links in your Favorites menu. In the next lesson, you will learn how to use the variety of search tools located on the Internet to find information.

Searching the Internet

In this lesson, you learn about search engines and the search utilities that are available on the Internet.

Understanding Search Engines

The Internet is like a large library full of books, but it lacks anything remotely similar to the Dewey decimal system to organize these piles. Anyone that wants to can walk in and toss another book on a pile. Now add to that more than 50 million people attempting to find information. From a browser's point of view, this is a nightmare.

Fortunately, thanks to a few innovative people and organizations, the Internet has developed a card catalog of sorts. Using a series of massive indexes, sites created by these people enable you to search the Net. Not all Internet sites are listed with all of the search engines. Not all Internet sites are listed with even one search engine. But there are enough sites available to find anything you might be interested in.

There are two distinct types of search sites: search engines and site directories. Search engines (which often have such unusual names as crawler, spider, or worm) do periodic sweeping searches of all the sites they can find on the Internet, recording specific site information like titles, topics, summaries, subjects, and headings. The worm gathers all of the information and reports it back to the main database where the information is stored.

To allow browsers to access this information, a form is provided as part of an Internet page. The form gives you access to do both simple and complex searches. Let's say you wanted to find information on children's toys. You could perform a search on **toys**. But this would get you information on all toys, both for younger children and older teens. A better search might be **children** & **toys**. This would narrow down the search to just those sites that have both the words children and toys on them. By narrowing your search parameters, you can make better use of your time and the search engine's capabilities, and you'll find your information faster.

Site directories provide an indexed list of sites organized under a few specific headings such as computers, entertainment, regions, business, arts, recreation, and sports. Each of these headings is then broken down further. In the case of the regional heading, you might see a listing for North America, South America, Europe, and Asia. Of course each of these would be broken down into countries, and then states or provinces, and so on.

Using Internet Explorer's Search Button

Microsoft has tied its Internet search page directly to Internet Explorer, making it extraordinarily easy for users to find a search utility to help them find the information they need. This page provides a listing of many of the main search pages: AltaVista, Excite, Yahoo!, Infoseek, Lycos, and HotBot. You can enter your search criteria on the Microsoft site, and the results appear as if you were on the search engine's home page.

Follow these steps to search from the Microsoft site:

1. From any Web page, click the **Search** button on Internet Explorer's toolbar.
2. When the Microsoft Search column appears, open the **Select Provider** drop-down list and choose a search engine. For this example, select **AltaVista**.
3. Place your cursor in the AltaVista **Search** field and type **Toys**, as shown in Figure 10.1.
4. To run the search, click the **Submit** button.
5. When the AltaVista results page appears, click a link that looks interesting.

When AltaVista's results page loads, pay special attention to the number of *hits*, or links, that match the term "Toys." Take special notice that AltaVista found 100,000 matching entries. All of the entries that were returned contain the term you were searching for.

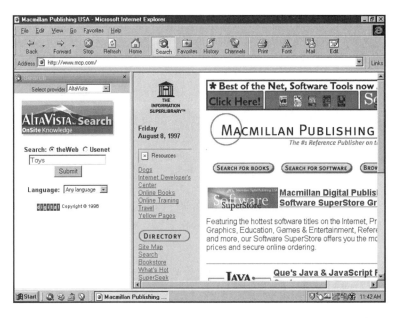

Figure 10.1   Internet Explorer provides you with an automatic link to AltaVista's search features.

Searching with Lycos

Lycos (**http://www.lycos.com**) is another great search engine that provides you with an advanced search tool. Lycos enables you to control the number of sites you will find, set a minimum score, and provides you with short summary results of each site. Lycos is one of the largest search engines, adding thousands of sites to their database each day.

Lycos does have one small problem. Because of its popularity and size, it is often quite slow. There are times when you won't get any response other than your browser telling you that the server is busy. Other times you may have to wait an extended period of time for the search page to load.

To search with Lycos, follow these steps:

1. In Microsoft's Search column, select **Lycos** from the **Service Provider** drop-down list (or type **www.lycos.com** in the Address box of Internet Explorer and press **Enter**).

2. Type your search term, such as **Children Toys**, in the search field, as shown in Figure 10.2. To run this search, click the **Go Get It** button.

Figure 10.2   Lycos enables you to search for multiple terms in a single search.

3. When the search is complete, you see a list of the sites that were found to contain those words. For each entry in the list, there is a very brief summary and the address of the page. Click a listing to go to that site.

 TIP   **Lycos Scores Pages**   Each site in Lycos is scored on a percentage scale, with 100% meaning that all of the words you searched for were found in the document. A score of 50% indicates that only half of the search words were found in the document.

Searching with E!Net Galaxy

E!Net Galaxy (**http:www.einet.net/**) is another directory-like search site. It offers a large list of sites broken down by major areas. One of the main differences between E!Net Galaxy and Yahoo! lies in the results it provides. E!Net Galaxy doesn't have nearly as large a site base as Yahoo, so you might find fewer hits. On the other hand, it provides detailed summaries of the sites that it does have. These summaries help you decide which sites you want to look at; you're not deciding based on the site name alone.

To search E!Net Galaxy, follow these steps:

1. From your current Web page, type **www.einet.net** in the Address field of Internet Explorer and press **Enter**.

2. The Galaxy directory is organized similarly to Yahoo. It has a series of main categories broken down into smaller subsections. Scroll through the page and click the **Community** link.

3. Scroll down through the community list until you find the **Family** heading. Notice that under this heading you have a list of topics that are related to family. Find the **Children** topic and select it.

4. Galaxy shows you a list of related topics (similar to the one shown in Figure 10.3), some articles, and a series of related collections of information. You can click a link to access the information that E!Net Galaxy makes available.

Figure 10.3   E!Net Galaxy provides you with a series of organized articles discussing a variety of topics.

E!Net also has a built-in search engine similar to the other search sites. Follow these steps to use it:

1. Click the **Advanced Search** link to open the form.
2. To perform a word search, type the search term (such as **children toy**) in the **Search For:** field and click the **Search** button.

E!Net Galaxy's word searches return a detailed summary of all the sites that were found (see Figure 10.4). Each site is listed, along with its score, the size of the site, a short excerpt of the text found on that page, the frequency of the most common words, and a quick outline of the site. You can't beat that type of information when you want to find the best site with the least amount of work.

Figure 10.4 E!Net provides search capabilities on all of its articles.

Searching with Infoseek

Another search engine that's accessible directly through the Internet Explorer Search page is Infoseek (**http://www.infoseek.com/**). Infoseek is very similar to Yahoo!. It provides both a search form and an indexed directory of sites to browse through. Infoseek also provides a link to Big Yellow (a national yellow pages directory), the latest national news, and even your local news.

Infoseek, although not as large as many of the search pages discussed in this lesson, has some very convenient features that make it useful for many individuals. Follow these steps to use Infoseek:

1. In Microsoft's Search column, open the **Service Provider** drop-down list and select **Infoseek**, or type **www.infoseek.com** in the Address field of Internet Explorer and press **Enter**. The main Infoseek screen appears, loaded with search forms and a site directory.

2. You can explore what Infoseek has to offer by clicking a category heading. For example, click the **Entertainment** heading. Infoseek provides a list of the other subtopics available under this heading (see Figure 10.5).

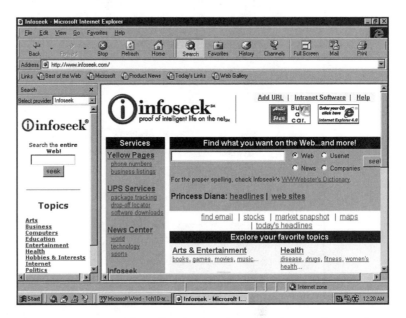

Figure 10.5   Infoseek provides a list of subtopics under the one that you have selected.

3. To look at Infoseek's word search utility, scroll to the bottom of your first search results screen. In the search field, type **Children's Toys**. This asks Infoseek to find only sites that have the phrase "Children's Toys," as opposed to sites with the individual words.

4. Click the **Seek** button. Infoseek runs the search and displays the search results. For each site it finds, it offers a short description of the site.

No Results If you don't get any hits for a search you perform, just go to another search engine and try again. You also can check back with each engine at a later date to see if they have added any new sites dealing with your **CAUTION** topic.

Searching with Yahoo!

Yahoo! (**http://www.yahoo.com**) is a large directory of Internet sites. Because Yahoo! has gained such popularity, other search sites have adopted its unique method of organizing information. Yahoo! uses a list-based index system that sorts information by main topics. Each topic is then broken into subtopics, and each subtopic is broken into sub-subtopics. You get the idea. Eventually you reach the specific pages you are looking for, without having to sort through thousands of Web sites that aren't really related to the information you're looking for.

Like the other search utilities, Yahoo! also has a standard search form that provides you with a method of reaching documents that might not be organized under appropriate headings. Follow these steps to use the Yahoo! search form:

1. From your current Web page, type **www.yahoo.com** in the Address field of Internet Explorer and press **Enter**, or select **Yahoo!** from the **Service Provider** drop-down list of search engines.

2. When Yahoo!'s search page loads, you see both a search field and a series of options to choose from (see Figure 10.6). For this example, select the **Intelligent Default** search method and select **Yahoo! Categories** as the search area.

3. Type **Kids Toys** in the search field and click **Search**.

TIP **Yahoo! Icons** Yahoo! uses a series of icons to give you information about sites. For example, a sunglasses icon notes cool sites with things that will interest most readers, and a New icon marks headings or sites that have been added or updated recently.

4. When you perform a word search, the results screen shows a series of links broken down into Yahoo! Categories, Yahoo! Sites, and AltaVista Web Pages. The Yahoo! Sites list shows you which categories the information was retrieved from, making it very easy to tell which main categories the information was found in. To see the rest of the list of sites, use the scroll bar.

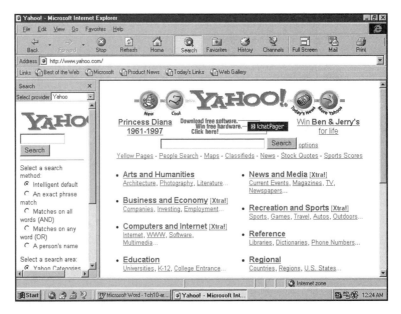

Figure 10.6   The Yahoo! search page.

5. All of the articles that are part of the Yahoo! system show the Yahoo! headers. This enables you to easily return to the main Yahoo! site in order to perform more searches. Click the **Yahoo!** link to return to the Yahoo! home page.

6. At the bottom of a list of Yahoo! sites, you may see a **Next Matches** link. This link specifies the number of other matches on the next page. Keep exploring these links until you find the information you want.

CAUTION

Too Many Hits!   Sometimes you will have thousands of matches, and scrolling through them 20 at a time is tiresome at best. Just remember that Yahoo! organizes the information by a scoring system. The highest scoring sites are, therefore, the ones most likely to have the information that you are looking for and are placed at the top of your results list.

Searching with Webcrawler

Webcrawler was one of the first search engines to appear on the Internet scene, and it is currently one of the most popular. Webcrawler is one of the few search engines you find that is consistently fast and rarely busy. It is one of the largest search engines in use, even though it (like other search engines) carries links to only a portion of the Web pages available on the Internet. The following steps show you how to use Webcrawler:

1. Place your cursor in the Address field below Internet Explorer's toolbar. Enter the address **www.Webcrawler.com** and press **Enter**. This loads the main Webcrawler search page.

2. In the Search field, type the words you want to search for, such as **toys**. You can narrow your search by using the & (ampersand) sign to combine search terms. If you want to look for complete phrases, enclose all of the words in quotation marks. For example, **children & toys** finds all pages that have both the words children and toys on them, but the words do not have to be next to each other or even in the same portion of the page. If you use **children's toys**, you only get the pages that have the phrase "children's toys," which narrows down your search dramatically. Once you have entered your search parameters, click **Search**.

3. The results of your search are displayed for you on a separate page. Each match is scored between 0 and 1000. A score of 1000 signifies the best matches and is located at the top of the list. To open any of those pages, simply click its link.

 TIP   **How Documents Are Scored**   The search engine scores the document by noting the number of times the search phrase is found in the document and whether the search phrase was found in the document title. Remember that even a document with a high score might not be useful for you.

In this lesson, you learned how to use a variety of the more popular search engines to find information. In the next lesson, you will use some specialized Internet directories to find specific types of information.

Searching Specialized Internet Directories

In this lesson, you learn how to use some of the specialized Internet directories to find specific types of information.

Finding Your Way with the Lycos Internet Roadmap

When the World Wide Web was first becoming heavily populated, search engines were simply used to track down other Web sites. Today's Web hosts a series of specialized search engines that provide specific information about people, places, or things on or off the Internet. One such search tool is the Lycos Internet Roadmap. Lycos provides detailed maps containing streets, highways, lakes, and rivers that can you can search to find a domain name, a ZIP code, or a specific street address.

CAUTION **Domain Name** A domain name is an address assigned to a computer on the Internet. Domain names are an easily recognizable form of Web site addresses, which are normally listed as numbers.

To use the Lycos Internet Roadmap, follow these steps:

1. Open the following address in Internet Explorer:

http://www.lycos.com/roadmap.html

2. Type **Redmond, WA** in the **City/State/ZIP** text box and press **Enter**. The map shown in Figure 11.1 appears on your screen.

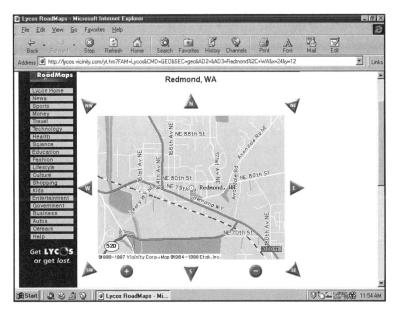

Figure 11.1 The Redmond, WA map shows the major streets in that fair city.

You can use the direction buttons located around the map to navigate to more locations around your destination. Each time you click a direction button, a new map is loaded in Internet Explorer to display your requested information. Follow these steps to try it out:

1. Click the + sign under the map. A new map is loaded, showing you more specific location information about Redmond.

2. Click the **S** button under the map to display a new map location just south of the one currently displayed.

When a new map is loaded off of a direction button, it is exactly one map grid away from the original destination. If you print multiple maps that are one grid away from each other, you can connect the maps to form a complete map of the area for easy directions.

A variety of other services also provide roadmaps to various locations. These include the following sites:

Yahoo! Maps (**http://www.yahoo.com/yahoo/**)

MapQuest (**http://www.mapquest.com/**)

69

InfoSeek StreetMaps (**http://www.infoseek.com/Facts?pg=maps.html**)

MapBlast (**http://www.mapblast.com/**)

MapsOnUs (**http://www.mapsonus.com/**)

Etak Guide (**http://www.etakguide.com/**)

Searching BigYellow: Yellow Pages Online

Microsoft's headquarters are located in Redmond, WA. Now that you are more familiar with the area around their offices, you might want to call there and ask them a question about Internet Explorer. If you don't have a copy of the yellow pages for the Redmond/Seattle area, you might want to use BigYellow (yellow pages online) as a quick and easy alternative. Here's how:

1. Open the following address in Internet Explorer:

   http://s11.bigyellow.com/home_infobutton.html

2. Enter **Microsoft** in the **Business Name** field, and the form shown in Figure 11.2 appears.

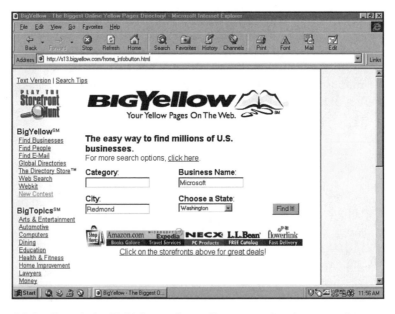

Figure 11.2   Search the BigYellow online yellow pages for phone numbers outside of your area.

3. Type **Redmond** in the **City** field, and then click **Find It!**. The results screen displays information about the Microsoft Corporation, including detailed listings for address, phone number, and yellow pages classifications.

You can also search BigYellow for a heading category or a product name. This can be useful if you're not sure exactly what you're looking for.

Finding Individuals with Four11

Have you ever wondered what happened to some old college buddies, or a former coworker, or that high school flame? If so, Four11 is for you. Four11 makes it easy to search for an individual's e-mail address with little information. Remember when you loaned Bill Gates lunch money in high school? Well, it's time to collect the interest!

Follow these steps to use Four11:

1. In Internet Explorer, go to the site located at **http://four11.com** (shown in Figure 11.3).

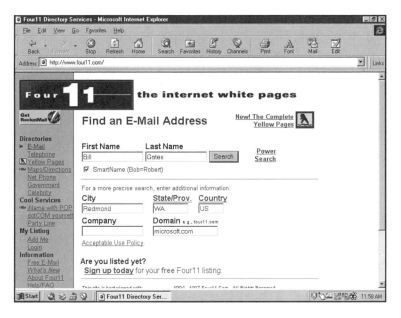

Figure 11.3 Four11's search engine.

2. In the text boxes, enter as much information as you can for the person you're looking for. For this example, enter the following:

First Name	**Bill**
Last Name	**Gates**
Domain Name	**microsoft.com**
City	**Redmond**
State	**WA**
Country	**US**

3. Click **Search** to obtain the results.

4. If you find the person you're looking for and you want to send him or her e-mail, simply click the link that applies to your search criteria the best.

Four11 has many advanced search features for members. Becoming a member of Four11 is free and enables you to search by high school or college attended, as well as to perform other specific searches.

Finding Individuals with the Switchboard

Just as you use Four11 to track down an individual's e-mail address (among other things), you can use the Switchboard to find a mailing address or a phone number. Switchboard seems to have one of the largest lists of both business and individual names available on the Internet. The following steps walk you through an example of how to use Switchboard:

1. Open Internet Explorer and go to **http://www.switchboard.com/**.

2. Click the **Find Business** link.

3. Type **Microsoft** in the **Business Name** field.

4. Type **Redmond** in the **City** field (as shown in Figure 11.4).

5. Click the **Search** button. When the search is complete, you see a full listing of information for the Microsoft corporation.

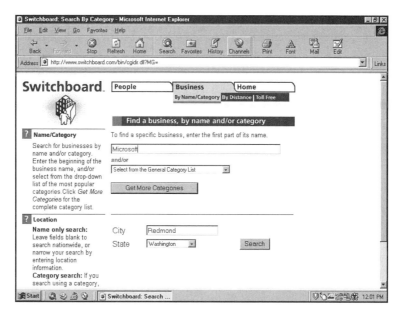

Figure 11.4 The Switchboard's Business search screen.

In this lesson, you learned how to find maps of locations on the Internet, look up yellow pages listings, and search for an individual's e-mail address with very little information. In the next lesson, you will learn how to download and save software from the Internet for your enjoyment and productivity.

Downloading Software with Internet Explorer

In this lesson, you learn how to find software on the Internet and download it onto your computer.

Saving Downloaded Files

Millions of users use the Internet to download files every day. There are hundreds of sites solely devoted to providing information and files for downloading. These sites provide either FTP or HTTP connection to the files, enabling you to make a copy of them on your computer. Most of these files are stored in one of a variety of compressed formats that reduce downloading time.

HTTP The HyperText Transport Protocol is used to define how information is passed between World Wide Web servers and Web browsers. This protocol identifies how that data is formatted and transmitted, and includes instructions for the actions Web servers and Internet Explorer should take in response to specified commands. For example, when you type an URL into Internet Explorer's Address field, an HTTP command is sent to the Web server, directing it to find and transmit the requested page. Many versions of HTTP are currently available. Most Web browsers and servers support HTTP 1.0; Internet Explorer supports the new version HTTP 1.

FTP File Transfer Protocol servers provide users with a wide range of files. FTP provides for both registered users and anonymous users. On anonymous systems, a user can log in using "anonymous" as his or her username. These sites do ask users to enter full e-mail addresses as passwords, and it is polite to cater to their request.

Before you download any software to your computer, you might want to check on a few things. First, you need a specific directory in which you can place your downloaded files. This directory shouldn't be used for any other purpose. Second, you will want to have some sort of virus detection software on your computer that checks your files when you download them and especially when you extract them.

The following steps assist you in creating a temporary download directory. If you already have a folder for downloading files, use its name in place of **temp** in the rest of this lesson.

1. Open the **Start** menu, select **Programs**, and select **Windows Explorer**.
2. Select the root of your C: drive.
3. Right-click the right pane and choose **Folder** and then **New** from the shortcut menu, as shown in Figure 12.1.

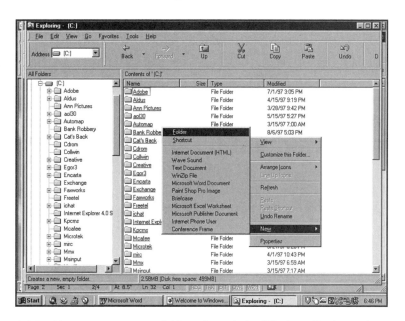

Figure 12.1 You can create new folders through the Windows Explorer shortcut menu.

4. Name the folder **Temp**, and then press **Enter**.

When you click a link to download software, a dialog box appears, asking for the location to which you want to save the file. Select the **Temp** directory that you created and choose **Open** to begin the download process.

If you don't already have a virus protection program, you can find a number of shareware programs (trial versions) at the sites listed in Table 12.1. You also can find a variety of other software packages available there.

Table 12.1   Software Download Sites

Site Name	URL Address
Alberts Ambry	www.alberts.com
Incredible Shareware Center	home.pi.net/~tuur/
Jumbo	www.jumbo.com
Shareware Central	www.q-d.com/swc.htm
shareware.com	www.shareware.com
The Software Shak	www.iminet.com/software/shak/
The Software Site	www.softsite.com/
The Ultimate Collection of Winsock Software (TUCOWS)	www.tucows.com
WinZip	www.winzip.com
ZD Net Software Library	www.zdnet.com/software/

Using Windows95.com

Windows95.com is a Web site dedicated to shareware and freeware for the Windows 95 and Windows NT 4.0 operating systems. Windows95.com contains links to thousands of games, device drivers, Internet-related software packages, and more. The managers of this site update it on a daily basis, so you can always be sure that you have access to the latest 32-bit software programs.

Shareware and Freeware   These are types of programs that are generally available for download and evaluation. Shareware programs aren't free. You do have to pay to use them past their preset trial limits. Shareware is generally 100 percent functional, but it contains time restrictions that stop the program from running after a specific date unless the program is registered. Freeware programs are free. They don't require registration and are fully functional when you download them.

Follow these steps to use Windows95.com:

1. Open Internet Explorer and go to **Windows95.com**.

2. Click the **32-bit Shareware** link in the middle of your screen (see Figure 12.2).

Figure 12.2 The Windows95.com home page.

The Windows95.com software directory is broken down into a variety of groups, including the following:

- **Newest Software.** This list, updated daily, provides you with a look at the newest software on the Internet.

- **Newest Icon's, Themes, etc.** This is a list of the latest desktop themes and icons to be used with the Microsoft Plus Pack's Desktop Theme generator.

- **Games.** Interested in Windows 95 entertainment? In this section, you can find every type of game from card games, to action games, to simulation and strategy games.

- **Utilities.** You can look for everything from anti-virus utilities to security systems.

- **Multimedia Tools.** In here, you can find a variety of utilities that enable you to work with videos, graphics, and sounds.

- **Productivity Tools**. This portion of the site contains a large number of applications that help you perform practically every task from faxing to creating birthday cards.

- **Personal Information Managers.** This section provides you with a variety of calendars, alarms, and computerized post-it notes to help you organize your day.

- **Network and Internet Tools**. This section provides you with immediate access to Internet- and Network-related files, such as Web browsers, e-mail clients, and Java resources.

As mentioned earlier, many of the files available for downloading off the Internet are compressed, or zipped up. To access these programs, you must have a decompression tool. One of the best shareware tools for performing this service is WinZip, an easy-to-use zip file program. WinZip takes the hassle out of the command line zip program PKZIP, giving you quick and easy one-button access to compressing and decompressing files.

 Zipped or Compressed Files   Zip refers to a specific method of compressing a file to achieve minimum file size and download time.

Follow these steps to download and install WinZip:

1. Select the **Utilities** link, and then choose **Compression Utilities** from the list of software types.

2. Scroll through the list of software and select the link for **WinZip for Windows 95**. This begins the download.

3. The file download wizard starts. Select the **Save This Program to Disk** option and click **OK**.

4. Select either your normal download directory or the Temp directory you created earlier in this lesson, and click **Save**.

5. After the file is downloaded, click **OK**. Then open the **Start** menu, select **Programs**, and select **Windows Explorer**.

6. Change to your **Temp** directory or another download directory.

7. Double-click **wzbeta32.exe** to begin the installation of WinZip.

WinZip provides you with a nice installation program that takes you step by step through the entire process. After the installation is complete, all of the compressed files that you download are associated to WinZip in your Windows 95 File Association chart. This saves you an extra step when you want to decompress a file. All you now have to do is download the compressed software. When you try to run it through Windows Explorer, WinZip automatically opens and shows you the contents of the file. This makes for very easy decompression of zipped files.

You can remove all of the files related to WinZip from your Temp download directory. After the program is installed, you don't need those files anymore. However, you might want to keep a copy of the wzbeta32.exe file in case something goes wrong later.

Take a few moments to look around Windows95.com and all of the software it makes available to you. If you like what you find there, you can add it to your list of favorite sites for easy access later.

Using Shareware.com

Shareware.com, like Windows95.com, provides you with access to thousands of software programs that you can download. Unlike Windows95.com, this site isn't limited to Windows-based software. From here, you can download Macintosh, OS/2, and even Atari shareware. Shareware.com uses a search engine to help you quickly locate files and programs that interest you. Follow these steps to use Shareware.com:

1. Open Internet Explorer and go to **http://shareware.com**.
2. Type **Games** in the Quick Search field, select the platform that you want to look in, and click the **Search** button.
3. Shareware.com provides you with a long list of programs that run under the operating system you specified. To download a game, click the link for the program you want.
4. You are taken to a list of FTP or HTTP sites from which you can download the game (see Figure 12.3). Select a download site near your present physical location. By using the servers located closest to you, you will be following netiquette and reducing the stress on other servers that might receive heavier use.

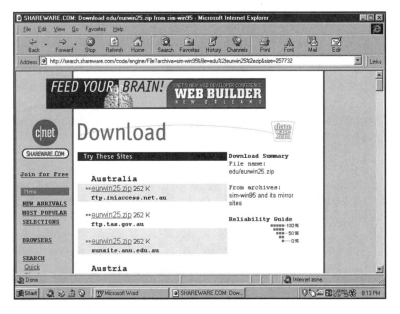

Figure 12.3 Select an FTP site from the list that Shareware.com provides you.

5. Internet Explorer's Download Wizard runs, just as it did when you down-loaded WinZip. You can install the game whenever you want by selecting its executable file from your Temp download directory.

6. To go back to the main page to begin a new search, click the **Back** button until you reach the main page, or click the **Shareware.com** home link located in the left-hand bar of your screen.

Shareware.com also has a link from the main page called "Most Popular Selections." You can click it to go to the most popular downloaded software. Here's how:

1. On the Shareware.com home page, click the **Most Popular Selections** link.

2. Select the operating system for which you want to look at software. For example, select **MS-Windows 95**.

3. Scroll through the list of popular software, and see if there's anything you would like to have. If you find something, click its link to download it.

Using TUCOWS

TUCOWS, which is short for The Ultimate Collection of Winsock Software (**www.tucows.com**), provides you with access to a wide variety of Internet-related software. Shown in Figure 12.4, TUCOWS offers many mirror sites to choose from. Each of these mirrors is organized slightly differently, but they all provide essentially the same software. Scroll through the main TUCOWS page and select the mirror site closest to you. You can then use that site's menus and search forms to find the software you want.

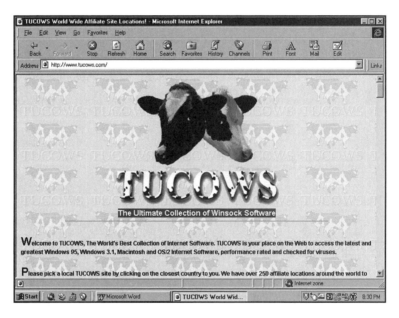

Figure 12.4 The main TUCOWS page provides you links to a wide variety of Internet-related software.

In this lesson, you learned how to find and download shareware from a variety of Internet software archives. In the next lesson, you will learn to download software from FTP sites.

Using Internet Explorer for FTP Downloads

In this lesson, you learn how to download files and other information directly from FTP sites using Internet Explorer.

An Introduction to FTP

Although it's one of the oldest services on the Internet, FTP (File Transfer Protocol) is still one of the most popular services. FTP servers are strict file servers. They aren't connected to any other computers on the Internet, and you can only connect to them if you know their addresses. The sole purpose of an FTP server is to store files that other individuals can copy to their computers. Most FTP servers have thousands of files available for users to access.

FTP servers generally break users into two groups: members and guests. Because you must log onto every FTP site, you have to provide the computer with a name and password. If you are a member, the site manager provides this information. FTP site members generally get access to more information than the guests. If you are a guest, you can still access information, but it probably won't be everything on the server.

Guests generally log in as *anonymous*. On an anonymous FTP site you can usually access services, but they ask one courtesy of you in return. Because you are an anonymous guest, most FTP sites ask you to use your full e-mail address as a password. Although this takes away the opportunity for the user to work under total anonymity, it makes it easier for the FTP manager to track who is using the site and what types of files that person likes. The more information about the user that the site manager has access to, the better he or she can meet the needs of the user.

Opening an FTP Site

Internet Explorer enables you to view FTP sites without any other software. There are actually several ways you can access these sites. The first and easiest is to select a link on a Web page that connects to the FTP server. When you retrieve files from the Internet you are often downloading them from FTP sites.

The second method you can use is to enter the address directly into Internet Explorer via either the Address field or the Open dialog box (shown in Figure 13.1). When you want to access an FTP site using this method, you have to enter an **ftp://** in front of the address you are accessing. For example, if you wanted to open Microsoft's FTP site (**ftp.microsoft.com**), you would type **ftp://ftp.microsoft.com**.

Figure 13.1 Internet Explorer enables you to open an FTP site from its Open dialog box.

TIP **Need a Prefix?** You don't have to type the prefix ftp://. Internet Explorer understands that any site address beginning with ftp is an FTP site, and it configures itself accordingly.

Retrieving an FTP File

FTP servers make thousands of files available to you on thousands of computers throughout the Internet. Most of these files are shareware or freeware programs, graphics, software applications, or informational files you can download. You will often need to download a file, but you might not have access to an FTP client. Internet Explorer provides you with an immediate way to access those files.

Although there are files on FTP servers that are readable only by MAC or UNIX machines, there are plenty available for your Windows machine. Follow these steps to download a file from an FTP site:

1. Open Macmillan Computer Publishing's FTP site by entering the URL **ftp://ftp.mcp.com/** in either the **Address** box or the Open dialog box. When this site opens (see Figure 13.2), you see the list of files at the root directory of Macmillan Computer Publishing's site.

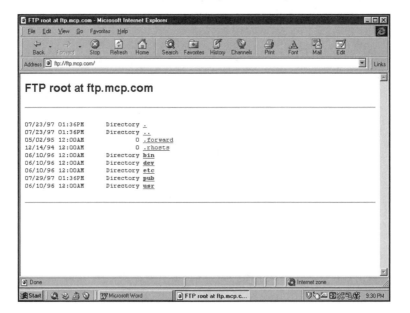

Figure 13.2 You can search Macmillan's archives for software.

TIP **Index.txt** Well-organized FTP sites provide an index file you can use to easily locate the file you're looking for. With this file at your fingertips, you don't have to worry about guessing which file is the right one for you or downloading the wrong file.

2. Select the **pub** link. This opens a list of the files in the /pub/ directory. To continue to download the software file, click the **software** link.

3. Click **Windows 95**.

4. To download the **htmlasst.zip** file, click its link. The Internet Explorer File Download Wizard starts to copy the file from the FTP server onto your computer (see Figure 13.3).

Figure 13.3 The File Download Wizard controls all of your download operations.

5. Click **OK**. Then select your **Temp** directory to store the file in and click **Save**.

6. When the file is completely downloaded, click **OK**.

Downloading an FTP file is just like downloading a file from a Web page. Simply click the file name and tell Internet Explorer where to save the file. After the file is downloaded, you can extract and install it by double-clicking its file name in Windows Explorer.

Almost all major software companies have an FTP site for product updates. Companies like Symantec and MacAffee use their FTP sites for distributing new virus lists for their anti-virus programs. Many times, new software is put into an FTP site for downloading before it is made available on the Web. You can be the envy of your office when you own the newest copy of Internet Explorer before your coworkers can even find it on the Web!

In this lesson, you learned how to use Internet Explorer as an FTP file retrieval client. In the next part, you will learn about ActiveX controls, plug-ins, and helper applications that you can use to enhance your Internet Explorer Web browser.

ActiveX Controls, Plug-Ins, and Add-Ons

Using Add-Ons and Plug-Ins

In this lesson, you learn about Web browser add-ons and plug-ins and how you can use them to enhance Internet Explorer's capabilities.

Enhancing Your Web Browser's Capabilities

Internet Explorer provides you with a robust, full-featured Web browser as you saw in Part 1 of this book; it's great for surfing the World Wide Web, searching for your favorite Web sites, and downloading great files and software. Believe it or not, you can extend and enhance the capabilities of Explorer with browser add-ons, and plug-ins (a third enhancement possibility—ActiveX Controls—are covered in Lesson 2 of this part).

Add-ons and plug-ins can function as Explorer enhancers, increasing the capabilities of the browser, or they can function as helper applications to provide support for things that Explorer cannot do, such as view certain file types, or play certain types of Web files, such as sound, video and multimedia files, within the browser window.

 Browser Add-On A mini-program that runs in conjunction with the Browser and supplies you with additional Internet tools, such as a special communication interface like Microsoft NetMeeting.

TERM   **Plug-In**   A mini-program that usually provides your Browser with the ability to play special content in the Web browser window, such as certain video, audio, and multimedia files.

You will find that add-ons and plug-ins can do a variety of things. For instance, add-ons such as NetMeeting, and Microsoft Chat enhance Explorer's communication abilities. Both of these add-ons provide you with the ability to communicate in real time with other users on the World Wide Web. Other add-ons and plug-ins like DirectShow, ShockWave (shown in Figure 1.1), and RealPlayer help Internet Explorer play video, audio, and multimedia files you can find on the Web.

Figure 1.1   Some add-ons and plug-ins, like ShockWave, enable you to play special Web files in the browser window.

 TIP   **Plug-In Evolution**   At one time, plug-ins were strictly associated with the Netscape Navigator Web browser. Now plug-ins have become synonymous with any program that helps your Web browser play special content within the browser window.

You will also come across add-ons and plug-ins that function outside of Internet Explorer as self-contained mini-programs. Microsoft DirectShow (shown in Figure 1.2) and NetShow play special Web files in special players outside of the Explorer Window.

Figure 1.2 Some add-ons and plug-ins, like DirectShow, play special Web files outside the browser window.

Microsoft FrontPage Express is an Explorer add-on that provides you with a HTML editor you can use to design your own Web pages. Web Server add-ons like the Microsoft Publishing Wizard and the Personal Web Server help you publish your FrontPage Express content and get it onto the Web.

Popular Explorer Add-Ons

Microsoft offers several excellent add-ons for Internet Explorer 4. These add-ons range from the highly visual and fun Microsoft Chat to Microsoft Wallet, an add-on you can use to make secure purchases over the Internet with your Explorer Web browser.

As far as Explorer add-ons go, which ones you need depends on the type of Explorer installation that you did. When you use Active Setup to download the files for Internet Explorer 4, you're given the option of three different installations:

Minimal: (14M) Includes Internet Explorer 4.0, Java Support, and the Microsoft Internet Connection Wizard.

Standard: (15M) Adds Microsoft Outlook™ Express and Microsoft Wallet to the Minimal installation.

Full: (22M) Adds Microsoft NetMeeting, NetShow, FrontPage Express, Microsoft Web Publishing Wizard, and Microsoft Chat 2.0 to the Standard installation.

Can't remember which installation you used? No problem, Microsoft offers a special Active Setup page for the various Internet Explorer add-ons that actually can tell you which components you have installed.

1. Connect to your Internet service provider or online service and open **Internet Explorer**.

2. In Internet Explorer's Address box, type: **www.microsoft.com/ie/ie40/ download/b2/x86/en/download/addon95.htm**.

3. Press **Enter**, and the Explorer Components Download page opens. The page asks you to wait while initialization takes place. Then the Active Setup dialog box appears and asks you if you want it to determine which Explorer components are installed on your computer, as shown in Figure 1.3.

4. Click **Yes** to continue. Active Setup determines the status of each of the Explorer add-on components listed on the page. Add-ons already installed on your computer are marked "Already Installed" in the status area to the right of the particular component's name.

Once you determine which add-ons aren't installed on your computer, you can use this Web page to select them and install them. For more information about downloading and installing a particular Explorer add-on, see the specific chapter in this part that covers it.

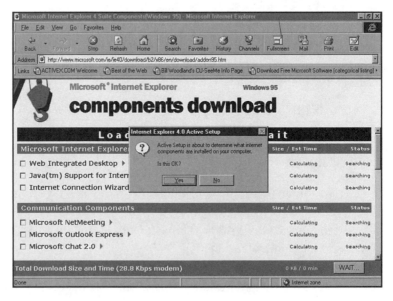

Figure 1.3   The Internet Explorer Components Download page will help you determine which Explorer add-ons you currently have installed.

Table 1.1 lists a number of popular Internet Explorer add-ons.

Table 1.1 Popular Internet Explorer Add-Ons

Add-On	Description
Microsoft NetMeeting	A communication program that provides an online environment for meetings. NetMeeting enables users to send audio and video information and communicate via an online Whiteboard.
Microsoft Outlook Express	The e-mail client software for Internet Explorer 4. Check out Section 3 of this book for all the ins and outs of Outlook Express.
Microsoft Chat	A fun chat environment that you can use to "talk" to other users in real time.
Microsoft NetShow	A multimedia tool that enables you to send or view online multimedia presentations.
DirectX	A multimedia add-on that provides support for highly graphical web environments and DirectX games.
Microsoft FrontPage Express	A web design tool that enables you to create your own Web pages.
Microsoft Publishing Wizard	A tool that helps you publish your Web pages on a computer network that uses Microsoft NT Server and the Internet Information Server software.
Personal Web Server	This Web publishing tool enables you to turn any computer into a Web server so others can access your Web pages.
Microsoft Wallet	A utility program that provides you with an easy and secure way to pay for online transactions over the Web.
Task Scheduler	An add-on that schedules common Windows maintenance programs such as ScanDisk and Disk Defragmenter and runs them automatically.

Popular Explorer Plug-Ins

Plug-ins also are a great way to enhance the abilities of Internet Explorer. A number of popular plug-ins exist and are described in Table 1.2.

Table 1.2 Popular Explorer Plug-Ins

Plug-In	Description
ActiveMovie	Microsoft's entry in the special Web content player category, ActiveMovie enables you to play audio and video files in a number of different formats.
ShockWave	Used to view and interact with special multimedia Web content that has been created in Macromedia Director or AuthorWare and then "shocked" for the Web.
Real Player	Access tons of Web audio and video using this popular player tool, including live broadcasts.
Apple QuickTime	Plays QuickTime movies from the Web. QuickTime is one of the most popular formats for Web video files.

Finding Add-Ons and Plug-Ins

A number of Web sites provide you with a library of Explorer add-ons and plug-ins. Because new add-ons and plug-ins are created constantly (sometimes there seems to be a total flood of new add-ons and plug-ins for a Web browser) it pays to check these sites periodically to see what new items have become available.

Obviously, the first place to check for new add-ons and news about Microsoft Internet Explorer 4 is its page at the Microsoft Web site. The address is **http:// www.microsoft.com/ie4/**.

Other sites that provide add-on and plug-in libraries include the following:

Stroud's Consummate Winsock Applications has a huge library of Internet related software. The add-ons and plug-ins on the site are updated often. The address for Stroud's is **http://cws.internet.com/**.

TUCOWS: The Ultimate Collection of Winsock Software has many mirror sites that you can use to download Internet-related files such as Web browser plug-ins. The main TUCOWS site is at **http:// www.tucows.com**. A TUCOWS mirror site sponsored by Sams Publishing can be found at **http://tucows.mcp.com/at**.

Shareware.com is another site where you can find plug-ins and add-ons and tons of other shareware and free ware. This site has a huge library of all the latest and greatest software available on the Web. You can connect to this site at **http://www.shareware.com**.

 TIP **Internet Search Engines**   You also can use any of the Internet search engines such as Yahoo (**www.yahoo.com**) and WebCrawler (**www.Webcrawler.com**) to find additional Explorer add-ons and plug-ins.

In this lesson, you became familiar with Internet Explorer add-ons and plug-ins—software programs that enhance and add to the capabilities of the Explorer Web browser. In the next lesson, you'll learn about ActiveX controls, another great way to extend the capabilities of Internet Explorer.

Using ActiveX Controls

In this lesson, you learn about ActiveX controls and how you can use them to expand the capabilities of the Internet Explorer Web browser.

Understanding ActiveX Controls

ActiveX controls supply you with another avenue for playing special Web files or running mini-applications inside the Internet Explorer window. ActiveX technology is not unlike the object linking and embedding (OLE) technology that you use to link and share information between applications in the Windows Environment. A specific ActiveX control links Internet Explorer to specific content or information in a special environment too—the World Wide Web.

The ActiveX controls that you install link Internet Explorer to the various helper applications that play the special Web content files or run certain mini-applications. It is the ActiveX control that turns the Internet Explorer into a container where the special Web content is seen or mini-applications are played.

ActiveX controls come in three types: controls that help the Web browser play special content, controls that run mini-programs on the Web, and special controls that are used by Web developers. For end-users like you and me the first two types of controls are the most important.

The ActiveX control for Adobe Acrobat is a good example of a control that's used to access special Web content. Acrobat enables you to view special Acrobat files, which are desktop published document files (.pdf files) used for many online manuals (see Figure 2.1). Acrobat files are often used because they can easily display special text formatting and graphics that would be difficult using HTML.

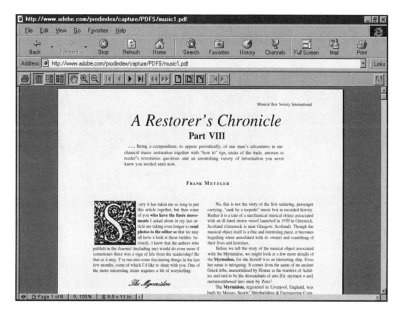

Figure 2.1 The ActiveX control for Adobe Acrobat allows you to open Acrobat files you find on the Web.

An example of another mini-application that plays special content in the browser window is the VRML ActiveX Control. This control enables you to navigate three-dimensional worlds inside the Internet Explorer window (see Figure 2.2).

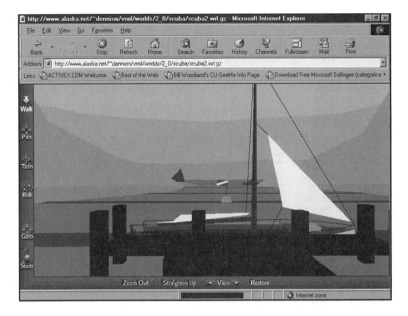

Figure 2.2   The VRML ActiveX Control works with Internet Explorer to place you in three-dimensional Web worlds.

Popular ActiveX Controls

A large number of ActiveX controls already exist for Internet Explorer. Some of the most popular controls are listed in Table 2.1

Table 2.1   ActiveX Controls

Control	Function
VRML ActiveX Control	This control enables you to explore three-dimensional Web sites and objects using Internet Explorer.
Adobe Acrobat	Access special desktop published Web content in the form of Adobe Acrobat files
ichat	This control turns the Internet Explorer window into a real-time chat environment.
ActiveX Uninstaller	This control utility enables you to remove unwanted ActiveX controls from your Internet Explorer installation.
Citrix Winframe Control	Enables you to share Windows-based information over the World Wide Web.

Where to Find ActiveX Controls

New ActiveX controls seem to appear almost daily. Fortunately, several sites that will help you keep up-to-date on your install base of ActiveX controls exist on the Web.

Microsoft provides an ActiveX site that serves as a good starting place in your search for ActiveX information and new and improved ActiveX controls. You can access this site at **http://microsoft.com/activex/gallery**.

Two other sites that are definitely worth checking out are ActiveX.com at **http://www.activex.com** and SoftSeek at **http://www.softseek.com/**. ActiveX.com houses a rapidly growing library of ActiveX controls that you can download. This site also provides excellent descriptions of the ActiveX controls that it houses. SoftSeek has a large library of ActiveX controls and gives you detailed descriptions of each of the controls. There are numerous links for downloading the listed ActiveX, providing you with more than one avenue to get the control onto your machine.

 TIP **ActiveX Control Files** TUCOWS and Stroud's also house libraries of ActiveX control files. For TUCOWS use the Brady Publishing mirror site at **http://tucows.mcp.com/**. For Stroud's go to **http://www.stroud.com**.

In this lesson, you found out what ActiveX controls are and where to find them on the Web. You also had an opportunity to learn about some of the more popular ActiveX controls for Internet Explorer. In the next lesson, you will download and install NetMeeting, a powerful Web communication tool add-on for Internet Explorer.

NetMeeting

In this lesson, you learn how to download, install, configure, and use NetMeeting, the Internet conferencing add-on.

Introducing NetMeeting

Microsoft NetMeeting is a conferencing add-on for Internet Explorer that enables you to share voice and video communications with others on the Internet in real-time. NetMeeting also offers a chat mode for users without audio or video capabilities and has a whiteboard that can be used and viewed by all the participants of the meeting.

Whiteboard An electronic version of a blackboard or whiteboard that can be viewed and used by all the participants in a "netmeeting."

Downloading and Installing NetMeeting

NetMeeting is available for free download on a number of sites on the World Wide Web, such as Stroud's Consummate Winsock site (**www.stroud.com**) and the TUCOWS site (**www.tucows.com**). Probably the easiest place to obtain the most current version, however, is Microsoft's Internet Explorer Component Download page.

The Component page uses Active Setup (the same type of setup that you experienced when downloading and setting up Internet Explorer 4). This page provides a list of the add-on components currently available.

1. Connect to the Internet via your Internet service provider or online service.

2. Double-click the **Internet** icon on the Windows Desktop to start Internet Explorer. In the Explorer Address box, type: **www.microsoft.com/ie/ie40/ download/b2/x86/en/download/addon95.htm**. Press **Enter** to continue. Allow active setup to determine which Explorer components you have installed on your computer by clicking **Yes**.

 TIP   **Add the Site**   You should definitely make the Component add-on site one of your Internet Explorer Favorites. Click the **Favorites** menu, and then click **Add to Favorites**.

3. To download NetMeeting, locate it in the add-on list under the Communications Components heading. Click the **NetMeeting** check box to select the software.

4. Click the **Next** button in the lower-right corner of the component download page.

 TIP   **Downloading Components**   If you want to download all the components available on this page, click the **Upgrade All** button on the upper-right corner of the download page.

5. Click the **Next** button in the lower-right corner of the component download page. The Component Confirmation and Installation page appears.

6. Select a download site near you using the site selection drop-down box.

7. Click the **Install Now** button. The Active Setup dialog box appears, showing the status of the download. Once the download is complete, this box shows the status of the installation of the add-on component, in this case NetMeeting.

8. An Active Setup Engine box appears, letting you know that the installation of NetMeeting was successful. Click **OK** to close the box. You are taken to the success page, a site that offers a number of links related to Internet Explorer.

Configuring NetMeeting

You must start NetMeeting to configure it. Because NetMeeting runs outside of Internet Explorer, you can close the Explorer window if you want.

TIP   **Offline Configuration**   You don't have to be online to configure NetMeeting.

To start NetMeeting for the first time and configure it, follow these steps:

1. Click the **Start** button and point to **Programs**, then point to the **Internet Explorer** group icon. Click the **NetMeeting** icon to start the software.

2. The NetMeeting Setup box appears. To continue, click the **Next** button. The next screen asks if you wish to connect to a directory server when you start NetMeeting. Directory servers provide a list of all the users that are connected to them—the means you use to "contact" other users when you "call" a meeting.

3. Click the directory server box and select one of the directory servers, as shown in Figure 3.1. Once you've selected the server, click the **Next** button to continue.

 TIP   **Use the Same Directory**   If you regularly communicate with other users, you should make sure that you all log onto the same directory server when you use NetMeeting. This makes it easier for you to find them and connect with them. You can also contact someone not on your server by switching to one of the other directory servers and double-clicking the name of the person you want to contact.

Figure 3.1   You must select a directory server to use as your home base when you connect with NetMeeting.

4. The next screen asks you to provide information about yourself, such as your name, e-mail address, and location. Fill in each of the boxes as shown in Figure 3.2, then click **Next**.

Figure 3.2 Providing your name and e-mail address for publication on the directory server makes it easier for others to contact you and set up meetings.

5. The next screen lets you know that the personal information you provided will be visible when you're logged onto the directory server. You are asked to categorize your information using a series of option buttons:
- For personal use (suitable for all ages)
- For business use (suitable for all ages)
- For adult-only use

6. Click the appropriate option button, then click **Next** to continue.

7. The next screen asks you to close all the programs that play or record sound so that NetMeeting can tune your computer's audio settings. Close any open sound programs and click the **Next** button.

8. The next screen asks you to specify the connection speed that you will use when connecting to the directory server—14400 bps modem, 28800 bps or faster modem, ISDN, or Local Area Network. Choose the appropriate option button and click **Next** to continue.

9. The next screen asks you to turn on your microphone and read aloud so that NetMeeting can set your audio settings. Click the **Start Recording** button when you're ready to begin reading and read the text on the screen (see Figure 3.3). When the tuning process is complete, the time remaining counter will register 0:00. Click **Next** to continue.

10. The next screen verifies that you have turned your settings and tells you to run this Wizard again if others have trouble hearing your audio when conferencing with NetMeeting. Click **Finish** to complete the NetMeeting configuration.

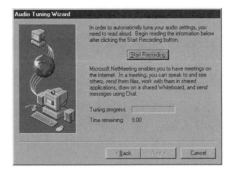

Figure 3.3   The NetMeeting audio tuning process makes sure that your outgoing audio is loud and clear when you communicate with others using NetMeeting.

TIP   **Retuning Audio Settings**   You can retune your audio settings at anytime, even when you're connected in an online meeting. In NetMeeting, click the **Tools** menu, then select **Auto Tuning Wizard**.

The main NetMeeting window opens after you complete the configuration. If you were online during the setup process, NetMeeting connects you to the directory server that you chose. If you were offline during the setup process, a message box appears, letting you know that NetMeeting could not connect. The next section discusses how to get online with NetMeeting and hold a meeting.

Holding an Online Meeting

You can hold an online meeting that has two or more participants (the number of participants is up to you). All the participants in the meeting can share the NetMeeting whiteboard, chat window, and software applications that have been designated for sharing.

To connect to a current meeting or initiate a new meeting with another individual, you use the NetMeeting Directory. This directory shows you all the people who are currently logged onto a particular name list server (see Figure 3.4).

Figure 3.4 The directory list shows you everyone currently online on a particular server.

Follow these steps to use the NetMeeting Directory:

1. Connect to the Internet and open **NetMeeting**. You will connect to the default directory server. Choose a name from the directory server. To invite a person to a meeting, double-click his or her name.

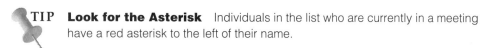

TIP **Look for the Asterisk** Individuals in the list who are currently in a meeting have a red asterisk to the left of their name.

2. NetMeeting attempts to connect you to the individual. If they accept your request for a meeting, the Current Call window opens and displays the name of the current participants (you and the other individual), as shown in Figure 3.5.

3. Once in the Current Call window, you can communicate via audio, the Chat window, the Whiteboard, or even video if your computer is equipped with a video camera.

4. If you have a microphone you can chat with the other participants via audio. Slide bars are available under the toolbar for increasing volume for you or the other participant's.

105

Figure 3.5 When the connection is made between meeting participants the Current Call window opens.

5. You also can converse with the other participant or participants via the Chat window. Click the **Chat** button on the toolbar to open it. When you open your Chat window it becomes available to all the users currently in the meeting (see Figure 3.6).

6. Type your text entry into the Message box and then press **Enter**, or click the **Send** button to the right of the Message box.

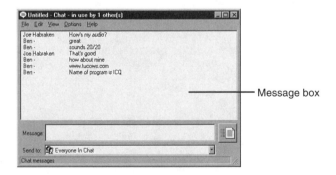

Message box

Figure 3.6 The Chat window provides users who don't have audio a way to communicate during the meeting.

7. The Whiteboard also provides another way of communicating. You can draw images, type text, or paste items onto the Whiteboard from other applications. To open the Whiteboard, click the **Whiteboard** button on the toolbar (see Figure 3.7).

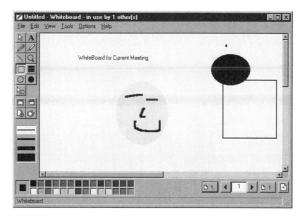

Figure 3.7 The NetMeeting Whiteboard provides another avenue of communication for your online meetings.

8. The Whiteboard also includes a remote pointer that you can use to point out items; all the participants can see this special pointer on their Whiteboards.

9. You also can share applications, such as Microsoft Excel (see Figure 3.8), with participants in your meeting. Open the application you want to share and then click the **Share** button on the NetMeeting toolbar.

10. Select the application that you wish to share. The application appears on the screen of all the meeting's participants, including your own. Changes can be made to the application by any of the participants.

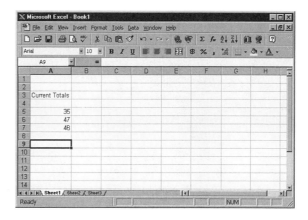

Figure 3.8 You can share applications during your meetings.

Online Video

NetMeeting is an extremely robust communication software package, offering a number of ways for you and others to communicate over the Internet. NetMeeting also supports video communication.

To take advantage of video communication all you need to do is outfit your computer with some type of video capture device, such as a digital video camera. Video from you and another participant will appear on the right side of the Call window when you're connected to a meeting (see Figure 3.9).

 TERM   **Video Capture Device**   This can be any device that provides a video feed to your computer. You can purchase a small inexpensive digital camera to connect to your printer port. Or you can buy a video input card to which you connect your home video camera.

You can only send or receive video information from one participant at a time (the same goes for NetMeeting audio). However, you can switch from participant to participant with the Tools menu's Switch Audio and Video command.

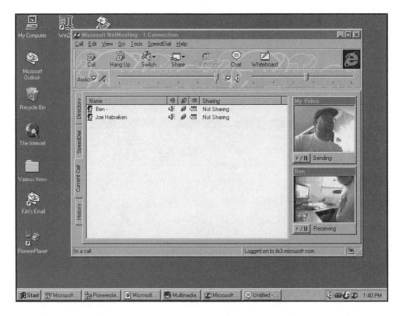

Figure 3.9   You can send and receive video using NetMeeting.

The great thing about NetMeeting is that you can receive video from another participant even if you don't have your own video device. You may notice, however, that sending and receiving video has a negative effect on the audio quality of the meeting.

Changing Configuration Settings

You can change any of your NetMeeting configuration settings while you're online and involved in a Meeting. The configuration settings are reached via the Tools menu and the Options command.

The Options dialog box contains six tabs:

General   This tab is where you set your communication speed. It also enables you to include a NetMeeting icon on the taskbar and set NetMeeting to automatically answer incoming calls.

My Information   This tab is where you can edit the information, such as your name and e-mail address, that you entered when you first configured NetMeeting.

Calling   On this tab, you can change the server that you log onto and have NetMeeting automatically create SpeedDial entries for all the users with whom you're in contact.

Audio   You can run the Audio Tuning Wizard from this tab, or you can set your audio sensitivity manually. Users without audio capability will not have the Audio tab available in the Options window.

Video   This tab enables you to change the size of the video windows and change the video parameters associated with your video source.

Protocols   Choose the communication protocols that you use with NetMeeting. You can choose to connect directly via modem, use TCP/IP over the NetMeeting servers, or connect through your local area network using IPX.

CAUTION   **Changing Settings**   NetMeeting does a pretty good job of configuring itself for use on your computer. You should only change option settings if you fully understand what the change will do to NetMeeting's performance and ability to communicate.

When you're ready to complete an online meeting, inform the other participants. The rules of courtesy that you follow for an online meeting should be the same as those you would follow for a face-to-face meeting. Upon concluding the meeting, click the **Hang Up** button. To close NetMeeting click the **File** menu, and then select **Exit**.

In this lesson, you learned how to download, configure, and use Microsoft NetMeeting. In the next lesson, you will learn how to download, install, and use Microsoft Chat, which is the chat client for Internet Explorer.

Microsoft Chat

In this lesson, you download and configure Microsoft Chat. Then you connect and participate in a real-time chat with other users.

Introducing Microsoft Chat

Microsoft Chat is a chat client that enables you to communicate in real-time with other people on the Internet. The ability to chat on the Internet has been around for a long time. In most cases, you enter a chat room using chat software and the text messages that are sent between the various participants are displayed in a text window. Microsoft Chat adds a visual (and often humorous) aspect to the chat environment. All the participants are represented by comic strip characters.

The chat session takes the form of a comic strip. The text messages from each of the participants are displayed as word balloons over the character that they are using to represent themselves.

You also can run Microsoft chat in a text only mode if you find the comic strip characters too distracting. However, their presence can take a chat session about nuclear physics and turn it into a humorous event.

The great thing about Microsoft Chat is that it's free. Microsoft provides it free and clear for anyone to use as his or her chat client.

Downloading and Installing Microsoft Chat

You can download Microsoft Chat from its own Home Page. The Microsoft Chat page also provides you with information about recent developments and tips and tricks involving their product.

1. Log on to the Internet via your Internet service provider or online service and then start Internet Explorer.

2. In the Internet Explorer Address box, type **http://www.microsoft.com/ie/ chat/** and press **Enter**. The Microsoft Chat Home Page opens, as shown in Figure 4.1.

TIP   **Another Download Method**   You also can use Active Setup on the Internet Explorer 4 component page at **http://www.microsoft.com/ie/ie40/ download/b2/x86/en/download/addon95.htm** to download and install Microsoft Chat.

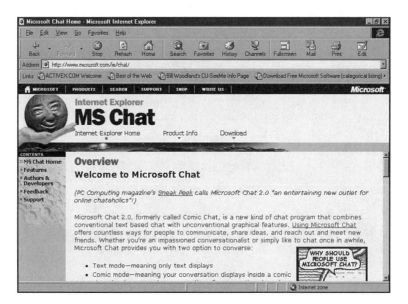

Figure 4.1   The Microsoft Chat Home Page provides you with information about this chat client software and links for downloading the product.

3. Click the **Download** link at the top of the page. A drop-down box will list items available for download.

4. Select the **Microsoft Chat** link in the Download drop-down box. The Microsoft Chat Download page appears. Scroll down the page until you see the version drop-down box. You can download Microsoft Chat as a stand-alone product or as an add-on for Internet Explorer.

5. To download Microsoft Chat as an Explorer add-on, select **Microsoft Chat for Internet Explorer Windows 95 and NT 4.0** in the drop-down box, as shown in Figure 4.2. Click the **Next** button to continue.

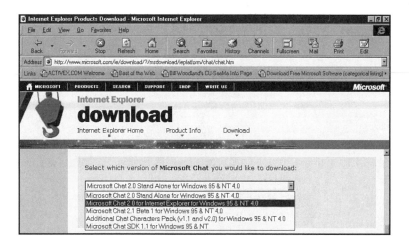

Figure 4.2 Select the version of Microsoft Chat you want to download.

6. The next page contains a drop-down box that enables you to select the language version of Microsoft Chat you want to use. The default choice is English, so click the **Next** button.

7. The next page offers a list of download sites for Microsoft Chat. Select the site nearest you and click the link.

8. An Internet Explorer file download box appears. If you want to download the Microsoft Chat file and install it later, click the **Save This Program to Disk** option button. To install Microsoft Chat immediately after downloading the file, click the **Run This Program from the Internet** option button. Then click **OK** to continue.

9. The File download status box appears, showing the status of the download. Once the download is complete, a Security Warning message may appear on your screen. If so, click **Yes** to continue.

10. The Install Microsoft Chat 2.0 box appears; click **yes** to install the software. When the license agreement box appears, click **yes** to continue.

11. You will be asked where you would like to install the Chat software. You can choose a new folder using Browse or install to the default folder by clicking **OK**.

12. The files download to the folder. To complete the installation, click **OK** in the Microsoft Chat thank you box.

Configuring Microsoft Chat

Once Chat is installed you're ready to start the software. The first time you start the software you need to specify a nickname that you will use when you're logged onto a chat session. You also will need to choose a character that you will appear as when you're in Chat.

Follow these steps to configure Microsoft Chat:

1. To start Microsoft Chat, click the **Start** button, point at Programs, and then click the **Microsoft Chat** icon. Since this is the first time you've started Microsoft Chat, it asks you to choose a nickname to use during chat sessions, as shown in Figure 4.3.

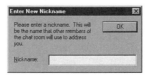

Figure 4.3   Type the nickname you want to use in your Microsoft Chat sessions.

2. Type your nickname and then click **OK**. The Connect box will appear. This box requires you to pick a server that you will use to log into chat sessions. Select one of the available servers from the drop-down list, as shown in Figure 4.4.

Figure 4.4   Select a server to log in to.

 Chat Server   A computer that you log on to for Microsoft Chat sessions. The server holds all the different chat rooms that you converse in.

3. After you've selected a server, click the **OK** button. You are connected to the server and placed in the default chat room, #Comic_Chat. If other users are in the chat room, you will notice that their chat input unfolds as a comic strip. The default comic character, Anna (see Figure 4.5), represents you.

Figure 4.5 The Chat window shows your current character and the comic strip for the current chat session, and it provides a list of the participants currently chatting.

Choosing a Character

Before you can really get involved in heavy-duty chatting, you will want to select your own character for use in the chat rooms. Setting the character and other Chat options are all done in the Microsoft Chat Options dialog box. Here's how:

1. Click the **View** menu, then select **Options**. The Options dialog box has tabs for personal information, the background used, settings for sounds and other chat parameters, and the character you wish to use.

2. Click the **Character** tab. Chat provides you with a number of character possibilities. To preview the characters, click each one's name, and the character appears in the Preview box, as shown in Figure 4.6.

3. Once you've selected your character from the list, you can also select their current expression from the Expression Palette. This Palette shows a range of emotions from happy to sad to angry. Click the expression you want to start your character with, and then click **OK** to return to the Microsoft Chat window. Your new character is displayed in the Character box.

TIP **Changing Character Expression** You can change the expression of your character using the Expression Palette below your character's identity box. Just click the expression you want to use.

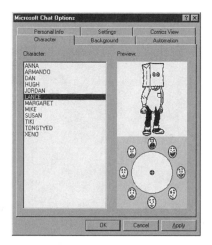

Figure 4.6 The Options dialog box enables you to choose your character for Microsoft Chat.

Chatting in Microsoft Chat

Once you've selected your character and edited any of the other options you want to change, you're ready to chat. Chatting is done by typing your message in the chat text box. You can then send the message by pressing **Enter** or clicking **Say with the Mouse**. Your character will appear in the comic strip and your chat entry will appear as a word balloon over your character's head (see Figure 4.7).

The other characters currently in the chat room are displayed in a participants list at the top right of the chat screen. You can scroll through the list of participants with the scroll bar. Your character appears in the box below the participant list, and beneath your character is the Expression Palette, which you can use to convey emotions as you chat.

Character box   Participant list   Expression palette

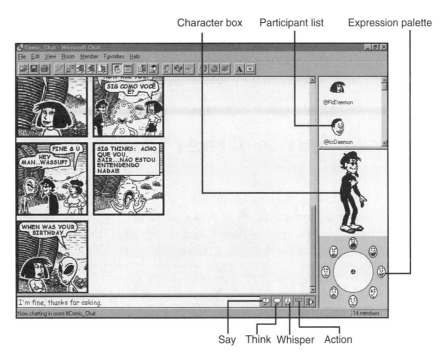

Say   Think Whisper Action

Figure 4.7   The Chat Room window is where all the comic action takes place.

You also can send your text messages so that they appear differently in the comic strip. You do this by clicking the appropriate send button to the right of the chat text box (see Figure 4.7). These are the possibilities:

Say displays your text as a word balloon over the character.

Think displays your text in a thought balloon over the character.

Whisper lets you send messages to selected characters. Select the character or characters in the participant list before sending the Whisper text. Whispered text will only appear in the cartoon viewed by the selected participants.

Action displays your chat text in the upper-left corner of the comic strip frame.

To start a new chat session, follow these steps:

1. Connect to your Internet service provider or online service. Start Microsoft Chat via the Start menu.

117

2. Once you're connected to the default chat room, type your text entries in the chat text box. Then select the **Say** button or another button to enter the text in the comic strip.

3. When you've completed your chat session, say your good-byes and then click **File, Exit** to close Microsoft Chat.

Connecting to Other Chat Servers and Rooms

You also can connect to a number of other chat servers that house many different chat rooms. To connect to a chat server other than your default, click the **File** menu and then select **New Connection**. The Connect box appears. Choose the server you want to log on to from the drop-down list provided and then click **OK**.

You will find that each of the chat servers available for Microsoft Chat also hold a large number of different chat rooms that you can access. It's easy to select a new channel using the Room list. Follow these steps:

1. Click the **Room** menu, then select **Room List**. This lists shows all the chat rooms available on the current chat server (see Figure 4.8).

2. Scroll down through the list. The name of a particular chat room will clue you into the subject matter and type of chatting that takes place there.

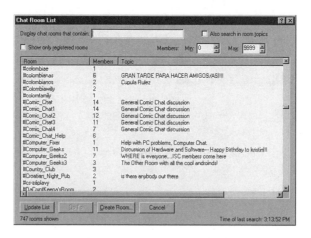

Figure 4.8   The Room list enables you to choose which chat room to enter.

3. When you're ready to choose a chat room, double-click the name. You are returned to the chat window and the chat session begins. Remember that others have already been in the room, so you are coming into things in the middle of the conversation.

When you've concluded a chat session, you can disconnect from the room via the Room menu, or you can exit Comic Chat.

When using Comic Chat, you should follow the general rules for Internet real-time communications.

- Don't type in uppercase; this is considered shouting.

- Choose your words carefully. Sometimes sarcasm and humor go right over peoples' heads. Use the character expressions to help make your chat entries clear.

- Don't deliberately insult other participants. It's not a bad idea to keep the Internet a kind and gentle place. Besides, insulting people on the Net can lead to retaliation that can be pretty unpleasant.

- Chat groups are places to talk and have fun. They're not a place to advertise. If you have a business or service, create a home page. Keep chat groups free of advertising.

In this lesson, you learned how to download, install, and use Microsoft Chat for real-time Internet chatting. In the next lesson, you will learn about DirectShow, an on-demand video and audio player add-on.

DirectShow/ActiveMovie

In this lesson, you download the Internet Explorer video and
audio player DirectShow (formerly known as ActiveMovie).
You learn how to install DirectShow and use it to play video and audio files on the World Wide Web.

Introducing DirectShow

The World Wide Web is chock full of special content—files that can't be opened or played directly by Internet Explorer. Much of the special content is audio and video files that you need an Internet Explorer add-on to play. One of the newest (and pretty close to the best) add-ons for playing audio and video files from the Web is Microsoft DirectShow (sometimes referred to as ActiveMovie).

DirectShow can play a number of files formats; it can handle the AVI, MPEG, and QuickTime video formats and the WAV, AU, AIFF, and MIDI sound formats. DirectShow plays the files in a special movie or sound window outside the Internet Explorer window.

DirectShow works with Internet Explorer because of an ActiveX control. The DirectShow control is initiated each time Internet Explorer comes across content specific to the control, such as video or audio files.

Downloading and Installing DirectShow

Microsoft DirectShow (as ActiveMovie) is available on several sites on the Internet, including Stroud's and TUCOWS. The easiest place to download DirectShow is the Microsoft Internet Explorer Components page.

TIP **Check for Installation** Use the Active Setup feature on Microsoft's Internet Explorer Component page to see if DirectShow is already installed on your computer. If so, you don't need to install it again, and you can skip ahead to the section on Using DirectShow in this lesson.

Follow these steps to download DirectShow:

1. Connect to the Internet and open Internet Explorer. In the Address box, type the following: **http://www.microsoft.com/ie/ie40/download/b2/x86/ en/download/addon95.htm.** Press **Enter**.

2. The Internet Explorer Download page appears . The Active Setup box appears and asks you if you want to have the currently installed add-ons identified. Click **Yes** to continue (or click **No** if you are sure that DirectShow is not installed).

3. Scroll down through the list of add-ons until you come to DirectShow. Click its check box to select it for installation, and then click **Next** to continue.

4. The Components Confirmation and Installation page appears, as shown in Figure 5.1. It lists the component you want to install, in this case, DirectShow. Choose a download site for the software from the drop-down box.

5. Click **Install Now**. DirectShow is downloaded and installed.

6. The Active Setup dialog box tracks the status of the download and installation process. When it's finished, you are notified that the download and installation was a success. Click **OK** to close the Active Setup notification box.

TIP **Background Information** If you would like to do some exhaustive reading on Microsoft DirectShow (ActiveMovie) and how it works, the Microsoft DirectX site is the place for you. You can find the site and all kinds of background info on DirectShow at **www.microsoft.com/DirectX/default.asp**.

CAUTION **Don't Download Older Versions** Older versions of ActiveMovie are avail-able at a number of download sites on the Internet. Don't download and install these versions of this ActiveX control. It will override your installation of DirectShow, and you won't be able to play video or sound files using Internet Explorer. To find the latest versions of Explorer add-ons, check the site **www.microsoft.com/ie4**.

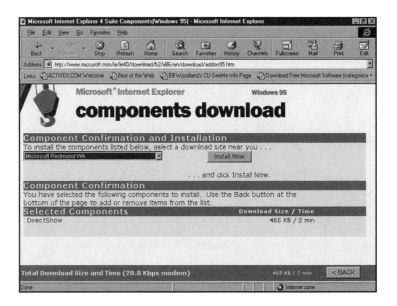

Figure 5.1   Choose a download site, and Active Setup downloads and installs the DirectShow component.

Using DirectShow

Now that DirectShow is installed, it will provide audio and video player support for Internet Explorer. DirectShow isn't the kind of software that you launch using the Windows Start menu or by clicking a particular button on the Internet Explorer toolbar. DirectShow is activated when you click a link for an audio or video file when you're browsing the Web using Internet Explorer.

This activation of DirectShow is accomplished because of the ActiveX control that ties Internet Explorer and DirectShow together and allows them to communicate. The great thing about this collaboration between DirectShow and Internet Explorer is that you will be able to play most of the video and sound files you encounter on the Web.

Playing Sound Files

The best way to test DirectShow is to go to some Web sites that contain special content files, such as audio or video files. Playing sound files can be a lot of fun, especially if the sounds are ones you want to hear. A very good place to test your Active Movie installation is The Sound America Home Page. This site has over 11,000 sound files on everything from television show theme songs to cartoon sound effects.

Follow these steps to test DirectShow by playing a sound file:

1. Type **http://soundamerica.com/** in Internet Explorer's Address box and press **Enter**.

2. The Sound America Home Page opens (see Figure 5.2). To play a particular sound file, select a category from the menu on the left of the page. For instance, click **Cartoons**.

Figure 5.2 The Sound America Home Page offers a huge library of sound files.

3. On the next page, select a cartoon favorite such as Bullwinkle. A list of Wav files are displayed for the cartoon you select. Click a WAV file to play it.

4. The DirectShow sound player appears and loads the sound file. Once the file is loaded, it plays. Figure 5.3 shows the screen while a DirectShow sound is being played.

Figure 5.3   DirectShow uses the sound player to play sound files you encounter on the Web.

Playing Video Files

You will find that a lot of Web pages contain links to video files in a variety of formats. DirectShow can play most of the video formats. The best way to test DirectShow's video playing abilities is to locate some video files on the Web and play them. A good place to put DirectShow through its paces is the Official X-Files Home Page, which contains a large number of video clips from the television show. Follow these steps:

1. In the Internet Explorer address box type **www.thex-files.com/** and press **Enter**. Click the **Case Files** link. The Case File page provides a link to the Episode Guide, which provides selected video promos from many of the episodes.

2. Click the **Episode Guide** link. Click any of the Episode links on this page. Each Episode offers a short video promo. Click the **Video camera** link.

3. DirectShow is activated and downloads the video file to the DirectShow player. Video files can be quite large, so you may have to wait for some time as the file is downloaded. Once the file is downloaded, DirectShow opens a video window and plays the video, as shown in Figure 5.4.

Figure 5.4   DirectShow uses the video player to play video files you encounter on the Web.

As you can see, DirectShow is an on-demand sound and video player add-on for Internet Explorer and is only used when sound or video file must be played. A number of the ActiveX control add-ons for Internet Explorer function in this manner, waiting in the wings until Internet Explorer needs them.

In this lesson, you downloaded and installed Microsoft DirectShow. You also used DirectShow to play sound and video files on the World Wide Web. In the next lesson, you will learn about Microsoft NetShow, a tool for sending and receiving multimedia presentations over the Internet.

NetShow

6

In this lesson, you download and install Microsoft NetShow. You also learn how to use NetShow to view multimedia presentations over the Internet.

Introducing NetShow

Microsoft NetShow is an online multimedia presentation broadcaster. It enables you to view and develop Web content that contains graphics, audio, video, and animation. Microsoft touts NetShow as the perfect tool for businesses and individuals who wish to broadcast multimedia content over the Web.

 TIP **Further Information** NetShow can be downloaded as a viewer, or you can download the NetShow server and tools software to develop your own multimedia content for the Web. For more about these two NetShow flavors, check out **http://www.microsoft.com/NetShow/**.

For end-users like us, however, NetShow is more importantly a viewer and player that enables us to see and hear these Web-based presentations. NetShow plays the multimedia content in streams, which means you don't have to wait for the whole presentation to download to your computer before it starts playing. This makes NetShow perfect for real-time presentations over the Net. NetShow presentations can even consist of synchronized audio and still pictures, making the old-fashioned slide show obsolete.

Downloading and Installing NetShow

NetShow is an add-on component for Internet Explorer. Therefore, it is available for download and installation from the Microsoft Internet Explorer Component Page.

Follow these steps to download and install NetShow:

1. Connect to the Internet and open Internet Explorer. In the Address box, type **www.microsoft.com/ie/ie40/download/b2/x86/en/download/ addon95.htm**. Press **Enter**.

2. The Internet Explorer Download page appears. The Active Setup box appears and asks if you want to have the currently installed add-ons identified. Click **Yes** to continue.

3. Scroll down through the list of add-ons until you come to NetShow. Click its check box to select it for installation, as shown in Figure 6.1, then click **Next** to continue.

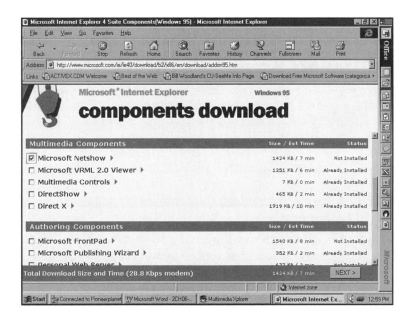

Figure 6.1 Click the NetShow check box and then click Next to have Active Setup download and install NetShow on your computer.

4. The next page provides you with a drop-down box of download sites. Select the download site nearest you and click the **Install Now** button.

5. The Active Setup dialog box tracks the status of the download and installation process. When it's done, you are notified that the download and installation was a success (see Figure 6.2). Click **OK** to close the Active Setup notification box.

Figure 6.2 Active Setup lets you know that the download and installation of NetShow was a success.

Using Microsoft NetShow

The NetShow player is now installed on your computer. NetShow can be used in two different ways. You can play NetShow files that have been stored on your computer, or you can play NetShow files and live content on the Internet.

Playing Saved NetShow Files

To play NetShow files that have been saved to your computer, you use NetShow like any other stand-alone audio or video player that you use in Windows. You start NetShow and then open the multimedia file you want to play. (NetShow plays NetShow multimedia files only in the .asf and .asx format.)

To start NetShow and play a file on your computer, follow these steps:

1. Click the **Start** button, then point to **Programs**. Point to the **Internet Explorer** group on the Program menu.

2. Click the **NetShow Player** icon to start NetShow. The NetShow Player appears on your desktop, as shown in Figure 6.3.

Figure 6.3 NetShow can be used to play saved multimedia files that you store on your computer.

3. To open a saved multimedia file, click the **File** menu, then click **Open File**.

4. In the Open dialog box, select the file and click **Open**. The presentation plays in the NetShow window, as shown in Figure 6.4.

Figure 6.4 NetShow plays presentation files in the NetShow window.

Playing NetShow Presentations on the Web

While it may be useful to save NetShow presentations to your computer for later play, the real power of NetShow is playing presentations directly from the Web. NetShow can play saved files on the Web or play live content.

You will find that NetShow operates in much the same way that DirectShow does when you use it as an Internet Explorer helper application. When you click on a link to multimedia files or a link to a live presentation, NetShow automatically starts, loads the content, and plays it for you.

One of the best places to find NetShow content is the NetShow Gallery at **http://www.microsoft.com/netshow/examples.htm**. This site contains examples of saved presentations and live presentations that you can play with NetShow.

Make sure you're online and have Internet Explorer open. Type **http://www.microsoft.com/netshow/examples.htm** in the Address box and then press **Enter**.

The NetShow Gallery page has a number of tabs that take you to pages containing links to NetShow content. You can choose from Samples, Live Events, Past Events, and Always Live events (see Figure 6.5).

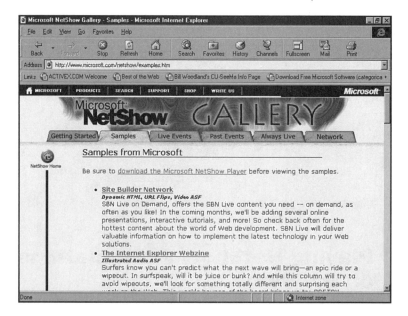

Figure 6.5 The NetShow Gallery page on the World Wide Web provides you with links to saved and live presentations that you can view with NetShow.

You can do any of the following things:

- Click the **Samples** tab to check out some of the saved presentations that you can play with NetShow. The Samples include presentations on how to make Espresso, how to get to Microsoft Headquarters from the Seattle Airport, and other presentations that show off NetShow's ability to deliver online multimedia content.

- Click the **How To Make Espresso** link. The NetShow window opens, and the Espresso presentation are played.

- Click the **Live Event** tab, and you can view links to upcoming live broadcasts on a variety of subjects. The date and the time for the broadcast is included for your reference.

- If you can't wait for one of the live events, click the **Always Live** tab. This page gives you links to a number of broadcasts that are always live.

- Click the **C-Span** link on this page to get a live video feed from Capital Hill. When you click the link you're taken to the AudioNet sponsored C-Span page. A C-Span Online box in the center of the page contains the link to a live NetShow broadcast.

- Click the **Click Here to View link**. NetShow opens and provides a live video presentation from the C-Span Network (see Figure 6.6). When you have concluded your viewing of the live feed, click the NetShow close button to close down the NetShow window.

The NetShow player provides you with an excellent tool for viewing all types of live and saved presentations. NetShow has the potential of becoming an exceptional educational delivery tool for Internet online courses.

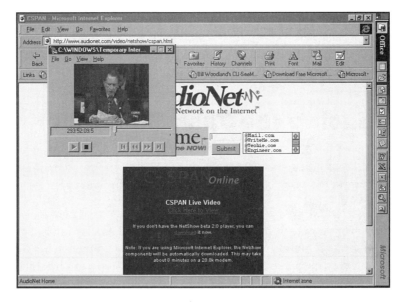

Figure 6.6 Live broadcasts are played by NetShow in streams, so you don't have to wait for large chunks of the broadcast to load before you see the video in the NetShow window.

In this lesson, you learned about Microsoft NetShow. You downloaded and installed the NetShow player and used it to play presentations on the World Wide Web. In the next lesson, you will learn how to download, install, and use the Task Scheduler, another Internet Explorer add-on.

Task Scheduler

In this lesson, you download and install the Internet Explorer Task Scheduler. You learn how to use Task Scheduler to maintain your computer using maintenance programs like ScanDisk.

Introducing the Task Scheduler

Task Scheduler is a program that enables you to schedule when system maintenance utilities, such as ScanDisk and Disk Defragmenter, are run on your computer. Task Scheduler also can notify you when your hard disk is low on space.

Now you may think that Task Scheduler seems like an unlikely add-on for Internet Explorer. However it's not as odd as it may appear; Microsoft is working very hard to integrate the Windows desktop with Internet Explorer. Their plan is to make your PC one with the Internet and provide a seamless interface that enables you to work on your PC and maintain it while also having quick access to the Internet (particularly the World Wide Web via Internet Explorer). So, to make a long story short, Task Scheduler helps you maintain you own little part of the Internet—your computer.

 TIP **Additional Utilities** Disk Defragmenter and ScanDisk are utilities that come with your Windows 95 operating system CD-ROM. You may wish to add these two utilities if you didn't install them when you installed Windows.

Downloading and Installing Task Scheduler

Task Scheduler can be downloaded from the Microsoft Internet Explorer Component Download page at **www.microsoft.com/ie/ie40/download/b2/x86/en/download/addon95.htm**. Because this page uses Active Setup, both the download and installation process are handled for you.

 TIP **Add the Page** Add the Internet Explorer Download page to your Favorites by clicking the **Favorites menu** and then clicking **Add to Favorites**. It will save you a lot of typing because nearly all of the Internet Explorer add-ons can be downloaded from this particular page.

Follow these steps to download and install Task Scheduler:

1. Connect to the Internet and open Internet Explorer. In the Address box, type **www.microsoft.com/ie/ie40/download/b2/x86/en/download/addon95.htm**. Press **Enter**.

2. The Internet Explorer Download page appears. The Active Setup box appears and asks if you wish to have the currently installed add-ons identified. Click **Yes** to continue.

3. The Components Confirmation and Installation page appears. It lists the component you wish to install, in this case Task Scheduler (see Figure 7.1). Choose a download site for the software from the drop-down box. Click **Install Now**.

Figure 7.1 Click Task Scheduler's check box, and Active Setup downloads and installs the Internet Explorer add-on for you.

4. The Active Setup dialog box tracks the status of the download and installation process. You will be notified that the download and installation was a success. Click **OK** to close the Active Setup notification box.

Using Task Scheduler

Task Scheduler doesn't require you to be online or running Internet Explorer when you add new tasks or edit the tasks that you've already scheduled. Task Scheduler is a stand-alone utility program that can be launched via the Windows Start menu.

Task Scheduler is used to start a particular program at a particular time. You can use it to schedule everything from maintaining your computer with tools like ScanDisk to checking your e-mail software for new mail.

Scheduling a New Task

The Task Scheduler enables you to schedule new tasks and edit the tasks already scheduled. Obviously, if you're running Task Scheduler for the first time, there won't be tasks currently scheduled.

To schedule a new task, follow these steps:

1. Click the **Start** button, point at **Programs**, point at **Accessories**, then point at the **System Tools** group. Click the **Scheduled Tasks** icon.

2. A Scheduled Tasks window appears on the Windows Desktop, as shown in Figure 7.2. Double-click the **Add Scheduled Task** icon in the window.

Figure 7.2 The Scheduled Tasks window is where you add a new task.

3. The Add Scheduled Task Wizard appears. This wizard helps you to schedule a new task. Click the **Next** button to move from the wizard's introductory screen.

4. The Scheduled Task Wizard lists all the programs that are on your Windows Start menu. Scroll down through the list until you find the program you wish to schedule (programs are listed in alphabetical order). As an example, select **ScanDisk,** as shown in Figure 7.3.

 TIP **Use Browse for Searching** If the program that you want to schedule isn't on the list you can use the Browse button to search for it.

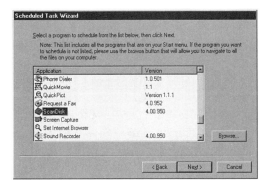

Figure 7.3 The Scheduled Task Wizard provides you with a list of all the programs currently found on your Windows Start menu.

5. Once you've selected the program to schedule, click the **Next** button. The Next screen offers you a list of scheduling options. You can schedule the program to run Daily, Weekly, Monthly, One time only, when your computer starts, or when you log on. Click the option button for the correct time frame. For the ScanDisk example, click **Weekly**.

6. This box also asks that you type a name for the scheduled item in the text box at the top of the screen. You can leave the name of the application in the box or type a new one. Click **Next** when you have completed the options on this screen.

7. The next screen asks you to set the time parameters associated with the scheduling of the program, as shown in Figure 7.4. Set the time, day of the week, and the beginning date for running the program. When you have entered the time information, click **Next**.

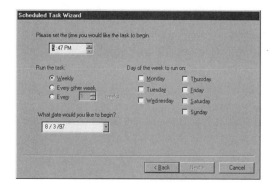

Figure 7.4 The Scheduled Task Wizard asks you to provide the time frame and frequency of the task you wish to schedule.

8. The final screen lists the task you wish to schedule and the time frame you wish to schedule it in. If any of the information is incorrect, you can click **Back** to edit the information. If all the information is correct, click the **Finish** button.

Editing a Task

You can edit the tasks that you schedule using Task Scheduler. You also can delete selected tasks. To edit an existing task, follow these steps:

1. Click the **Start** button, point at **Programs**, point at **Accessories**, and then point at the **System Tools** group. Click the **Scheduled Tasks** icon.

2. The Scheduled Tasks window appears, showing the Add Scheduled Task icon and icons for any tasks that you have already scheduled. Double-click a scheduled task to edit it.

3. A dialog box opens for the task you selected, as shown in Figure 7.5. To edit the time parameters for the task, click the **Schedule** tab. You can then edit the time, day of the week, or weekly cycle for the task. This dialog box also enables you to set parameters that tell the task not to run if the computer's batteries are low, or if you are currently working on the computer.

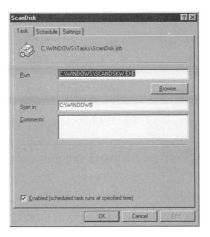

Figure 7.5 In the Scheduled Tasks window you can edit any of the tasks.

4. Click the **Settings** tab as shown in Figure 7.6. This tab enables you to set task parameters such as how long the computer should be idle before the tasks begins, and whether or not to run the task if the computer is operating on batteries. Select the **Delete the Scheduled Task** check box when finished to delete the task after it runs for the first time.

5. When you have edited any or all of the parameters associated with the task, you can close the task dialog box by clicking **OK**.

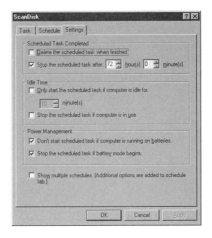

Figure 7.6 The Settings tab enables you to set conditions such as low battery to keep a task from running as scheduled.

Deleting a Task

The easiest way to delete a task is to open the Scheduled Tasks window via the Start menu. Select a task you want to delete and then press the **Delete** key. You will be asked if you want to place the selected task in the recycle bin. Selecting **Yes** removes the task from the Scheduled Tasks window.

Task Scheduler can be very useful for running routine maintenance on your computer by scheduling programs like ScanDisk and Disk Defragmenter. You also can use Task Scheduler to check your e-mail or log onto the Internet at specified times.

CAUTION

System Agent Users   If you installed Microsoft Plus on your computer, you've already had access to System Agent, a program very much like Task Scheduler. System Agent provides the same type of program scheduling that Task Scheduler does. If you're happy with System Agent, you may not want to install Task Scheduler as well.

In this lesson, you downloaded and installed the Task Scheduler. You also learned how to schedule and delete tasks using the Task Scheduler. In the next lesson, you will learn how to use Microsoft Wallet when making payments for goods and services on the World Wide Web.

Microsoft Wallet

In this lesson, you learn how to configure and use Microsoft Wallet, an Internet Explorer add-on that makes online transactions easier and more secure.

Introducing Microsoft Wallet

The Microsoft Wallet is used to hold information about you and the payment methods you want to use for online transactions on the World Wide Web. Payment information kept in the Wallet controls which credit card you use for a particular purchase. Address information provides shipping and billing information needed during the online entry.

All the information in the Microsoft Wallet is secure and is protected during the online transaction using industry standard encryption schemes. Once you configure Microsoft Wallet, you're ready to buy on the Web without agonizing over the risk of making online purchases.

Downloading Microsoft Wallet

Microsoft Wallet is an add-on for Internet Explorer and works integrally with the Web browser. It is installed on your machine with Internet Explorer when you do the standard and full installation. If you downloaded and installed Internet Explorer using the Minimal configuration, you'll need to download Microsoft Wallet from the Microsoft Internet Explorer Component Page.

 TIP **Further Information** If you would like to learn more about Microsoft Wallet, it has its own home page at **http://www.microsoft.com/commerce/wallet/**.

To download Microsoft Wallet, follow these steps:

1. Connect to the Internet and open Internet Explorer. In the address box type **www.microsoft.com/ie/ie40/download/b2/x86/en/download/addon95.htm**. Then press **Enter**.

2. The Internet Explorer Download page appears. The Active Setup box appears and asks you if you wish to have the currently installed add-ons identified. Click **Yes** to continue.

3. Scroll down through the list of add-ons until you come to Microsoft Wallet. Click its check box to select it for installation and then click **Next** to continue.

4. The Components Confirmation and Installation page appears. It lists the component you want to install—Microsoft Wallet. Choose a download site for the software from the drop-down box. Then click **Install Now**.

5. The Active Setup dialog box appears. It tracks the status of the download and installation process. When it's finished, you are notified that the download and installation was a success. Click **OK** to close the Active Setup notification box.

Configuring Microsoft Wallet

Once you've installed Microsoft Wallet, you're ready to configure it for use. Wallet is fully integrated with Internet Explorer. You configure Wallet with the Internet Explorer Options dialog box. Follow these steps:

1. Click the Internet Explorer **View** menu, and then click **Internet Options**. The Internet Explorer Options dialog box appears.

2. Click the **Content** tab. The Content tab holds the settings for various features involving the content that the Internet Explorer can access. This tab also houses the Microsoft Wallet settings (see Figure 8.1).

3. In the Microsoft Wallet area of the Content tab, click the **Addresses** button. The Address Options dialog box appears, as shown in Figure 8.2. This box holds your address information after it's entered.

Figure 8.1 Use the Content tab on the Internet Explorer Options dialog box to configure Microsoft Wallet.

Figure 8.2 The Address Options box holds your address information.

4. Click the **Add** button to add an address to the Address Options dialog box. The Add a New Address dialog box appears. Enter your personal information in the appropriate boxes in this dialog box.

5. Once you enter your personal information, you're asked to click a button designating this address as Home or Business. You're also required to give the information a Display name (one will be automatically assigned based on your first name and the location chosen; you can edit the name).

6. Once you've completed the entry of the information (as shown in Figure 8.3), click the **OK** button. The new personal profile appears in the Address Options dialog box in the Display Name text box. Click **Close** to close the Address Options box.

Figure 8.3 Type your address information into the Add a New Address box.

TIP **Configuring Multiple Profiles** You can configure multiple personal profiles, one for home and one for business. You also can configure different profiles if you want one address sent billing information and another address sent the goods that you purchase during your online shopping.

Once you configure your personal information, you can configure the payment information that Microsoft Wallet needs during online transactions. This is again done with the Content tab of the Internet Explorer Options dialog box. Here's how:

1. In the Microsoft Wallet area of the Content tab, click the **Payments** button. The Payments Options dialog box appears. This box is similar to the Address Options dialog box and contains the name of the credit cards that you enter into Microsoft Wallet.

2. To enter a new credit card and the associated information, click the **Add** button. A drop-down menu appears, giving you three choices: Add a New Visa Card, Add a New MasterCard, or Add a New American Express. Click the option for the type of card that you want to add.

3. The Microsoft Wallet license agreement appears. Click **I Agree** to continue. An Add a New Credit Wizard appears and walks you through the steps of inputting the information that you need to use this credit card online (see Figure 8.4).

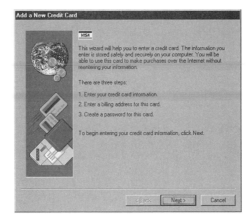

Figure 8.4 The Add a New Credit Card Wizard will help you enter your credit card information for online buying.

4. Click the **Next** button to continue. The first screen asks you to enter the card name, expiration date, and card number. A display name for the card is also required (this is automatically entered as your first name and the credit card type, but you can change it).

5. Once you've entered the information related to the card, you can continue the process by clicking **Next**.

6. The next screen asks you to select an address from your address list to serve as the billing address for the card. Select the appropriate address using the drop-down box provided and click **Next** to continue.

7. The last step in the process of adding a credit card to the Microsoft Wallet is to password-protect the credit card. This password is needed during online transactions using the credit card. Enter a password in the **Password** box and then re-enter the password in the **Confirm Password** box, as shown in Figure 8.5. Click **Finish** to complete the credit card profile entry.

The credit card appears in the Credit Card Options box under the card's display name. You can add additional cards to the Options box by repeating the above process.

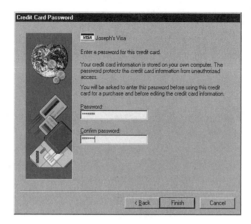

Figure 8.5 The final step in setting up your credit card information is the selection of a password.

Don't Forget the Password   Make sure that you write down your password and keep it in a safe place. If you don't have the password to give Microsoft Wallet the go ahead for using your credit card information, making online purchases impossible.

CAUTION

If you're finished configuring Microsoft Wallet, close the Internet Explorer Options box. Now you're ready to use Microsoft Wallet for online transactions.

Online Purchases with Microsoft Wallet

If you want to use Microsoft Wallet, you need to be ready to shop online. Tons of online shopping Web sites exist for everything from fly fishing equipment to computer software and hardware. For the information you placed in Microsoft Wallet to do you any good you must do your shopping on a Web site that supports the protocols that accept data from Microsoft Wallet.

Wallet Payment   Microsoft Wallet only works for transactions that occur on sites that support the Wallet payment method.

CAUTION

Because the Microsoft Wallet add-on for Internet Explorer is relatively new, a definitive list of sites that use the Wallet control isn't available. However, one site that boasts use of Microsoft Wallet for payments is the Internet Shopping Network at **http://www.isn.com/**. Microsoft has plans to announce additional Web shopping sites that adopt the Microsoft Wallet control in the future. You can keep up-to-date with Microsoft Wallet information at the Microsoft Wallet home page at **http://www.microsoft.com/commerce/wallet/**.

In this lesson, you learned how to download and configure Microsoft Wallet for Internet Explorer. In the next lesson, you will learn about Macromedia ShockWave, an interactive multimedia player helper application for Internet Explorer.

ShockWave

In this lesson, you download and install the ShockWave ActiveX control for Microsoft Internet Explorer. You also learn how to use ShockWave to access interactive multimedia on the Web.

Introducing ShockWave

You already know that you can play and view audio, video, and multimedia files on the Web with Internet Explorer add-ons like DirectShow and NetShow. Going to the next step and adding interactivity to special content on the Web increases the possibilities for learning and fun on the Web a thousandfold.

Macromedia, the company that developed interactive multimedia authoring tools like Macromedia Director and AuthorWare, has developed a way to get interactive multimedia onto the Web: a product called ShockWave.

When you have the ShockWave ActiveX control for Internet Explorer installed on your computer, you can interact with multimedia content on Web sites. This content is regular interactive multimedia (developed in Director or AuthorWare) that has been "shocked" for the Web. Shocked content can be used to provide interactive games, even educational content on the Web.

 Shocked Refers to multimedia programs that have been converted to Web content using ShockWave.

Downloading and Installing ShockWave

You can find the ShockWave ActiveX control for Internet Explorer at several sites, including Stroud's (**www.stroud.com**) and TUCOWS (**www.tucows.com**). Probably the best place to find the most recent version of ShockWave and obtain additional information about the software is the Macromedia Web site at **wwww.macromedia.com**.

To download ShockWave, follow these steps:

1. Connect to your Service Provider or Online Service and then open Internet Explorer. In the Address box, type **www.macromedia.com**, and then press **Enter**.

2. As soon as your Browser accesses the site, a Security Warning box appears, and you are asked if you want to download the ActiveX control for ShockWave Flash. ShockWave Flash is a control that allows Internet Explorer to play very short shocked content on a Web page. You need to download this control to navigate the Macromedia site and download the full-blown version of ShockWave.

   Click **Yes** in the Security Warning box. The control only takes a moment to load. Now the small multimedia items on the Web page play in your Web browser window.

 TIP **Accepting Downloads** The great thing about ActiveX controls is that if a Web site uses them and you don't have the control installed, the appropriate control is downloaded and installed at that moment. Whenever you access a new site and a control download box appears, go ahead and accept the control download to view the special content.

3. The Macromedia Web page appears in all its multimedia glory, as shown in Figure 9.1. To go to the ShockWave page, click the **ShockWave** link in the lower center of the current page.

4. The ShockWave page (**http://www.macromedia.com/shockwave/**) provides information on ShockWave and links to other pages that contain shocked content. To download ShockWave, click the **Get ShockWave** link on the left side of the ShockWave page.

5. The ShockWave download page appears. Enter your name and e-mail address in the appropriate boxes. Then scroll down and click the **AutoInstall Now** button. ShockWave is downloaded and installed.

Figure 9.1   The Macromedia Web page loads the ShockWave Flash ActiveX control and provides you with a link to the ShockWave page.

CAUTION

Security Warning   The ShockWave download and installation looks like the loading of any other Web page on your Web browser. A save file box or installation status box doesn't appear during the process. You may get a Security Warning box during the download process, and if you do, click **Yes** to continue. Now just sit back and relax and the control will be downloaded and installed.

You don't have to do anything else. The ActiveX control is now attached to your Web browser and ShockWave is now available to play interactive multimedia in the Internet Explorer window.

TIP   **Successful Installation**   If your ShockWave installation was a success, a ShockWave movie sample and a ShockWave Flash sample start playing in the boxes at the bottom of the ShockWave download page.

Using ShockWave

Using ShockWave can be a ton of fun. There's some great interactive shocked content on the Web. A good place to start viewing and interacting with shocked content is the Macromedia's Shockzone. You can find a link for the Shockzone on the Macromedia home page and the ShockWave home page. The site's address is **www.macromedia/shockzone**.

Follow these steps to use ShockWave:

1. Open the Shockzone site using an appropriate link or by typing **www.macromedia/shockwave** in the Internet Explorer Address box. The Shockzone has links to Spot Lights (interesting ShockWave sites), Site of the Day, Arcade, Jukebox, and other links to hot ShockWave content sites, as shown in Figure 9.2.

Figure 9.2   The Shockzone is a good place to go to find shocked content on the Web.

2. Click the link for **Site of the Day**. Obviously, the site of the day will vary. This is a good way to get your feet wet with some of the latest and greatest shocked content on the Web.

149

The Staff Picks link also is another good way to take a look at some very good shocked sites. When you click this link, each staff member's name appears with his or her site choice.

My favorite link on the Shockzone page is the Arcade link. This link provides you with a list of interactive games on the Web. The first link provided on the Arcade page is to the Celebrity Slugfest at **www.slugfest.kaszen.net**. This shocked arcade game enables you to engage in fisticuffs with your least favorite celebrity. Choose the celebrity boxer by clicking his or her picture (see Figure 9.3).

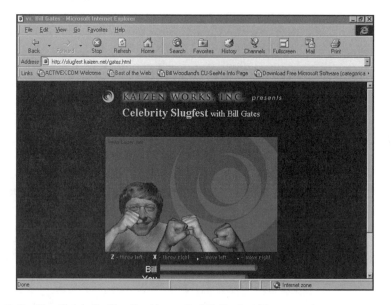

Figure 9.3 The Celebrity SlugFest is pretty idiotic, but it's a good way to try out interactive multimedia using ShockWave.

Another excellent site for putting ShockWave through its paces is the Boris Yeltsin Operation Game (**www.comedycentral.com/boris.html**) at the Comedy Central Web site. See if you can cure Boris without setting off the buzzer in this excellent knock-off of the original Operation game.

 TIP **Patience** Some shocked content can take a seemingly long time to load into your Web browser window; at times you will have to be very patient.

Shocked content can be used for online games, interactive educational sites, and other applications where the provider wants the user (you) to interact with the material on the Web site. You also can find additional shocked sites by using your favorite Web search engine and searching for ShockWave.

In this lesson, you learned how to download, install, and use ShockWave. In the next lesson, you will download and use the RealPlayer video/audio player.

RealPlayer

In this lesson, you learn about an audio and video player called RealPlayer. You also learn how to download, install, and use RealPlayer.

Introducing the RealPlayer

The RealPlayer from Progressive Networks is a combination audio and video player that can play on-demand audio and video files on Web sites or play live broadcasts containing audio and video information. RealPlayer plays video and audio content in streams so that you don't have to download the entire file before the player broadcasts the audio or the video.

In many respects, RealPlayer is similar to Microsoft NetShow. RealPlayer, however, uses a different broadcast protocol and so can access Web audio and video content that NetShow cannot. A great deal of audio and video content and live broadcasts are available on the Web when you use the RealPlayer to access them.

RealPlayer offers you a variety of content. You can listen to National Public Radio broadcasts, listen to Web radio stations, and even view several short films by filmmaker Spike Lee. Two versions of RealPlayer exist: RealPlayer Plus, which can be purchased online or in computer software stores, and the RealPlayer 4.0 free version, which can be downloaded. RealPlayer Plus offers several enhancements not found on the free version.

Downloading RealPlayer

The best site for downloading the most current version of RealPlayer is the Progressive Networks RealPlayer Web site.

To download RealPlayer, follow these steps:

1. Connect to your service provider or online service and then open Internet Explorer. In the Address box, type **http://www.realaudio.com/**, and then press **Enter**.

2. The Progressive Networks RealAudio Web site provides a link for downloading the retail and free versions of the RealPlayer. This Web site also provides links to sites that contain RealPlayer content. To download the RealPlayer (free version), click the **RealPlayer 4.0** link. The download link takes you to the RealPlayer and RealPlayer Plus download page (see Figure 10.1).

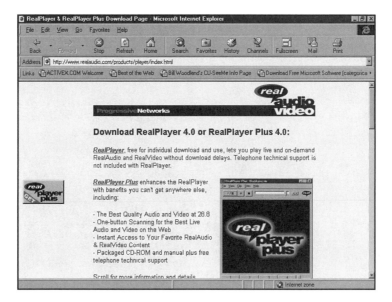

Figure 10.1 The RealPlayer and RealPlayer Plus download page provides you with links to download both of the player versions.

3. Click the link for the RealPlayer. You are taken to a registration page where you select the operating system, processor, and connection speed that you will use when connected to the Internet. You also are asked to provide your name and e-mail address (see Figure 10.2). Once you select the correct items and enter the appropriate information, click the **Download Now** button.

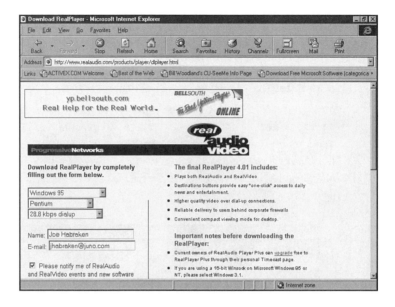

Figure 10.2   The RealPlayer download page asks you to enter information about your computer and yourself before you download the software.

4. A list of servers for the download appears on the next Web page. Click a server location to begin the download. A download box appears. You can choose to save the file or open it. Save the file and then it will be available if you ever need to reinstall it.

5. Make sure the **Save This Program to Disk** option button is selected, and then click **OK**. A Save As dialog box appears. Select a folder on your computer that you wish to save the RealPlayer file to, as shown in Figure 10.3. Then click **Save**. The RealPlayer installation file is saved to your computer. When the download is complete, a completion box appears. Click **OK** to close it.

Figure 10.3   Select a folder where you can save the RealPlayer installation file.

Installing the RealPlayer

Now that you've downloaded the installation file for the RealPlayer, you're ready to install this Internet Explorer add-on. To do so, follow these steps:

1. Use the Windows Explorer to open the folder that you downloaded the RealPlayer installation file into. Locate the file **rp32_401.exe** and double-click it to install RealPlayer (see Figure 10.4).

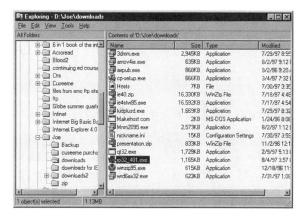

Figure 10.4 Double-click the rp32_401.exe file to begin the RealPlayer installation.

2. The RealPlayer installation begins. The installation process is handled by a series of screens. After reading the opening screen, click **Next** to continue. You are asked to read the license agreement; after reading click **Next**.

3. The next screen asks you to enter your Name, company, and e-mail address. After doing so, click **Next**. The next screen asks you to select your Internet connection, as shown in Figure 10.5. After selecting your connection, click **Next**.

4. The next screen asks you to designate a folder where you would like the RealPlayer software installed. Click **Next** after designating a folder.

5. The Next screen shows the browsers you have installed on your computer, such as Internet Explorer. A selected check box next to the Internet Explorer version number installs RealPlayer so that it runs with Internet Explorer. Click **Finish** to complete the setup. An installation complete box appears; click **OK** to close it.

6. Upon completion of the installation, the RealPlayer opens and plays a sample video. Close the RealPlayer box to exit the application.

Figure 10.5 Select a connection mode and speed for your Internet connection.

Using the RealPlayer

Now that the RealPlayer is installed, you're ready to use it to play on-demand and live video and audio content on the World Wide Web. The RealPlayer operates outside of your Web browser, playing the special content in a RealPlayer window. The best place to find RealPlayer content is on the Progressive Networks RealAudio Web site at **www.realaudio.com**.

1. Go online and open Internet Explorer. In the Address box, type **www.realaudio.com** and press **Enter**. You are taken to the Progressive Networks Web site.

This site provides a directory of links to RealAudio content. Among the links are those for C-Span and National Public Radio. This page also provides special links to RealVideo and RealAudio showcases that enable you to test RealPlayer's video and audio abilities.

2. Click the link for **RealVideo Showcase**, as shown in Figure 10.6. The links on the next page range from video footage of the syndicated television series BayWatch and the Arts and Entertainment Networks Standup Comedy Archive, to links for C-Span and the Fox News Network. Click the link for **Fox News Network**. To see a list of available videos, click the **Video** link at the top of the page.

3. Links to RealPlayer video content take the form of still pictures containing the RealPlayer logo at the bottom. These photo-links also have a start button with a video insignia, as shown in Figure 10.7. Click the **Start** button, and the RealPlayer opens a window and plays the video content (see Figure 10.8).

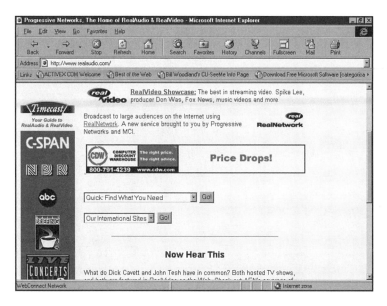

Figure 10.6 The RealPlayer video showcase provides a number of links to RealPlayer video content.

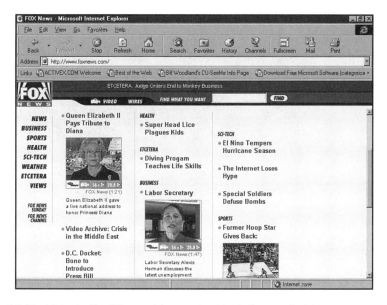

Figure 10.7 Links to RealPlayer video content look like small video screens.

Figure 10.8   RealPlayer video plays in a special video player.

The RealPlayer also can play audio content that you find on the Web. A great site to check out for audio programs is the National Public Radio site at **http://www.real.com/contentp/npr/atc.html**. This site has links to your favorite NPR programs like All Things Considered and Science Friday. Click any of the links to enjoy audio content with the RealPlayer (see Figure 10.9).

TIP   **Starting from Windows**   You also can start the RealPlayer via the Windows Start menu. If you're online you can use the News, Tech, Sports, and other buttons to access audio and video content without opening the Internet browser.

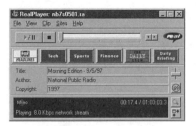

Figure 10.9   RealPlayer audio plays in a special audio player.

The real purpose of on-demand and real-time audio and video players like RealPlayer is two-fold. They supply you with a player that enables you to play special Web content when you happen upon it on the Web. The RealPlayer also makes it easy for you to listen to regularly scheduled programs and specific content as you would on your television or radio.

In this lesson, you downloaded and installed the RealPlayer: an on-demand and live video and audio player. You also used the RealPlayer to access video and audio content. In the next lesson, you will learn about VRML as you explore 3-D virtual worlds on the Web using the Microsoft VRML Viewer.

Microsoft VRML Viewer

In this lesson, you download and install Microsoft VRML Viewer for Internet Explorer. You then explore three-dimensional worlds and objects on the Web.

Introducing VRML

VRML—Virtual Reality Modeling Language—is a programming language that has enabled programmers to turn the Web into a three-dimensional wonderland. VRML can be used to create three-dimensional objects and three-dimensional worlds that you can view as you browse the Web. You can not only view these worlds, but, with VRML, move three-dimensional objects and navigate through a three-dimensional world.

 VRML Virtual Reality Modeling Language is used to create virtual worlds and objects that can be viewed with a special VRML add-on for Internet Explorer.

Internet Explorer alone won't get you into these Virtual Web worlds. You need a VRML add-on for Internet Explorer that enables you to view the three-dimensional objects inside the browser window.

A number of VRML browser add-ons exist. Microsoft has developed their own VRML add-on for Internet Explorer in the form of an ActiveX control; it's called the Microsoft VRML Viewer.

Downloading and Installing the VRML ActiveX Control

The Microsoft VRML Viewer is considered one of the core add-on components for Internet Explorer (like Outlook Express and NetMeeting). It can be downloaded and installed from the Microsoft Internet Explorer Component Page. Because this page uses Active Setup, the downloading and installation of the file are both handled for you. Follow these steps:

1. Connect to the Internet and open Internet Explorer. In the Address box, type **www.microsoft.com/ie/ie40/download/b2/x86/en/download/ addon95.htm**. Press **Enter**.

2. The Internet Explorer Download page appears. The Active Setup box appears and asks you if you want to have the currently installed add-ons identified. Click **Yes** to continue.

3. Scroll down through the list of add-ons until you come to the Authoring Components category. Microsoft VRML 2 Viewer is listed in the Multimedia Components section. Select the **Microsoft VRML Viewer** check box. Click **Next** to continue.

4. The next page provides you with a drop-down box of download sites. Select the download site nearest you and click the **Install Now** button.

5. The Active Setup dialog box tracks the status of the download and installation process. When it's finished, you are notified that the download and installation was a success. Click **OK** to close the Active Setup notification box.

6. The proper installation of the VRML viewer requires that your system be restarted. Close your current applications (save your work if necessary) and click the **Yes** button to restart.

Using the VRML Viewer

To use the VRML viewer, you must locate a Web page that contains VRML content. VRML objects on the Web range from entire worlds to movable objects. A good site to test out your VRML viewer is the VRML Model Catalog at **http:// www.ocnus.com/models/models.html**. This page has links to a number of VRML objects grouped by category.

To test the VRML viewer, follow these steps:

1. Open the **www.ocnus.com/models/models.html** site using Internet Explorer. Scroll down the page that appears, as shown in Figure 11.1.

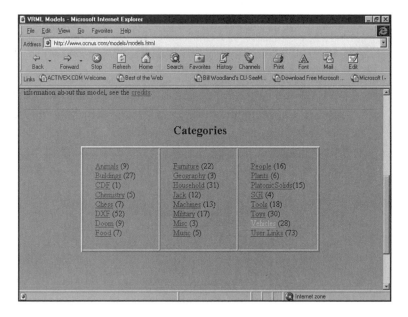

Figure 11.1 Ocnus.com offers a page of links to a number of VRML objects.

2. In the Categories box, click **Vehicles**. Scroll down through the list and select the **Porsche**. The VRML Viewer interface loads, and then the object (the Porsche) appears in the middle of the browser window.

3. Place the mouse on the object, press the left button, and then push the mouse toward the object. Your view zooms in toward the three-dimensional automobile (see Figure 11.2).

4. You can rotate the vehicle by clicking the **Study** tool on the left side of the VRML Viewer. Place the Study tool on the car and drag the car using the mouse. You can rotate the car and even flip it so the bottom of the car is visible.

5. When you tire of the Porsche, press the **Back** button on the Explorer toolbar and try out some of the other VRML objects listed in the catalog.

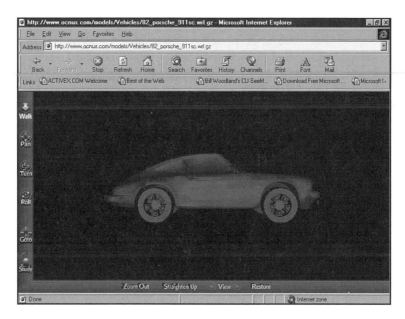

Figure 11.2 The VRML Viewer enables you to zoom in on the 3-D Porsche, rotate it, tilt it, and even flip it upside down.

Controlling Movement in 3-D Space

To get a really good feel of how sophisticated VRML can be, it makes sense to visit one of the three-dimensional VRML worlds. A three-dimensional world also is a good place to try out all of the VRML Viewer's tools and learn how to control your movements in 3-D space. Follow these steps to try out a three-dimensional VRML world:

1. Use Internet Explorer to go to **www.tristero.com/coffee/vrcoffee/ coffee.wrl**. This site provides a virtual coffee shop (see Figure 11.3). You can use the VRML Viewer movement controls to walk around the shop. All of the controls are used by selecting the control and then dragging the mouse (holding the left mouse button down) in a particular direction. The following list describes how to use each of the movement controls:

   - The **Walk** control enables you to move forward and backward with the mouse.
   - The **Pan** control enables you to slide to the left or the right.
   - The **Turn** control enables you to swing to the left or the right.
   - The **Roll** control enables you to rotate the VRML object (in this case, it turns the room upside down).

163

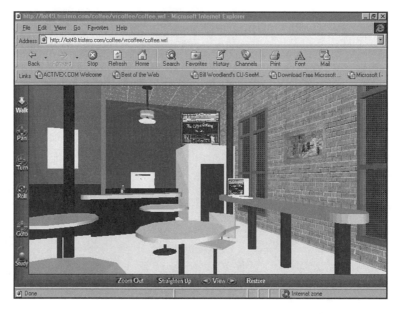

Figure 11.3   The Virtual Coffee Gallery is a good place to practice moving in 3-D space.

- The **Goto** control enables you to click on a part of the VRML space. You are moved toward the item until you click somewhere else in the space.

- The **Study** control enables you to rotate a VRML object in any direction.

- The **Zoom Out** control enables you to zoom out to see the entire virtual world.

- The **StraightenUp** control puts you back on an even keel, as if you were standing upright (things can get pretty tilted with some of the controls).

- The **View** control enables you to totally shift your perspective to either the left or right.

- The **Restore** control gets the view back to where you started (this can be helpful, especially if you flipped your virtual world upside down).

2. Once you've gotten a good feel for how to move in 3-D space, you're ready to tackle other worlds. As an extra treat, the Coffee Shop Virtual World has hidden links to other Web pages and to various other objects. Try clicking on the wall art and other signs in the room to see what happens.

VRML Problems VRML files can be very large and aren't always completely compatible with every VRML viewer available. You may find times when a VRML world or object doesn't appear correctly. In the worst case scenario, a VRML file can lock up Internet Explorer.

CAUTION

Cool VRML Sites

As you can see, VRML worlds can be a lot of fun. A number of excellent virtual world sites exist on the World Wide Web. You can use any of the Internet search engines, such as Yahoo or WebCrawler, to search for VRML worlds. If you do this search every once in a while, you will find that new VRML sites pop up all the time.

An excellent list of VRML Web sites is provided by Silicon Graphics at **http://webspace.sgi.com/Repository/** and is called VRML Worlds. This site lists the Virtual worlds in categories like Architectural spaces and Art spaces. Under Historical spaces you can visit Stonehenge. In the Geographical spaces, you can take a walk around Freeport. In the Commerce spaces, you can sit a spell on the Silicon Graphics patio.

Another good list of VRML links can be found at **http://www.autonomy.com/virtual.htm**. This site has links to VRML worlds and links to other resources involving virtual reality.

A very cool site that you should visit is the Ziff Davis Terminal Reality site located at **http://www5.zdnet.com/zdwebcat/content/vrml/outside.wrl**. This 3-D world lets you walk around a futuristic landscape and enter the Terminal Reality building, which contains links and other virtual world surprises (see Figure 11.4.).

You should also check out the Proteinman's Top Ten VRML Worlds at **http://www.virtpark.com/theme/proteinman/**. This site offers links to a number of very enjoyable virtual worlds. For instance, you may need a virtual vacation. If so, check out the Proteinman's link to **www.alaska.net/~dennism/vrml/worlds/2_0/scuba/scuba2.wrl.gz**. You'll see a sailboat bobbing on the water as the waves roll in (see Figure 11.5).

VRML worlds are becoming more sophisticated all the time. And while that usually makes them a lot more fun and interesting, it probably means that the files will take a while to load on your Web browser. You can find all sorts of VRML projects on the Web, everything from games to educational material.

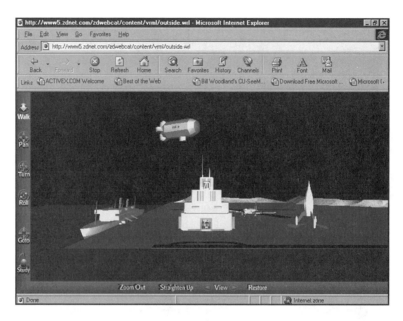

Figure 11.4   Test your ability to move about in a virtual world.

Figure 11.5   The Alaska vacation virtual world has a sailboat that bobs on the waves.

In this lesson, you learned about VRML and the Microsoft VRML Viewer for Internet Explorer. In the next lesson, you will learn about the Adobe Acrobat reader, which is used to read special file types on the World Wide Web.

Adobe Acrobat ActiveX Control

In this lesson, you download and install the special Web document reader Adobe Acrobat. You also use Adobe Acrobat to read specially formatted Acrobat documents on the Web.

Introducing Adobe Acrobat

A number of special content types reside on the Web: audio files, video files, and multimedia files. Another type of special content that you run across on the Web is Acrobat. Acrobat documents (.pdf files) are print-ready (meaning they are laid out and desktop published) files that have been converted into a special file format. Any Acrobat documents you find probably originated in Adobe PageMaker or some other desktop publishing software package (PageMaker is also from Adobe, the company that makes Acrobat).

Acrobat File   A special desktop published file (.pdf) that can be read like a book using the Acrobat Reader.

TIP   **Create Your Own**   Adobe makes a full-blown version of Adobe Acrobat that you can use to create and edit your own Acrobat files. It's not a free product like the Acrobat Reader, however.

Acrobat documents make wonderful online manuals and booklets because they can contain graphics, photos, and diagrams just like a printed book. To view these special Acrobat files you need the Adobe Acrobat Reader. Adobe distributes an ActiveX control version of the Acrobat Reader that you can use with Microsoft Internet Explorer.

Downloading Adobe Acrobat

The best place to get the most recent version of Adobe Acrobat for Internet Explorer is the Acrobat Web site (**http://www.adobe.com/prodindex/acrobat/ readstep.html**).

1. Connect to the Internet and open Internet Explorer. In the Address box, type **http://www.adobe.com/prodindex/acrobat/readstep.html** and press **Enter** to go to the Acrobat reader download page.

   Once you're on the page you're asked to go through three steps: Register with Adobe, select the version of Acrobat you want to use, and then download the software.

2. To register with Adobe, click the register link. You are asked to provide your name, e-mail address, and other personal information. Once you've completed the registration you are returned to the download page.

 TIP   Trouble Downloading?   If you're having trouble downloading Acrobat at the main Adobe site, try some alternative download sites at **http:// www.adobe.com/prodindex/acrobat/alternate.html#mirror**.

3. Scroll down the download page and select the Acrobat Reader you want to install in the appropriate drop-down box; also select your operating system and language preference, as shown in Figure 12.1. Once you've completed your selections, click the **Download** button.

4. You are taken to a download information page that explains that Adobe Acrobat can be installed as an ActiveX control for Internet Explorer. This page also provides additional information about Acrobat. Scroll down the page and click the link for the current version of Acrobat, in this case, **ar32e30.exe**.

5. When the Internet Explorer File Download box appears, click **OK** to continue.

6. A Save As box appears on your screen. Choose an appropriate folder for the Acrobat installation file and click **Save**. The file is downloaded to your computer and placed in the folder you selected.

 TIP   Creating a Download Folder   It may make sense to create a "downloads" folder on your computer so that you always have a place where you can place the files that you download off of the Web with Internet Explorer.

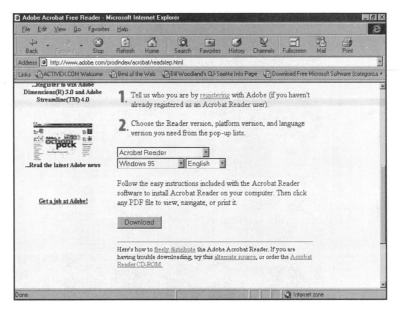

Figure 12.1 The Acrobat download page requires some information from you and then you're ready to download the software.

Installing Adobe Acrobat

Once the Acrobat Installation file has been downloaded you're ready to install the software. You can use the Run command on the Windows Start menu or use the Windows Explorer to run the Acrobat installation file. Follow these steps:

1. Open the **Windows Explorer**. Open the folder that you downloaded the Acrobat Installation file (ar32e30.exe) into. Double-click the file to begin the installation process.

2. A box appears, asking you if you want to install Acrobat. Click **Yes**. The Acrobat 3 Installation screen opens. Click **Next** to continue.

3. Read the license information, and then click **Yes** to agree. The next screen asks you to select a directory for the Acrobat software (see Figure 12.2). Once you've selected the directory (or left it at the default) click **Next** to continue.

4. The software is installed to the directory you selected. Click **Finish** to complete the process. The Reader opens a readme file. When you finish reading the file, close the Windows Notepad. A dialog box appears, saying that Setup is complete. Click **OK** to close it.

169

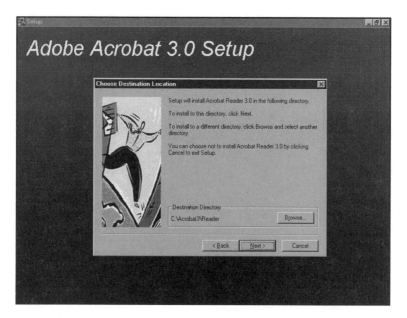

Figure 12.2 Select the directory that you wish to install the Acrobat Reader software into.

Using Adobe Acrobat

Using the Acrobat Reader is really a matter of coming across Acrobat files on the World Wide Web when you are browsing Web sites using Internet Explorer. You will find that may Web sites use the .pdf Acrobat files for long documents that would be unwieldy if they had been created using Web pages. To view an Acrobat file using Acrobat Reader, implement the following steps:

1. Go online and start Internet Explorer. Adobe provides some great examples of Acrobat files at **http://www.adobe.com/prodindex/capture atwork.html#samples**. Type this URL into the Address box and press **Enter**.

2. Scroll down through the page until you come to the various links to Acrobat samples, as shown in Figure 12.3.

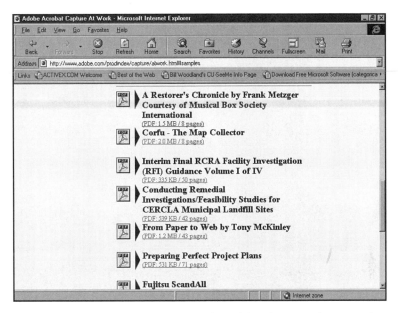

Figure 12.3 Adobe provides links to a number of Acrobat sample pages that you can view using the Acrobat Reader.

3. Click any of the links (you may want to pick one of the smaller files so you don't have to wait a long time for downloading). Explorer loads the .pdf Acrobat file.

Once the file has been loaded, the Acrobat Reader software loads. Because the latest version of the Reader is fully integrated with Internet Explorer as an ActiveX control, the Acrobat file actually appears inside the Internet Explorer Window, as shown in Figure 12.4.

4. The Acrobat toolbar also appears in the Explorer window. You can use the various tools to zoom in and out on the document, print the document, move the document in the current window, and move forward or backward a page.

5. Once you've finished working with the Acrobat file you can switch to another Web page and continue your Web browsing.

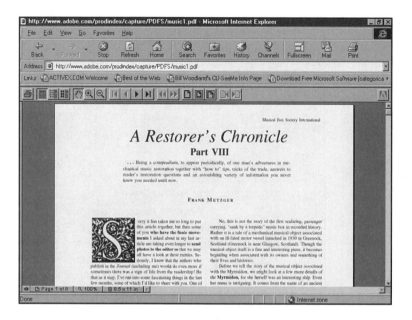

Figure 12.4 Acrobat documents appear in the Internet Explorer window.

CAUTION

Don't Close the Window When you load an Acrobat file into Internet Explorer, the Acrobat Reader opens a blank window. This is how the Reader's abilities are transferred into the Internet Explorer window. If you inadvertently close this empty Acrobat Reader window, Internet Explorer can no longer show the document in the Acrobat format.

The Acrobat format has really caught on; more and more Acrobat files appear on the Web every day. The great thing about Acrobat files is that you can view them, or download and save them for later use. You will even find that some software you purchase includes manuals made up of Acrobat files. It's a great way to save paper and avoid printing hard copy manuals.

In this lesson, you downloaded and installed the Adobe Acrobat Reader. You also used the Reader to view Acrobat files on the Web. In the next lesson, you will learn to download and install DirectX 2.

DirectX

In this lesson, you download and install the DirectX component for Internet Explorer. You also learn how DirectX technology is used to enhance Web page content.

Introducing DirectX

DirectX is a new interactive multimedia technology from Microsoft. This technology was initially developed to provide a platform for game development and other multimedia software programs.

In some respects DirectX is similar to and can be considered a companion technology to ActiveX. The use of DirectX and its sound, graphics, and interactive abilities are just starting to be exploited in Web applications. Microsoft has made it a point to include tools in the most recent version (5.0) of DirectX that are useful to Web developers. You will find Web sites that require DirectX components to run special multimedia applications; some of the new 3-D virtual world software browser add-ons take advantage of DirectX technology.

One application of DirectX technology that you're probably familiar with is the DirectShow audio and video content viewer for Internet Explorer. DirectShow was developed using ActiveX controls and DirectX components (see Part 5, Lesson 6 for more on DirectShow). Although you won't find or need DirectX on all the Web sites you visit, its use is growing and so Microsoft provides a DirectX add-on component for Internet Explorer.

 TERM **DirectX**   A group of programming technologies that provide excellent interactivity and make it easier (if programming was easy in the first place) to develop three-dimensional objects and virtual reality worlds.

TIP **For More Details...** Microsoft hosts a DirectX site for developers where you can learn everything you wanted to know and more about the DirectX technologies. Check out this site at **www.microsoft.com/DirectX/default.asp**.

Downloading and Installing DirectX

DirectX is one of the core components for Internet Explorer, and you can download it from the Microsoft Internet Explorer Components page. This page uses Active Setup, which downloads and installs a selected Internet Explorer component for you. Follow thses steps:

1. Connect to the Internet and open **Internet Explorer**. In the Address box, type **www.microsoft.com/ie/ie40/download/b2/x86/en/download/ addon95.htm**. Then press **Enter**.

2. The Internet Explorer Download page opens. The Active Setup box appears and asks you if you want to have the currently installed add-ons identified. Click **Yes** to continue.

3. Scroll down through the list of add-ons until you come to the Multimedia Components; this is where you can find DirectX (see Figure 13.1). Click its check box to select it for installation, and then click **Next** to continue.

4. The Components Confirmation and Installation page appears. It lists the component you want to install, in this case DirectX. Choose a download site for the software from the drop-down box. Then click **Install Now**.

5. The Active Setup dialog box tracks the status of the download and installation process for the DirectX component When it's finished, you are notified that the download and installation was a success. Click **OK** to close the Active Setup notification box.

Using DirectX

DirectX isn't really an application in and of itself; it's more a set of protocols that you need to have installed so that you can take advantage of other add-ons and tools for Internet Explorer that require help from DirectX to get their job done. Like the ActiveX controls that you have worked with in this section, DirectX doesn't really do anything until you come across content or applications on the Web that need it.

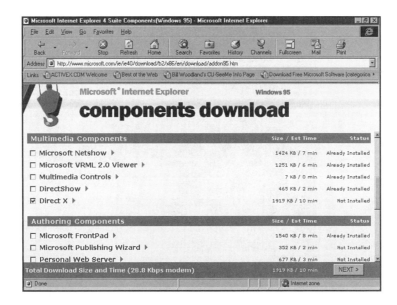

Figure 13.1 Click the DirectX check box on the Internet Explorer Component page to start the download process.

To get a good handle on what DirectX can offer, you should probably check out some of the DirectX technology samples offered by Microsoft at their DirectX Theater site (**http://www.microsoft.com/directx/default.asp**). This page has links to audio, virtual reality, and game samples that use DirectX (see Figure 13.2).

Another huge application of DirectX technology can be found in the PC game market. Many new games that you can download from the Internet require that DirectX be installed on your computer.

TIP **Games Using DirectX**   You can find a number of games developed using DirectX that you can download and try at **http://www.dreamscape.com/frankvad/free.games.nz.html** (the Virtual Free Stuff Game site).

DirectX on the Web

A Web application that takes advantage of DirectX technology is the blaxxun Passport add-on for Web browsers. This software enables you to chat with other users of the software in three-dimensional worlds. It's a combination of chat and Virtual Reality all in one Web application.

175

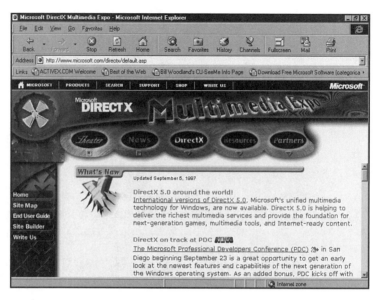

Figure 13.2 The DirectX Theater provides links to a number of DirectX samples.

Follow these steps to download the blaxxun Passport sofware so you can see DirectX in action.

1. You can download the blaxxun software from the blaxxun interactive Web page at **http://ww3.blacksun.com/index2.html**. Click the **Alice in Wonderland 3D link** and blaxxun takes you to a download page where you can download blaxxun Passport chat and VRML viewer. Once you've downloaded the software (pp2ieglms.exe) from the Web site, you can use the Windows Explorer to locate the file and install it by double-clicking it.

2. Once you've completed the installation of the blaxxun Passport, a screen appears, asking if you want to launch Passport automatically. Click the **No** check box, and then click **Finish** to end the installation process.

You have to beef up the DirectX components on your computer to run Passport. The DirectX add-on for Internet Explorer cannot run the sophisticated 3-D worlds that Passport can take you to by itself. There is a link on the blaxxun download page for the additional DirectX components needed to run the Passport software. Download the DirectX software (it downloads as dx5eng.exe). Run the DirectX installation. Now you're ready to run Passport.

TIP **Download the Latest Version** You also can download the latest version of the full-blown DirectX components from Microsoft at the DirectX Web site, located at **www.microsoft.com/DirectX/default.asp**.

Running blaxxun Passport

To start the blaxxun Passport software, follow these steps:

1. Click the **Passport** icon in the Black Sun Passport group on the Windows Start menu. Internet Explorer opens, and you are taken to the blaxxun Entry page, as shown in Figure 13.3.

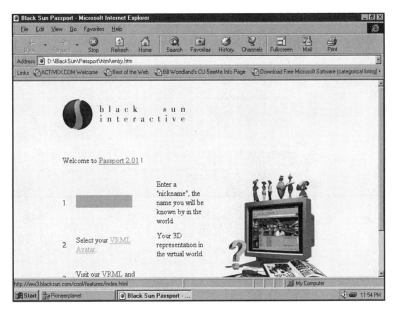

Figure 13.3 The blaxxun entry page enables you to select a nickname and avatar and then enter the VRML chat world.

2. This page requires that you complete three steps to enter the Virtual chat world: Choose a nickname, choose an avatar to represent you, and click the link to the virtual world. Click in the nickname box and type a nickname.

3. The next step is to select your Virtual avatar, which represents you in the virtual world. You can go with a default avatar or click **VRML Avatar** to select a new one. You are taken to a page that houses several different avatars. Choose an avatar and then click the **return** arrow to return to the Entry page.

177

Avatar   An avatar represents you in a 3-D virtual world. It can be a representation of a human, an animal, or just about any other image that you wish to use. Each virtual world has a set of stock avatars that you can use as your persona.

4. You're ready to enter the 3-D Chat world. Click the **VRML World** link on the Entry page. It takes a moment or two, but the blaxxun 3-D chat world loads in the browser window, as shown in Figure 13.4. A set of chat controls appear at the bottom of the Browser windows. They enable you to enter chat text and move your avatar to show certain expressions, such as smiling and waving.

5. You navigate the Chat world just like any other VRML world. Hold down the left mouse button and push the mouse in the direction you want to go.

6. To chat in the VRML world, type your chat text in the chat box at the bottom of the browser window, and then press the **Enter** key. You also can motivate your avatar by clicking buttons like Hello, Yes, and Bye.

Figure 13.4   Push the mouse in the direction that you would like to move in the 3-D chat world.

7. Other users present in the world are listed in the user box in the chat controls area. To quickly find another user's avatar, click his or her username in the user box, and then click the **Beam** button. You are "beamed" to the location of the particular user's avatar (see Figure 13.5).

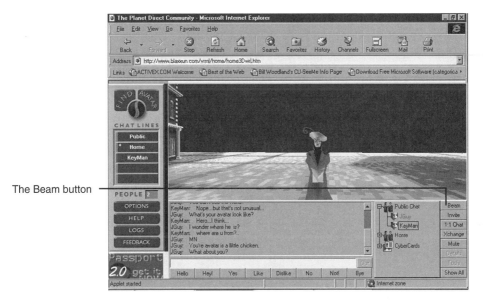

The Beam button

Figure 13.5 Use the Beam button to quickly find another user's avatar.

8. When you're done chatting, say your good-byes and either close the Internet Explorer window or switch to another Web page location.

This combination chat and VRML world from blaxxun is just one example of the VRML and multimedia potential of the DirectX technology. As time passes, additional Web applications of DirectX will be available.

In this lesson, you learned about Microsoft's DirectX technology and installed the DirectX components for Internet Explorer.

Outlook
Express Mail

Configuring Electronic Mail

In this lesson, you learn how to configure Outlook Express Mail so you can read your e-mail.

Introducing E-Mail

Electronic mail, or e-mail, is one of the largest rages in Internet communications. E-mail is the most used service on the Internet. Even individuals who don't have access to the Web have access to e-mail. Electronic mail has already become a primary communications system with a growing number of companies, government organizations, and individuals.

Let's look at some of the advantages that e-mail has over standard postal mail (snail mail) and long distance phone calls or faxes.

- *E-mail is fast.* Messages can be delivered around the world in minutes, with no worries about long distance phone charges, getting a busy number, or time zone differences. Time zones are rough on business situations. Sometimes you might need to contact someone about something important, but it would be after working hours or in the middle of the night in his or her time zone. By sending an e-mail message you can have your message in front of your business contact as soon as they get to work or check their mail.

- *You can be personable.* E-mail also enables you to be more personable with the people you're interacting with. The format enables you to write a quick note answering someone's question, without the fanfare expected of a formal letter.

- *You can work at your own pace.* Because you also have the opportunity to answer questions at your own leisure, you can avoid any hasty thoughtless remarks that you might have been tempted to make in the midst of a phone call.

- *Timely responses are more likely.* How many times have you received a letter in the mail that it has taken you two or three months to write and mail a response to? Because you have all the means of responding to e-mail at your disposal as soon as you read it, you're more likely to respond quickly.

- *E-mail can save you money.* What about those people that you need to talk to daily? Aren't those phone calls getting expensive? E-mail enables you to talk to your business partners and loved ones every day at little to no expense. E-mail even saves you the 32 cents for a stamp, the cost of the paper and envelope, and the time spent trying to remember to throw that envelope in the mailbox.

Learning E-Mail Etiquette

Just as everything else in life has a code of conduct, e-mail has its own set of rules that are generally accepted practices.

- *Read your mail!* People send your e-mail so you get information fast. If you don't read your e-mail, you might be missing something important. Besides, you're taking up extra space on your Internet service provider's server.

- *Always specify a subject.* Use a subject heading that summarizes what you're discussing in your message. This allows your recipient to prioritize the messages that they receive.

- *Always identify yourself.* Don't assume that the recipient knows you by your e-mail address. At the end of each message leave your name and contact information.

- *Know your recipient.* Don't use sarcastic remarks or rude humor unless you know that it won't offend your recipient.

- *Use proper English and be brief.* Just because you're writing to a friend doesn't mean that you want to shower him or her with pages of useless slang.

- *Avoid unauthorized copying.* Although we never count on e-mail being private, you need to make sure that you don't purposefully send another person's statements to someone else. The original author might not appreciate it.

There is one last thing you need to be aware of when sending e-mail messages. The legal issues that affect all other types of communications affect electronic mail as well. The real issue with electronic mail is copyrights. You cannot distribute copyrighted information in either a printed or electronic format without breaking copyright regulations. If you have scanned in a copy of a picture for your personal use and you decide to mail it to a bunch of friends, you could be in violation of copyright regulations. You own the copyright on images that you have created or photographs that you have taken, so you can distribute them in whatever manner you want. If a friend has taken a picture of you, he or she owns the copyright on the image, and you should get permission before distributing it. In addition, if you want to send a recognizable image of one of your friends through e-mail, you should also get the person's permission to distribute the image.

Federal laws prohibit distribution of other material. Items that would be considered pornographic or lewd are included in this list. Many countries have laws making the sending or receiving of this type of material illegal with a very heavy penalty, including jail time, so if you're sending information out of country, think about the regulations governing the recipient.

CAUTION

E-Mail Is Not Private   There are no laws that prohibit companies from reading the messages that are on their computers. So anything you send through electronic mail can legally be considered public information. It may also be interesting for you to note that a deleted e-mail may not truly be deleted. Servers all across the Internet do backups of their information either daily or multiple times a day. This creates a high likelihood that your messages could be stored on backup tapes across the world.

Configuring Your Account

When you're using Outlook Express Mail you must first configure it to work with your Internet service provider. Configuring Outlook Express Mail is easiest the first time you start the program due to the automatic configuration wizard that runs at that point. The wizard prompts you for all of the information you need to enter, making the configuration a snap.

Wizard Microsoft provides a series of helper applications, called wizards, that take you on step-by-step tours for making your software work in your particular situation. They ask you for all of the information needed to complete the procedure, and they tell you where to find the information if you don't have it.

When you're configuring your mail account, you need to have the following information available:

Mail Server Address

User ID

User Password

 TIP **Finding Information** When you first started your account, your provider most likely gave you a copy of all the information you need to connect to your mail. If you can no longer find this information sheet your service provider should be able to help you.

If you have run Outlook Express Mail before, the following steps will help you configure your mail client gather your correspondence. Without the server configured properly, you won't be able to reach the computer that holds your messages. If you haven't started Outlook Express, the wizard discussed in step 3 automatically appears and prompts you for the server address and your id and password.

1. With Outlook Express Mail running, open the **Tools** menu and select **Accounts**.
2. Click the **Add** button, then select **Mail** from the list of available account types.
3. As you can see from Figure 1.1, the server configuration screen requires you to enter all the information needed to recover your mail. Type your full name in the **Display Name** field. Click **Next**.
4. Enter your full e-mail address in the **E-Mail Address** field. Click **Next**.
5. Select the type of **Mail Server** that your provider uses. This will most likely be a POP3 system, although some use IMAP.
6. Enter the address of your incoming mail server in the **Incoming Mail (POP3 or IMAP) Server** field. The name of the server should be in a format similar to **mail.domain.net**.

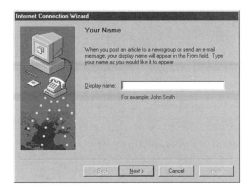

Figure 1.1 The Internet Connection Wizard helps you configure your mail account mail server from which you get your Internet e-mail.

7. In the **Outgoing Mail (SMTP) Server** field, enter the full address of your outgoing mail server. Click **Next**.

8. When you prepare to enter your logon information, be sure that both the case and spelling of your password is correct. Type your **POP Account Name** and **Password** in the fields provided for them. Click **Next**.

9. Give your account setup a name that's easy to remember, type it in the **Internet Mail Account Name** field, and then click **Next**.

10. There are three ways to connect to your service provider. Outlook Express Mail enables you to select the method that's most appropriate for you. Select from the **Phone Line**, **Local Area Network**, or **Manual** options shown in Figure 1.2. Click **Next**.

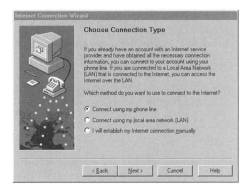

Figure 1.2 The Choose Connection Type configuration screen enables you to control how you connect to your service provider.

11. If you have selected to use a phone connection, you also will need to select a Dial-Up Networking connection. If you haven't ever connected to the Internet, you need to create a new dial-up connection. If you have been using the Internet previously, you probably already have a connection to use. In this case, select the **Use an Existing Dial-Up** connection, and then select a connection to use. Click **Next**.

If you selected either the Local Area Network or Manual connection, you're done configuring your account and you see the Congratulations screen. Click the **Finish** button and start using Outlook Express.

 TIP   **Dial-Up Networking Connections**   If you don't have any Dial-Up Networking connections configured, open the **Start** menu, select **Accessories**, and select **Dial-Up Networking**. When the group window opens, double-click the **Add New Connection** icon and follow the wizard's prompts.

12. After you have completed all the configuration options necessary, click the **Finish** button. If you want to make changes to your settings, click the **Back** button until you find the option you want to adjust, make the adjustment, and use the **Next** button to return you to the final screen.

Configuring Your Message Windows

As you use Outlook Express Mail you might find that you have trouble reading the messages in the default font or that the colors being used are difficult to see. You also may want to configure a specific set of stationary to use with your messages. The following steps show you how to configure your message screen so that you can read your mail with ease.

1. With Outlook Express Mail running, open the **Tools** menu and select **Options**.

2. Click the **General** tab.

3. Check the **Make Outlook Express My Default E-Mail Program** check box, as shown in Figure 1.3.

4. Click the **Send** tab.

5. If you want to use HTML in messages (which are readable by users of many of the most popular mail clients), select the **HTML** option button in the Mail Sending Format section.

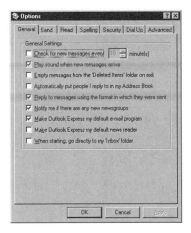

Figure 1.3 This configuration screen enables you to configure your e-mail client to perform to your specifications.

6. If you plan to send images with your mail, click the **Settings** button. Check the **Send** pictures with messages check box. Click **OK**.

7. If you want to send all your messages using Plain Text, select that option button. The Settings button enables you to send your messages using either MIME encoding, or using UUencoding. MIME is the default option.

8. Click the **OK** button to close the Options dialog box.

9. Open the **Tools** menu and select **Stationary**.

10. Click the **Mail** tab.

11. From this dialog box, you can control which font and font color is used in your messages. Click the **Font Settings** button in the Compose Font section to change your screen font.

12. Figure 1.4 shows the font options that you have available. Select the font style and size that you want to use, and then click the **OK** button.

13. If you want to use stationery with your messages, select the **This Statio-nery** option button, then click the **Select** button and choose a stationery form to use. For your convenience, a sample is shown of each background. Once you have selected the stationery you want to use, click **OK**.

14. Click the **OK** button on the main Stationery dialog box.

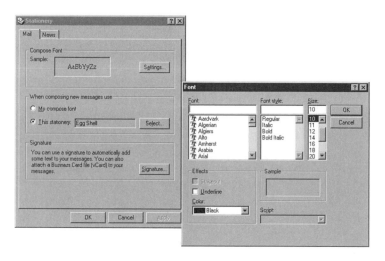

Figure 1.4   Configure your fonts through the Font dialog box.

Creating and Configuring Your Signature File

Signature files are just one of the many ways that Internet e-mail users save time when sending messages. Signature files appear at the bottom of every message. They inform everyone about who you are, and what e-mail address you use. Some people often put their favorite quotations at the end of their signature files. Others put their position and the name of the company that they work for in theirs. Signature files can add a sense of personality to a message, or add a sense of official protocol to the message.

1. With Outlook Express Mail open, open the **Tools** menu and select **Stationery**.

2. When the Stationery dialog box opens, select the **Mail** tab, and then click the **Signature** button.

3. Select the **Text** option button and enter the information that you want to appear at the bottom of each of your messages. If you want to have your signature information appear on each message, check the **Add This Signature to the End of All Outgoing Messages** check box at the top of the dialog box. Once you're done configuring these settings, click **OK**.

4. If you want to attach a virtual business card to your e-mail messages, you can select an Address Book entry to be attached to each message that you mail. Select the **Address Book** entry from the drop-down list. Click the **Edit** button if you want to make changes, or click **New** if you want to create a new entry.

5. Click **OK**. Next time you start a new message, your signature file automatically appears at the bottom of your message. Close the Stationery dialog box by clicking **Apply** and then **OK**.

 TIP   **Editing Your Signature**   If you need to make a one-time edit to the message, you can make the changes on the letter. If you want to make a permanent change, make those changes in the Options dialog box.

In this lesson, you learned how to configure your Outlook Express Mail client to retrieve electronic messages off of your Outlook Express Mail server. In the next lesson, you will learn how to work with the Windows Address Book.

The Windows Address Book

In this lesson, you learn how to use the Windows Address Book with Outlook Express for storing and managing your e-mail addresses.

Understanding E-Mail Addresses

E-mail addresses are often used as an individual's personal identifier on the Internet. They enable users to send and receive information all across the Internet. An e-mail address serves as a phone number, but instead of identifying a particular house, it identifies a particular person (or company). E-mail addresses use a variety of formats depending upon the network that you're using, but Internet e-mail addresses follow one main form.

A typical e-mail address consists of two distinct parts. The first part identifies a unique user (userid) on the network, and the second identifies the specific system (host) that user belongs to. On some networks, userid's are case sensitive. On these systems jack, Jack, and JACK are three separate userid's or individuals. The Internet uses a system of Domain Name specifications to track specific hosts and their classifications. Table 2.1 shows you the main top-level domains, or extensions, that are available.

 Domain Names Every computer has its own address on the Internet that other computers use to find it. These addresses are used to identify the computers and the networks that are permanently attached to the Internet. Your personal computer does not have a domain name because you connect through your service provider (who does have a domain name).

Table 2.1 E-Mail Address Extensions and Their Intended Origins

Extension	Origin
EDU	universities, colleges, all school systems
COM	commercial businesses
MIL	military bases and organizations
GOV	government agencies
ORG	organizations
NET	networking units such as Internet service providers

Most host systems outside of the United States tend to be registered under both a country code and a domain extension. Although this is a good rule of thumb, hostnames aren't always indicative of their source of geographic location. A good example of this is microsoft.com that is composed of a series of hosts located throughout the world, not just in the United States.

There are many different computers or networks registered under a specific domain. For example, a company might have the domain catsback.com. This would tell you that they are a commercial business organization. They are then responsible for managing any other hostnames that fall within their domain. For example, **www.catsback.com** might represent the computer hosting Cat's Back's Web site, just as **ftp.catsback.com** would represent the computer hosting their FTP archives. And, as you might guess, **mail.catsback.com** would be the name of their mail server.

Internet e-mail addresses consist of a userid, followed by an "at" symbol and the hostname in this format: **userid@computer.subdomain.domain**. Following this model, an e-mail address for this company might be catsback@ mail.catsback.com. Because there's no limit to the size of an address, you could possibly send mail to an individual with an address resembling this: **jaque_b_tourlebouland@otime.cntrinvbur.ak-dpt.staterept.paris.mil.fr**.

Internet Address Directories

There are a wide variety of internationally accessible e-mail address books located on the Internet. By using these LDAP (Lightweight Directory Access Protocol) e-mail address books, you can quickly and effortlessly add the addresses that you find to your Windows Address Book.

TERM

LDAP The Lightweight Directory Access Protocol was originally designed as an Internet client server protocol for accessing the preexisting X.500 directory services. Since its origination, LDAP has evolved to become a standard means of accessing online directory systems.

Outlook Express provides you with immediate access to the most popular LDAP directories, including Four11 (**http://www.four11.com**), Switchboard (**http://www.switchboard.com**), InfoSpace (**http://www.infospace.com**), BigFoot (**http://www.bigfoot.com**), and Who/Where (**http://www.whowhere.com**).

When you need to look up an individual on these systems, you can use the following steps:

1. Open the **Start** menu, select **Programs**, **Internet Explorer**, and then **Address Book**. If you already have Outlook Express running, you can click the **Address Book** button, or you can open the **Tools** menu and select **Address Book** (Ctrl+Shift+B).

2. Click the **Find** button, or open the **Edit** menu and select **Find** (Ctrl+F).

3. Select the directory service that you want to use from the **Search** list (see Figure 2.1).

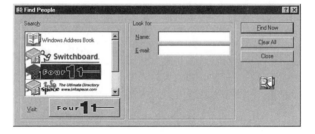

Figure 2.1 The Find People dialog box enables you to search both your local Address Book and a variety of Internet directories.

4. Enter the information that you want to search for, whether it is a user's name, e-mail address, postal mail address, or phone number in your local Address Book. If you selected one of the directory services, enter either a name or e-mail address.

5. Click the **Find Now** button. If the individual that you're looking for is listed with that service, his or her name appears in the search results window shown in Figure 2.2.

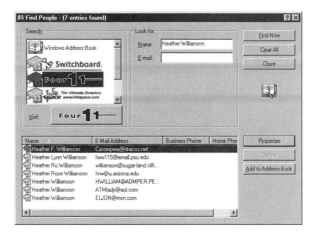

Figure 2.2 The results of a search using Four11.

6. Select the name that you want to add to your Address Book, and then click **Add to Address Book**.

7. Click **Close**.

Using the Windows Address Book

The Windows address book places everything at the tip of your fingers. You have access to all of its key features directly from the main toolbar. With the click of a button you can add a new contact to your local address book, edit an existing contact, or simply group some of the contacts you already have.

Adding a Contact

To create a new address book entry, follow these steps.

1. Open the **Start** menu, select **Programs**, **Internet Explorer**, and then **Address Book**. If you already have Outlook Express running, you can click the **Address Book** button, or you can open the **Tools** menu and select **Address Book** (Ctrl+Shift+B).

2. Click the **New Contact** button, or open the **File** menu and select **New Contact** (Ctrl+N).

3. Enter the individual's first, middle, and last name in the appropriate fields, shown in Figure 2.3. These names are combined to create an automatic display name. You also can choose to fill in a nickname for the individual you're adding.

195

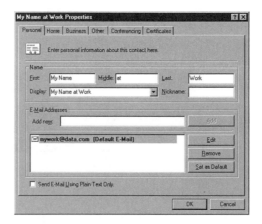

Figure 2.3 The Properties dialog box, from which you can add a new contact.

4. In the E-Mail Addresses section, click in the **Add New** field and type in the full address you want to use, such as **jack@whitehouse.gov**.

5. Click the **Add** button.

6. If you want to send only plain text messages to these individuals, check the **Send E-Mail Using Plain Text Only** check box at the bottom of the screen.

7. Click the **Home** tab. On this tab you can store the personal mailing information about your contact. Included on this page is space for the individual's Personal Web Page address. Be sure to leave **http://** attached to the front of the page address.

8. Click the **Business** tab. This screen enables you to store all of the business information for your contact, including an address for his or her business Web site.

9. Click the **Other** tab, and you can store notes about this particular individual.

10. Click the **NetMeeting** tab. If you have installed Microsoft NetMeeting, you can use this tab to store the connection information for your NetMeeting contacts.

11. From the **Select or Add New** drop-down field, select an e-mail address to use to find the contact.

12. Enter the address of the directory server you want to use to find this person.

13. When you finish entering the contact information that you want to track, click the **OK** button.

Editing a Contact

The following steps walk you through editing an entry in your Contact list.

1. With the Address Book open, select the entry you want to edit.
2. Click the **Properties** button, or open the **File** menu and select **Properties** (Alt+Enter).
3. Click the tab that stores the information you need to edit. Most likely this is the Personal tab because you probably want to edit the e-mail address.
4. To edit the e-mail address, click the **Edit** button.
5. Place your cursor in the highlighted e-mail field, and then edit the entry to reflect the necessary changes to the e-mail address.
6. When you finish making your changes, click the **OK** button.

Adding a Group

Groups are used to organize mass delivery of e-mail messages. As you develop groups of friends on the Internet, you may find yourself sending those individuals the same e-mail messages. To make this process easier, simply collect those names under a single nickname and then send your messages. The following steps help you with this task.

1. Open the **Start** menu, select **Programs**, **Internet Explorer**, and then **Address Book**. If you already have Outlook Express running, you can click the **Address Book** button, or you can open the **Tools** menu and select **Address Book** (Ctrl+Shift+B).
2. Click the **New Group** button, or open the **File** menu and select **New Group** (Ctrl+G).
3. Create an easily identifiable name and type it into the **Group Name** field (shown in Figure 2.4).
4. Click the **Select Members** button. If you want to create a New Contact, you can do so by clicking the **New Contact** button.
5. From the Select Group members dialog box, click the names of the individuals that you want to include in your group from the left-hand window. Hold down the **Control** key to select multiple names.
6. Click the **Select** button, and the names you chose appear in the list on the right (see Figure 2.5).

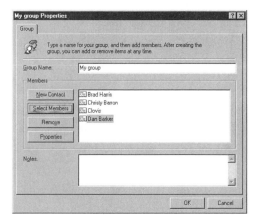

Figure 2.4 The Group Properties dialog box enables you to create personal groups for distributing mass mail messages.

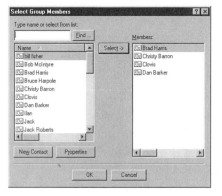

Figure 2.5 The Select Group Members dialog box enables you to add members to your groups.

7. When all of your names have been added to the Members list, click **OK**.

8. Click **OK** on the Group Properties dialog box. You see your new group listed below the main Address Book icon on the left side of your Windows Address Book screen.

Deleting an Entry

Addresses change often, and sometimes the time comes when you no longer want to correspond with a specific individual. In this case, you may want to delete a Contact. Follow these steps to do so.

1. With the Windows Address Book open, select the entry that you want to delete.

2. Click the **Delete** button on the toolbar, or open the **File** menu and select **Delete**. The entry immediately disappears from your Contact list and all of your groups.

Importing Addresses

As you continue using Internet e-mail, you may find that you have switched from one e-mail client to another or that you have a business associate or friend who wants to share his or her address book with you.

1. Open the **Start** menu, select **Programs**, select **Internet Explorer**, and then select **Book**. If you already have Outlook Express running, you can click the **Address Book** button, or you can open the **Tools** menu and select **Address Book** (Ctrl+Shift+B).

2. Open the **File** menu, select **Import**, and select **Address Book**.

3. Select the type of Address Book you want to import into your existing address book. The options are shown in Figure 2.6.

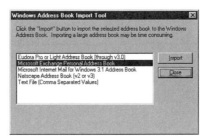

Figure 2.6 The Windows Address Book Import Tool provides you with a means of importing information directly into your existing address book.

4. Once you have selected the appropriate import type, you need to follow the instructions laid out for you in the wizard that runs. For the Netscape, Eudora, and Internet Mail imports, you are simply asked for the directory in which the address book is stored. If you are importing a Windows Explorer address book, you will be asked to select the specific profile from which you want to import addresses and then the specific address book to use.

In this lesson, you learned how to create and edit address book entries, create personal mailing lists, import address books from other programs, and use the variety of LDAP directories on the Internet to increase the size of your personal Address book. In the next lesson, you will learn how to create messages to be sent over the Internet.

Creating
Messages

In this lesson, you learn how to send messages with rich content and attached files.

Writing a Message

Creating a message to send through the Internet is a very simple process. You simply have to address the message and send it to your service provider. The following steps show you how:

1. With Outlook Express open, click the **Compose Message** button on the toolbar, or open the **Compose** menu and select **New Message** (Ctrl+N).

2. When the New Message dialog box shown in Figure 3.1 opens, enter the address of the individual to whom you are sending the message in the To field.

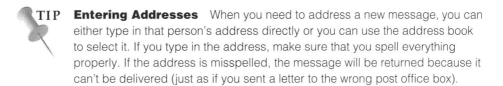

TIP **Entering Addresses** When you need to address a new message, you can either type in that person's address directly or you can use the address book to select it. If you type in the address, make sure that you spell everything properly. If the address is misspelled, the message will be returned because it can't be delivered (just as if you sent a letter to the wrong post office box).

3. If you don't know the address where you need to send the message, select an address from the Windows Address Book by clicking the rolodex card icon next to the To prompt, or by opening the **Tools** menu and picking **Select Recipients**.

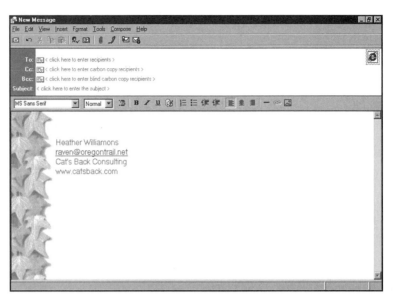

Figure 3.1   The New Message window, from which you can create a message to send to friends and associates across the Internet.

4. When the Address Book opens, as shown in Figure 3.2, select the name of the individual to whom you want to send a message.

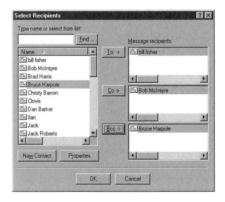

Figure 3.2   The Outlook Express Address Book, from which you can select your mail recipients quickly and easily.

5. Click the **To:** button to place that individual's name in the To list. Click the CC: button to add that individual to the carbon copy list. Click the **BCC:** button to add an individual to the blind carbon copy list.

CC: and BCC: If you carbon copy a message to someone, the main recipients of the message know that you are sending copies to the listed individuals. If you blind carbon copy a message to an individual, the main recipients don't know that the person will also be reading the message.

6. Once you have selected all the individuals that need to receive this message, click the **OK** button.

7. When you return to the New message window you find the names you selected in the To:, CC:, and BCC: fields. Place your cursor in the **Subject** field.

8. Type a short description of the message that you're sending in the Subject field.

9. Press **Tab** or click your mouse in the message body window. This takes you down to the body area of your message. Type your message here.

10. Once you're done typing your message, open the **Tools** menu and select **Spelling** (F7). No matter to whom you send a message, you need to make sure that you're using proper spelling and grammar.

11. The Spelling Checker, shown in Figure 3.3, enables you to add words to your dictionary, ignore your current spelling, or change words to the suggested spelling. When the spelling check is finished, you are returned to the message window.

Figure 3.3 Outlook Express Spelling Checker makes sending properly spelled messages easy for everyone.

Inserting Text from a File

As you have probably noticed already, it is often overly time consuming to write out every e-mail message. This frustrating situation does have a solution. If you already have the information typed in some other format, you can easily insert the text of that document into a message using the following steps. Unlike inserting or attaching a file, when you insert text from a file, you do not have a gold paperclip icon indicating that a file has been attached. Instead, you will see the text in the message, as if it were typed there originally.

1. Open the **Insert** menu and select **Text from File**. This opens the Insert Text File dialog box shown in Figure 3.4.

2. From this dialog box, select the text file that contains the information you want to add to your message.

Figure 3.4   Select a file to insert into your message.

3. Click the **Open** button. The message window opens, showing your inserted text.

TIP   **Alternative Insert**   If you're currently looking at the document that you want to use in your message, use the Copy and Paste commands on the Edit menu to move the text from your document to your message.

Inserting Stationery

Using Outlook Express, you can make all of your messages use a particular stationery that you like. Although this makes your messages larger, it gives messages a sense of individuality that other e-mail clients don't provide you. Follow these steps to use stationery:

1. Open the **Insert** menu, select **Background**, and then select **Picture**. The Background Picture dialog box opens.

2. Click the **Browse** button.

3. Select the background that you want to use, for example **festive.gif**. If you want to see what an image looks like before you use it, right-click the image's name and select **Open** from the shortcut menu. This opens the image in its associated program.

Program Associations When you install software onto your computer, it automatically tells Windows 95 what sort of files it can access. Windows 95 then adds those relationships to its file association list. This list is used to automatically open files when you browse both on your local computer and on the Internet.

4. Click the **Open** button.

5. Click **OK** to automatically update your message stationery with the new image shown in Figure 3.5.

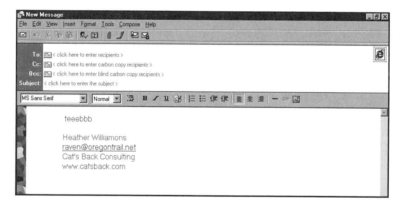

Figure 3.5 As soon as you change your stationery, the change is displayed in the message body window.

Attaching a File

Sometimes you need to send a file to an individual. Outlook Express makes that easy by providing you with all the tools you need to attach a file of any type directly to your messages. You also can attach virtually any number of files to your messages if you so want. Here's how:

1. Open the **Insert** menu and select **File Attachment**. This opens the Insert Attachment dialog box.

2. From this dialog, select the text file that contains the information you want to send along with your message.

3. Click the **Attach** button. The message window displays your attached file in a sub-screen, as you can see in Figure 3.6.

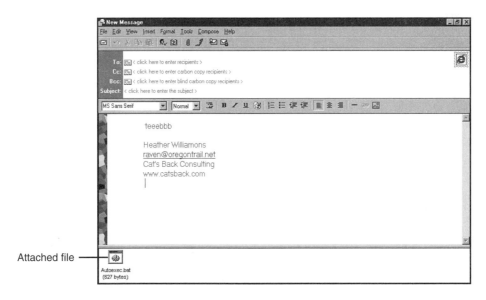

Attached file

Figure 3.6   After you attach a file to your message, it appears in a special section of the New Message window.

Writing with HTML

Outlook Express provides you with the ability to send rich HTML messages to your contacts. HTML gives you the ability to send elaborate messages containing pictures, sounds, colorful text, and artistic fonts.

> **TERM**   **HTML**   The Hypertext Markup Language is the standard language used to create Web pages all across the Internet. It uses a series of discrete instructions to tell your Web browser or Outlook Express how to display the information contained within your message.

The following steps show you how you can incorporate these features into your messages.

1. With Outlook Express open, click the **New Message** button on the toolbar, or open the **Compose** menu and select **New Message** (Ctrl+N).
2. In Lesson 1, you configured Outlook Express to automatically use HTML for the messages. To make sure that's still selected and you're going to create this message using HTML, open the **Format** menu and select **Rich Text (HTML)**.

TIP **HTML Formatted Messages** If you're creating a message that will be sent using HTML, you will be able to see the HTML toolbar located directly below the addressing section of the window and above the message body.

3. Address your message to whomever you want to send it to.

4. Place your cursor in the message body and type this short message:

> Hello everyone!
>
> I hope you are all having fun. I just installed Outlook Express.
>
> It is a pretty cool program.
>
> Catch you on the Internet sometime!
>
> Ciao… me!

5. As you can see in Figure 3.7, the text originally appears on your stationery in the default font and color. To change that, first highlight the first line you typed.

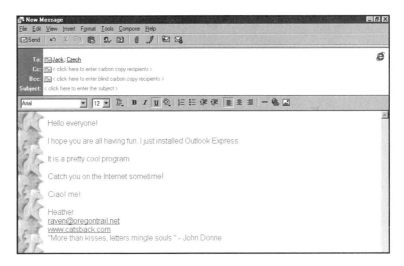

Figure 3.7 Creating a message using HTML is just as easy as formatting a standard text message.

6. Click the **Font Size** drop-down arrow and select **36**.

7. Highlight your closing statement.

8. Click the **Bold** button or press **Ctrl+B**.

9. With the closing line still highlighted, increase the font size to Larger, and then change the font to something a bit more festive, such as Comic Sans.

TIP   **Sending HTML Messages**   Not all of the e-mail clients that are being used can properly read HTML formatted messages. If you're sending a letter to an individual whose mail reader doesn't support HTML, he or she sees all of your HTML codes in the body of the message, which makes reading a message quite difficult.

10. Move your cursor to the empty line below your salutation.

11. Open the **Insert** menu and select **Picture**.

12. Click the **Browse** button to select a picture to use. This image needs to be either in GIF or JPG format. You can find some images to test on the Internet or in your Temporary Internet Files folder in your Windows directory.

13. Select the image and click **OK**. The image automatically appears in your message (see Figure 3.8).

Figure 3.8   Using HTML formatting enables you to adjust your fonts and add images directly into your message.

Adding a Web Page Address

As you correspond with individuals, you will see that they often send you addresses for Web pages, newsgroups, and FTP sites. Outlook Express automatically recognizes these addresses and enables you to open these sites by simply clicking the links. You can add these addresses to your messages also. These steps show you how.

1. With Outlook Express open to a message window, type the following Web address: **http:/www.catsback.com/**. As you finish entering this address, you see it automatically change color and become underlined. You have just created an active link to this Web site. Anyone to whom you send this message will be able to automatically open this Web site.

2. Type your e-mail address. As you complete this process you see your address turn into an active link also. If you add your address into your signature file, people will be able to immediately send you a message by clicking your e-mail address.

Setting Message Priority

Before sending a message, you should check a couple of things besides your spelling and grammar. One of these is message priority. This setting places a flag next to messages that you feel are of primary importance for your recipient to read.

To set priority on a message, open the **Tools** menu, select **Set Priority**, and choose the priority status that you want to use. The available priority levels are **High**, **Normal**, and **Low**.

In this lesson, you learned how to attach text and files to your messages and create colorful HTML-based messages to share with your contacts. The next lesson shows you how to send these messages through the Internet.

Sending E-Mail and Retrieving Your Mail Messages

In this lesson, you learn how to deliver messages you have written and retrieve messages that other people have sent to you—on your schedule, not the computer's.

Sending and Retrieving While Connected

The only way to get your messages off your service provider's computer is to download them with your Outlook Express client or another similar mail client. When you download your messages, they are removed from your service provider's computer and placed on your own. This saves space on your mail server so that it can be used later. By placing your messages on your computer you can read them offline, saving phone and connect time charges that are billed by your provider.

 Connect Time Charges The costs associated with connecting to your Internet service provider, based solely upon the amount of time that you use their services.

 E-Mail on the Road If you travel a lot and use multiple e-mail clients or multiple computers, you might want to configure your traveling computer so it doesn't delete e-mail messages from your server. This enables you to easily collect all of your messages on your home computer when you return. This may help you keep from losing important information while you're traveling.

There are two ways you can retrieve messages with Outlook Express. The first is to log into your service provider manually each time you want to gather messages. The other way is to set up a schedule that your mail client can follow on its own, enabling you to gather mail messages without any intervention on your part.

 Offline/Online When you're connected to your service provider through your phone line, you are online. When you're not connected to another computer, you are offline. These terms can refer to many different parts of the computing world, but in this case they refer to a state of connection between your computer and your service provider's computer.

If you don't keep your computer on all the time, or if you don't run your mail client constantly, you need to tell Outlook Express when to send your messages. The following steps show you how to do this:

1. With Outlook Express running, click the **Send and Receive** button on the Toolbar, or open the **Tools** menu and select **Send and Receive** (Ctrl+M) to send mail through all of your accounts. This opens the Connect To: dialog box shown in Figure 4.1.

2. Click the **OK** button.

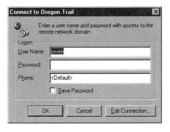

Figure 4.1 The Connection dialog box used by Outlook Express to connect to your service provider and exchange your messages.

3. After you receive notice of a connection, you can watch Outlook Express send and receive your messages.

4. When the messages have been transferred, click the taskbar button that opens your Connection dialog box. Click **Disconnect**.

Automatic Disconnect If you want to have Outlook Express automatically hang up your phone after you transfer your messages, open the **Tools** menu and select **Options**. Click the **Dial-Up** tab and make sure that the **Hang Up When Finished Sending, Receiving, or Downloading** check box is checked.

Scheduling Messages to Be Delivered

If you leave your computer and mail client running for long periods of time, you may want to configure Outlook Express to exchange your messages automatically. To do so, follow these steps:

1. With Outlook Express running, open the **Tools** menu and select **Options**.

2. Click the **Send** tab.

3. Check the **Send Messages Immediately** option.

4. Click the **General** tab.

5. Check the **Check for New Messages Every xx Minutes** check box. Thirty minutes is the default setting for this option. You can change it to whatever is most appropriate for your situation. In most situations, every hour is sufficient.

6. Click the **Dial-Up** tab.

7. Check the **Hang Up When Finished Sending, Receiving, or Downloading** check box.

8. Click **Apply**, and then click **OK** to activate and save your settings changes.

In this lesson, you learned how to control your mail transfers and schedule them for when they are convenient for you. In the next lesson, you will learn how to reply to the messages that you have received.

Reading and Replying to Messages

In this lesson, you learn to read and reply to messages you have received.

Opening a Message

There are many things you can do with the messages that you retrieve from your mail server. You have the option of reading messages and then replying to either the original author or all of the individuals to whom the message was sent. You also can forward the messages that you receive to anyone else. But before you can do any of that, you need to read the messages you receive.

Opening a message isn't the only way to read it, but it is one of the easiest. You can read through a message in the preview window, or you can open it in the full message display. Although you cannot print a message from the preview window, you can reply or forward a message to other individuals from there.

To open a message in the full message window (as shown in Figure 5.1), double-click the message line in the Inbox list. This opens the full message window and displays your selected message. From this window, you can make whatever changes need to be made before you process the message further.

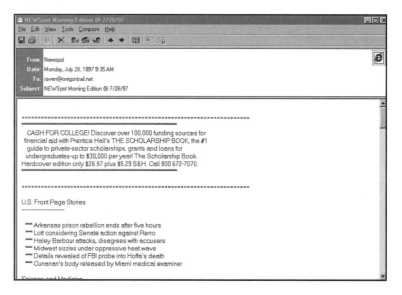

Figure 5.1   In the full screen message window, you can edit messages you have received.

Replying to a Message

When you reply to a message, your response is sent by default to the original author only, not to all the listed recipients. However, you can choose to reply to everyone who received the message. Just as you can read a message from either the preview window or the full message window, you can reply to it from either of these screens. Here's how:

- To reply to a message from the preview window, select the message, and then click the **Reply to Author** button on the Outlook Express toolbar (see Figure 5.2). Alternatively, you can open the **Compose** menu and select the **Reply to Author** option (Ctrl+R).

- To reply to a message from the full message window, double-click the message entry, wait for the full window to open, and then click the **Reply to Author** button on the message window toolbar.

Either way, a copy of the original message opens in another window with a greater than sign (>) before each line. To type your response, simply place your cursor in the original message text where you want your comments to go and start typing.

Reply to Author   Reply to All

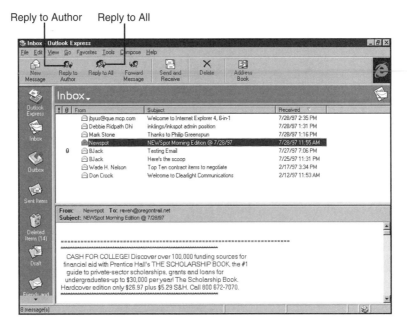

Figure 5.2 The Reply to Author button on the main Outlook Express toolbar.

When you finish adding your comments, click the **Send** button to add your message reply to the Outgoing message queue.

TIP **Replying with File Attachments**   If you reply to a message with a file attachment, the file won't be sent back with your reply. All that will remain of the file is a note letting you know that a file was once attached to this message. The same thing happens if you select Reply to All from a message with a file attachment.

Replying to All the Message Recipients

Replying to all the message recipients is essentially the same as replying to the original author, except you send your response to all the original recipients. From either the preview window or the message window, click the **Reply to All** button, or open the **Compose** menu and select **Reply to All** (Ctrl+Shift+R). This opens a message from which your response is sent to everyone listed in the To:, CC:, and BCC: address lines of the original message (see Figure 5.3).

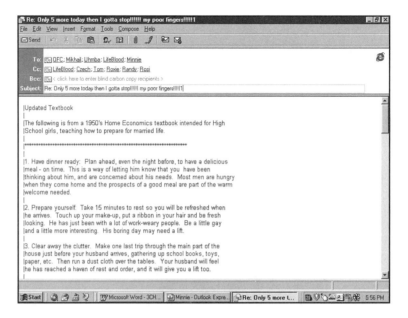

Figure 5.3 When you choose Reply to All, all original recipients are listed as recipients for your reply.

Type your response in the message at appropriate places, and then click the **Send** button to place the message in the Outgoing message queue.

Forwarding a Message

Forwarding is similar to replying to a message, except the recipient of the message is generally not the original author, nor is it one of the original recipients. When you forward a message to another individual, that person sees the original author, the original recipients, your responses, and any file attachments that were included.

Forwarding Messages Although electronic mail isn't considered private, it is still a violation to share information or images without the express written permission of the original author. You need to think of this when sending messages containing copied material to individuals not on the original mailing list.

To forward a message, click the **Forward Message** button (shown in Figure 5.4), which is available in both the Outlook Express window and the message window. Alternatively, you can open the **Compose** menu and select **Forward** (Ctrl+F).

Forward Message

Figure 5.4 The Forward Message button.

Forwarding as an Attachment

The fourth option for forwarding messages is to forward a message as an attachment. In this way, you can attach multiple pieces of information to a single message. Of course, you have to be careful to attach only as many messages as the recipient's e-mail client can receive properly. For example, if you're forwarding a message to an individual on the AOL network, that person can receive only one attachment per message.

To forward a message as an attachment, open the **Compose** menu and select **Forward as Attachment**.

In this lesson, you learned how to open, read, reply, and forward the messages you receive. In the next lesson, you will learn how to work with file attachments.

Working with Attached Files

In this lesson, you learn how to send and receive files through Internet e-mail.

Recognizing Attached Files

After you have used electronic mail for a while, you will find that friends or members of mailing lists send you files with your messages. These files might be word processing documents, graphic files, audio files, or even movie files. Files of any type can be sent through e-mail.

When you receive a message with a file attached, you see a paperclip icon to the right of the message header listing in the Inbox. This icon only symbolizes that there is an attachment. It doesn't specify the number of attachments or what file type the attachment is. So a message may have one or more messages or one or more files attached to it.

Common File Encoding Methods

Several methods are used to make encode files for transportation through the Internet. No matter which method you use, the encoding process takes an 8-bit binary file, translates it into standard 7-bit text, and then adds it to the end of the message you're sending. Many e-mail clients, including Outlook Express, automatically decode files sent to them in this fashion so you don't have to. The two main encoding techniques used by Outlook Express are MIME and UUEncode/UUDecode.

MIME stands for Multipurpose Outlook Express Extensions. This freely available specification enables you to exchange message text in languages with different character sets and to share multimedia e-mail among the different systems using Outlook Express standards. MIME enables you to read messages containing the following information:

- character sets other than US-ASCII
- enriched text
- images and sounds
- other encapsulated messages
- tar files
- PostScript
- pointers to Internet files

MIME has several predefined types of nontextual message content, and it also enables you to create your own types. MIME has been carefully designed to work with the most bizarre variations of SMTP, UUCP, and other mail transport protocols that treat the headers and bodies of e-mail messages in strange ways.

The following list shows some of the features of a good MIME-compliant mail client, such as Outlook Express.

- Displays GIF-, JPEG-, and PBM-encoded images
- Displays PostScript parts using a PostScript viewing or printing device
- Obtains external message body information through Internet FTP or a mail server
- Plays audio parts on systems that support digital audio

Although a fully MIME-compliant system would provide you with all the message bells and whistles, the minimal requirements are almost trivial. At a minimum, the MIME-compliant client must ensure that you don't see the raw data from a MIME message inappropriately.

 TIP **MIME FAQ** You can get a copy of the MIME FAQ at this Web site: **http://www.cis.ohio-state.edu/text/faq/usenet/mail/mime-faq/top.html**.

Finding the Files Attached to Your Messages

Messages with attached files can be identified in a couple of ways. Each of these methods gives you different information that you may need before saving the file to your hard drive.

- **Message Size**   Every message with an attached file shows the combined total size of the file and the original message. This value is apparent in the message list above the preview window.

- **Message List Icon**   When you're looking at the list of messages in your Inbox or another folder, you see a green paperclip icon next to messages with attached files.

- **Preview Icon**   When you select a message to preview, you see a gold paperclip icon in the upper-right corner of the preview window (see Figure 6.1). If you click this icon, you can see a list of the files that are attached to the message.

Click the paperclip icon to see this list of attached files

The paperclip icon

Figure 6.1   The Outlook Express preview window shows you a list of all the files attached to a message.

- **Attachment List** When you open a message in the message window, you see a series of file icons across the bottom of your message (as shown in Figure 6.2). The icons representing these files indicate which applications open them.

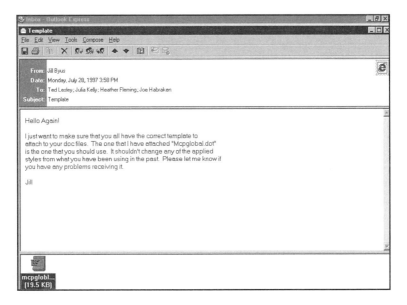

Figure 6.2 Once a message is open, you can see all the file attachments as icons across the bottom of the window.

Uploading Files with E-Mail

If you want to attach a file to an e-mail message you're sending, you must make sure your recipient is capable of receiving the file. Not all e-mail clients can work with MIME or UUencoded attachments. Some might have to use third-party decoders to read the file.

Once you know the recipient can receive the file, follow these steps to attach a file to a message you're sending:

1. With Outlook Express open, click the **Compose Message** button on the toolbar, or open the **Compose** menu and select **New Message** (Ctrl+N).

2. Address the message by typing the address of its intended recipient or by selecting his or her name from the Address Book.

3. Enter an appropriate subject in the **Subject** line.

4. Open the **Insert** menu and select **File Attachment**. This opens the Insert Attachment dialog box, from which you can select the files you want to send with your message (see Figure 6.3).

Figure 6.3   Use the Attach File dialog box to select the files you want to send with your messages.

5. Click the **OK** button. When this window closes, you see the file icon attached to the bottom of your message window.

6. Click the **Send** icon to send your message. Sending a message with an attached file is no different from sending a message by itself.

Downloading and Opening Attached Files

Of course, the ability to send files would be useless if you couldn't receive them yourself. Receiving a file is a simple process of opening the file after you have retrieved your messages. Because the files are attached directly to the e-mail messages you receive, you don't have to do anything special to receive them. All you have to do is open the attachment and save it to disk.

- **Preview Window**   When saving an attachment through the preview window, double-click the gold paperclip icon to open the list of attachments, and then click the name of the file. This automatically opens the file if it has an associated application; if it doesn't have an associated application, the Save Attachment dialog box appears, from which you can save it to one of your drives (see Figure 6.4).

- **Message Window**   When saving an attachment through the message window, simply right-click the icon and select **Save As**. If you want to open a file, double-click its icon.

Figure 6.4   From the Save Attachment dialog box, you can save your file attachments wherever you want.

In this lesson, you learned about file attachments: how to send them and how to receive them. In the next lesson, you will learn about the various methods you can use to organize your e-mail.

E-Mail Maintenance

In this lesson, you learn how to manage your incoming e-mail.

Sorting Your E-Mail

One of the most frustrating things about e-mail is the lack of organization. All of your messages automatically come into one folder and stay there until you have the time to do something about it. In Outlook Express, this problem is compounded if you have multiple e-mail addresses from which messages are collected. Fortunately, there's an easy way for you to have this information sorted and stored.

Outlook Express includes some useful tools for separating this information. You can easily retrieve mail for all of your personal and business accounts and keep it separate. Outlook Express enables you to create subfolders within the Inbox or any other folder that you want. This means you can easily filter all your incoming mail into specific areas—so personal messages can go into one folder, business-related messages can automatically be placed in another folder, and each of your mailing list messages can be sorted into a folder of their own. This can save you time, and it enables you to tackle the important messages and leave the rest for a later.

Creating Folders

The following steps walk you through creating a folder:

1. Open the **File** menu, select **Folder**, and then select **New Folder**. The Create Folder dialog box appears (see Figure 7.1).

Figure 7.1 You can create a new folder under any folder in Outlook Express, including those that are installed by default.

2. Type the name for your folder in the **Folder Name** field. For example, you might type **Personal Inbox** as the name of a subfolder in which you want to store your personal messages.

3. You can place your new folder wherever you want in your Outlook Express folder hierarchy. Simply highlight the name of the folder in which you want to create the subfolder. For example, click **Inbox**.

4. Click the **OK** button.

Moving Messages into Folders

Once you have created a series of folders, you need to organize your existing messages into them. Follow these steps to move your messages into the folders you have created:

1. Select the first message that you want to move to your new folder.

2. Right-click the entry and select **Move To** from the shortcut menu that appears. (Alternatively, you can open the **Edit** menu and select **Move to Folder**).

3. Select the folder that you want to place your message in, such as the Personal Inbox folder you created under the Inbox.

4. Click **OK**.

Filtering Messages

Once you have created some folders and most of your messages are sorted into them, you need to set up Outlook Express so that it takes care of this filtering process for you. When you're using Outlook Express, you have a lot of options for controlling where specific messages go and how they get there. If you're using multiple e-mail accounts, you can use Outlook Express's filtering system, as outlined in these steps:

1. Open the **Tools** menu and select **Inbox Assistant**.

2. Click the **Add** button. As you can see in Figure 7.2, you can sort messages based on the names in the To:, CC:, or From: lines, the Subject: lines of your message headers, the account through which you received the messages, or the messages' size.

3. There are a variety of ways that you can complete this information, so you can essentially sort each individual message into a separate folder. For example, if you're a member of a mailing list, you might enter the list name in the To: field (such as list@studiob.com). If you're using multiple e-mail accounts, you can sort your information into personal and business folders in your Inbox. To do so, click the **Account** check box, and select your personal account entry.

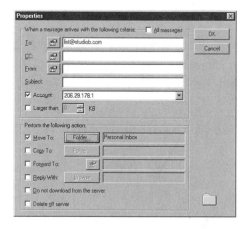

Figure 7.2 The properties for each Inbox Assistant filter give you the ability to sort information into specific filters.

4. In the Perform the Following Action section, click the **Move To** button.

5. Click the **Folder** button.

6. Select the **Personal Inbox** folder you created earlier.

7. Click the **OK** button.

8. Click **OK** again in the main Properties dialog box. You now have the first rule for your Inbox Assistant to follow (see Figure 7.3).

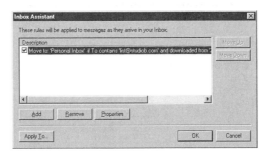

Figure 7.3 The Inbox Assistant shows the list of rules that have been created. Those with checked boxes are active.

9. Click **OK** to save the rule you created.

Once you have created a rule for your Inbox Assistant to follow, anytime you download messages, they are automatically sorted into the folders that you have configured.

Deleting Old E-Mail Messages

Part of maintaining a well-organized e-mail system is deleting the messages that you no longer need (the ones that are simply taking up important space). To delete a message, select its messages header from the list in your folder, and click the **Delete** button on your toolbar or press the **Delete** key on your keyboard.

When you delete a message, it automatically goes to your Deleted Items folder. It remains there until you empty that folder or your scheduled backup runs, whichever comes first.

Compacting Mail Folders

After moving and deleting messages, you will want to compact your mail folders. This might sound odd, but it's a necessary form of maintenance for keeping Outlook Express functioning well.

TERM   **Compacting Folders**   When you compact a message folder, you simply reorganize the files it contains so that they take up less space on your hard drive. This process also removes any messages that you have marked for deletion.

To compact *all* of your mail folders, open the **File** menu, select **Folders**, and then select **Compact All Folders**. The dialog box shown in Figure 7.4 appears, showing you the progress of your folders being compacted.

Figure 7.4   Outlook Express displays the name of each folder as it compacts it.

If you want to compact *only a single folder*, switch to the folder you want to compact, click the folder name heading, and select it from the list of available folders (see Figure 7.5). Then open the **File** menu, select **Folder**, and select **Compact**.

Figure 7.5   Use the folder heading to select a new folder to view.

Configuring Your E-Mail Options

As you compact your folders and delete your messages, you may want to set up your system to automatically remove messages you delete. These steps teach you how to configure this option.

1. Open the **Tools** menu and select **Options**.

2. Click the **General** tab.

3. Check the **Empty Messages from the "Deleted Items" Folders on Exit** option.

4. Click the **Apply** button, and then click **OK**.

In this lesson, you learned how to manually organize your e-mail messages into folders and how to automatically organize them by using filters. In the next lesson, you will learn about the variety of HTML news message services.

HTML Mailing Services

8

In this lesson, you learn about the variety of news services that send you HTML-enriched newsletters and articles on a regular basis.

About HTML News Mailing Services

There are many types of *broadcast news services*, organizations that send you messages in HTML format, providing you with immediate access to the information that you want when you want it. These services offer a wide range of information, often for free, that you can use in a variety of ways. Each service supplies a different type of information. Some services offer information strictly related to a single software company or product, while other news services focus on topical areas such as sports or computer sales and support. No matter where your interests lie, there is a mailing service that will send you the information you're looking for.

Microsoft's News Services

Microsoft wants to provide all of their customers with the most up-to-date information possible. In order for them to do so, they have created a series of newsletters that you can receive automatically in your Inbox. Each of these newsletters provides you with information about a specific area within Microsoft's hallowed walls.

- **MSDNFlash**   This biweekly newsletter features developer news, events, and information.
- **Windows Technology News**   This biweekly newsletter helps keep you up-to-date with the latest technical information dealing with Windows 95 and Windows NT systems.

- **Office News Service**   This monthly e-mail letter helps you get the most out of Microsoft Office.

- **BackOffice News**   This weekly newsletter provides you with information about Microsoft BackOffice and other business-related products.

- **Exploring Windows**   This biweekly newsletter provides announcements, tips, tricks, and techniques for all Windows Users.

- **Microsoft Games Monthly Mailer**   This monthly newsletter provides you with all the hints, tips, and traps for the upcoming and released Microsoft Games.

- **Insider's Update**   This monthly guide takes you on a tour through home computing with Microsoft software.

- **"Smallbiz" News Flash**   This weekly newsletter augments *Smallbiz*, a Webzine designed to assist small businesses in taking advantage of computer technology.

- **Technology Colloquium**   This newsletter serves as a forum for faculty and administrators at colleges and universities to share their experiences with integrating technology into their curricula.

- **Microsoft Press Pass**   This weekly newsletter and its corresponding Web site provide a great source of news and information for anyone who is interested in tracking developments at Microsoft.

- **Microsoft Press NewsWire**   This monthly newsletter provides the latest news about the developments in the publishing departments at Microsoft Press.

- **Partnering with Microsoft News**   This monthly newsletter provides you with a preview of each month's *Partnering with Microsoft* Webzine.

- **MCP News Flash**   This monthly news brief provides you with the latest information about the Microsoft certification program, including exam announcements and special promotions.

- **Training and Certification News**   This monthly guide offers you a look at what is new with the training and certification programs at Microsoft.

- **Mobile Worker Magazine Flash**   Although this letter doesn't appear to come out every month, you can still keep up-to-date with the latest developments on Microsoft Windows CE and the Handheld PC.

- **Local News (where available)**   For some areas, Microsoft can provide you with an e-mail version of all your local news.

Once you have read through some of these newsletter descriptions, you may find some you want to subscribe to. The following steps walk you through that process.

1. Open Internet Explorer to the page located at **http://www.microsoft.com/ regwiz/personalinfo.asp**.

2. Click the **Sign Me Up!** link in the upper-left corner of your screen.

3. On the first Personal Information screen (shown in Figure 8.1), you need to select the language in which you want to receive all your newsletters, the country in which you currently reside, your full e-mail address, and a password. The password must be at least six characters and can contain only letters, numbers, and the underscore.

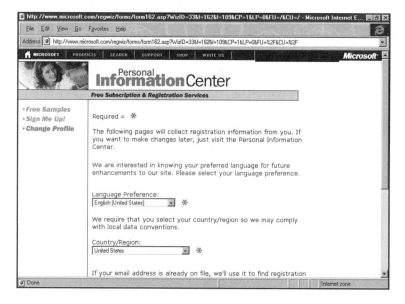

Figure 8.1 The Personal Information screens at Microsoft collect all the information they need to provide you with full newsletter delivery service.

4. When you have completed this information, click the **Next** button.

5. Type your first and last name in the appropriate fields. The remainder of the information requested on this screen is optional. Fill it in at your discretion.

6. Click **Finish**.

7. Next, you are asked to select the newsletters you want to receive. Click the check box in front of each newsletter you want to read (see Figure 8.2). You can change your newsletter selection at any time.

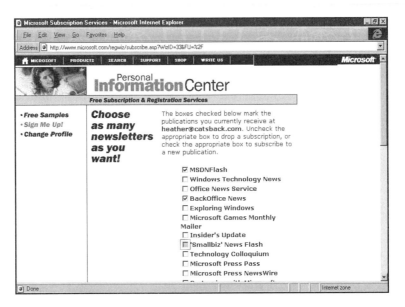

Figure 8.2 Choose from the list of available Microsoft newsletters.

8. Click **Next**.

9. Select the format for each newsletter you want to receive. The available options are Rich Text Format, Text Only, and Hyperlink.

10. Click **Finish**.

Other News Broadcast Services

Many other news broadcast services are available on the Internet. The following sections list just a few of them.

Business

- **Inc. Online (http://www.inc.com)**

    This news service brings financial service professionals news on events and industry information essential to doing business in today's market-place.

- **Entrepreneurial Edge Direct (http://www.edgeonline.com/)**

  Find solutions to your real-world business problems, as well as forward-thinking ideas. Get all the information on managing a thriving business in today's market, all through interviews with today's hottest entrepreneurs.

Entertainment

- **ELLE International Direct (http://www.elle.com)**

  Get the latest fashion news, beauty tips, cultural information, and trends from *ELLE* editions around the world.

- **HotWired (http://www.hotwired.com)**

  Receive the highlights of today's top stories and be directly connected to the news and entertainment information that interests you most.

- **SpotLite from InfoBeat (http://www.infobeat.com)**

  This free service from *InfoBeat* provides you with daily horoscopes, lottery numbers, movie reviews, TV listings, movies, videos, and music reviews all placed in your Inbox each day.

Home and Leisure

- **HomeArts Home Delivery (http://www.homearts.com)**

  Get immediate access to some of today's hottest recipes and cooking info, romance advice, gardening tips, pregnancy and family info, puzzles, and games.

- **National Geographic Online (http://www.nationalgeo.com)**

  Explore the world with *National Geographic*. Twice a month you can join explorers and adventurers as they look at the earth, sea, and sky.

- **The Kaplan Edge (http://www.kaplan.com)**

  Do you love games, math, logic puzzles, and brain teasers? Sharpen your skills with a daily dose of this newsletter.

News Services

- **Inkling: America's Stories (http://www.inkling.com)**

  Take Dave Barry, Mitch Albom, Carl Hiassen, Leonard Pitts, and Norm Chad, throw them into a pot, and stir. The result is a vibrantly flavored combination of sports columns, high technology, women's voices, and the weirdest stuff on the Web.

- **New York Times Direct (http://www.nytimes.com)**

  Using this service, you can select specific sections from the Web edition of the *New York Times* and have them delivered directly to your Inbox.

- **USA TODAY (http://www.usatoday.com)**

  Every morning, *USA TODAY* brings you the top news stories of the day direct from the front pages of the nation's newspaper.

Personal Finance

- **Closing Bell (http://www.merc.com/cbell2.html)**

  Have personalized market-moving news and closing prices for your stocks, mutual funds, or market indexes delivered directly to your computer every evening.

- **CMP's TechInvestor Direct (http://techweb.cmp.com/corporate/)**

  Receive financial news every day when the stock market closes.

Shopping

- **Gift ONE (http://www.giftone.com)**

  Never forget an important date again. Gift ONE delivers a reminder for those important days, helps you select the perfect gift, and even ensures that it arrives on time.

- **Internet Shopping Network (http://www.isn.com)**

  The Internet Shopping Network is the largest computer superstore, with more than 40,000 computer hardware, software, and downloadable software products in a single location. You can have the product promotions, specials, and news that interest you delivered directly to your e-mail Inbox.

- **Thunderbeam Kids' Software (http://www.thunderbeam.com)**

  Let Thunderbeam keep you posted on the latest free downloads and kids' software reviews.

Sports and Fitness

- **CBS SportsLine's Personal SportsPage (http://www.cbs.com/sports/)**

  You can have more than 80,000 pages of continuously updated sports news delivered to your Inbox every day.

- **Sports Illustrated Online (http://cnnsi.com/personal/index.html)**

  Let Sports Illustrated Online and SportsWrap bring you all the latest sports news and stories. You get the latest scores, game recaps, front page news, and links to insightful and interactive features.

Technology News

- **AnchorDesk, a Service of ZDNet (http://www.anchordesk.com)**

  Get a precise—and concise—look into today's top technology news with ZDNet AnchorDesk and Jesse Berst.

- **CNET Digital Dispatch (http://www.cnet.com)**

  The popular C!Net Web site provides you with a weekly look at the Internet and reviews some of the best computing products available.

- **PC Week Direct (http://www.pcweek.com/ibd/inbox.html)**

  Receive your computer industry news, lab product reviews, and special reports on your desktop each day.

- **The Wall Street Journal Interactive Edition Technology Alert (http://wsj.com)**

  The *Wall Street Journal* provides you with a daily overview of the top technology news.

- **Wired News (http://www.wired.com)**

  This daily service provides you with an insider's informed perspective on how technology is affecting today's business, culture, and politics.

Travel

- **Travel Discounts Direct**

  You'll get the most comprehensive and up-to-date information on airfare discounts, tours, cruises, car rentals, frequent flyer programs, and hotels delivered directly to your Inbox.

- **WeatherVane (http://www.infobeat.com)**

  This free e-mail service from the Weather Channel and *InfoBeat* brings you personalized weather forecasts for the cities you want. You get to pick as many weather regions as you want and then select the days and times for which you need the forecasts delivered to your Inbox.

Subscribing to These Services

When you want to access these services, all you need to do is subscribe to them. Most of them require only your full name and e-mail address, although some systems, such as Microsoft's, request much more detailed information. All of these services use an HTML-based form that gathers the information they need in order to send you your information.

In this lesson, you learned about HTML mailing lists and the information they make available to you. In the next lesson, you will learn how to make Outlook 97 interact with Outlook Express.

Using Outlook Express with Outlook 97

In this lesson, you learn how to use Outlook Express in conjunction with Outlook 97.

Introducing Outlook 97

Early in 1997, Microsoft released their Office 97 package. This software included Outlook 97, which is Microsoft's all-in-one desktop information manager. Outlook 97 includes an e-mail Inbox, a Contact list, a scheduling Calendar, a Task List, a contact Journal, and a location to which you can track notes on your communications exchanges.

Outlook 97 is organized in a fashion very similar to Outlook Express, but it has more features. Outlook 97 provides you with a short two- or three-line start to each of your messages so you can see what the first part of the message is and who it's from. Figure 9.1 shows the Outlook 97 window.

Importing Message Folders

If you use both Outlook Express and Outlook 97, you can import your mail message folders so you don't end up with messages scattered between two different programs. Although Outlook Express makes it very easy to import information from Outlook 97, it's very hard for you to reverse the process. The following steps show you how to import your messages from Outlook 97:

1. Open the **File** menu, select **Import**, and select **Messages**.
2. Select **Microsoft Outlook** from the list of available message formats.
3. Click the **Next** button.

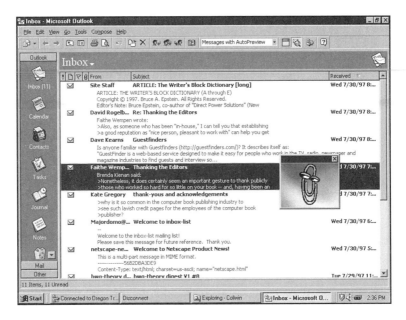

Figure 9.1 The Outlook 97 Inbox lets you look at the start of each message.

4. The location of your Outlook messages should have already been found for you. If not, click the **Browse** button and select the directory in which you have stored your message folders.

5. After you locate the message folders, you are asked to select the specific folders from which you want to import information (see Figure 9.2). Click the **Selected Folders** option button, and then select the **Inbox** folder.

6. Click **Finish**.

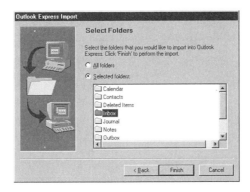

Figure 9.2 Select the specific folders you want to import into your new Internet mail client.

Importing Your Personal Address Book

When you're switching from Outlook 97 to Outlook Express you don't want to lose access to all the addresses you have stored. The easiest way to avoid this is to import all of your Outlook 97 addresses into Outlook Express. Follow these steps:

1. Open the **File** menu, select **Import**, and select **Address Book**.
2. Select **Microsoft Exchange Personal Address Book**.
3. Click **Import**.
4. Select the Outlook 97 Profile from which you want to import the Address book, and then click **OK**.
5. It only takes a moment for the Address Book import function to be completed. When you receive notification that the import was successful, click the **OK** button.
6. Click the **Close** (X) button to remove the remaining import window.

In this lesson, you learned how to share your message folders and your personal address book with Outlook 97. In the next part, you will learn how to use Outlook Express as a newsreader.

Outlook
Express News

Configuring Outlook Express for News

In this lesson, you learn how to connect Outlook Express to your News server.

Configuring Your Server

Before you can get started using Outlook Express, you have to get the software configured to use your News server. You will be asked to provide your e-mail account name and password, your News server name and password, and some information about your Internet service provider.

Internet Service Provider The generic term for the company that provides your Internet connection. Your service provider also provides the information you need to configure Outlook Express.

When you run Outlook Express, you need to make sure you're connecting to the proper News server. To do this, follow these steps:

1. Open the **Start** menu, select **Programs**, **Internet Explorer**, and then select **Outlook Express**.

TIP **Running the First Time** The first time you run Outlook Express, the configuration process starts automatically.

2. Open the **Tools** menu and select **Accounts**.

3. Click the **Add** button and select **News**. This opens a screen similar to the one shown in Figure 1.1.

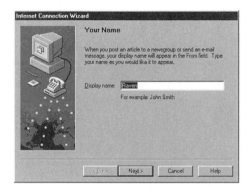

Figure 1.1   The first screen of the Internet Connection Wizard for configuring your News server.

4. Type your name in the **Display Name** field, and then click **Next**.

5. Enter your full e-mail address in the **E-Mail Address** field, and then click **Next**.

6. Type the full address of your News server in the **News (NNTP) Server** field, and then click **Next**.

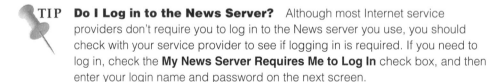

TIP   Do I Log in to the News Server?   Although most Internet service providers don't require you to log in to the News server you use, you should check with your service provider to see if logging in is required. If you need to log in, check the **My News Server Requires Me to Log In** check box, and then enter your login name and password on the next screen.

7. Type a name for your News connection in the **Internet News Account Name** field, and then click **Next**.

8. You now need to indicate how you connect through your provider to your News server. There are three ways to connect to your service provider. Outlook Express Mail lets you select the method that is most appropriate for you. Choose from the phone line, local area network, and manual options shown in Figure 1.2. Then click **Next**.

9. If you choose to use a phone connection, you need to select a Dial-Up Networking connection. If you have never connected to the Internet before, you need to create a new dial-up connection. If you have used the Internet

previously, you probably already have a connection to use; in that case, select **Use an Existing Dial-Up Connection**, and then select a connection to use. Click **Next**.

If you selected either the Local Area Network or the Manual connection, you're done configuring your account. When the Congratulations screen appears, click the **Finish** button, and you can start using Outlook Express.

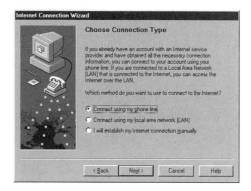

Figure 1.2   In the Choose Connection Type configuration screen, indicate how you connect to your service provider.

10. When you complete the configuration, click the **Finish** button. If you want to make changes to your settings, click the **Back** button until you find the option you want to adjust, make the adjustment, and use the **Next** button to return you to the final screen.

Configuring Your Message Windows

It's simplest to read your news articles in an easy-to-read font. To configure your message window font, follow these steps:

1. Open the **Tools** menu and select **Options**.

2. Check the **General** tab.

3. Check the **Make Outlook Express My Default News Reader** check box.

4. Check the **Send** tab to see the options shown in Figure 1.3.

5. In the News Sending Format section of the dialog box, select either **HTML** or **Plain Text** for your news articles.

6. Click the **OK** button.

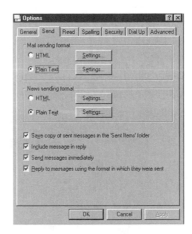

Figure 1.3 The Send tab of the Options dialog box allows you to control the format in which your messages are sent.

Creating and Using a Signature File

A *signature file*, or sig file, is text placed at the bottom of each of your messages. Sig files often include information about the author of the message, a favorite quote, or maybe even the score of your favorite football team's latest game.

If you want to use a signature on each of your news messages, you have to tell Outlook Express what you want it to say. The following steps walk you through configuring your signature lines.

1. Open the **Tools** menu and select **Stationery**. Click the **News** tab.
2. Click the **Signature** button. Figure 1.4 shows the signature options.

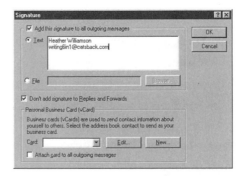

Figure 1.4 With a signature file, you can personalize the messages you send.

3. If you want to include a signature in all messages you send, click the **Add This Signature to All Outgoing Messages** check box, and then choose the type of signature you want to use:

- Select the **Text** option button and enter the information that you want at the bottom of your articles.
- Select the **File** option button, and then enter the name of the file you want to use or click the Browse button and select the file from the dialog box that appears.

4. (Optional) If you don't want the signature to appear in replies and forwarded messages, click the **Don't Add Signature to Replies and Forwards** check box.

5. (Optional) If you want to attach a virtual business card to your e-mail messages, you can select an Address book entry to be attached to each article that you send. In the **Card** drop-down list, select the **Address Book** entry. Click the **Edit** button if you want to make changes, or click **New** if you want to create a new entry.

6. When you finish setting the options in the Signature dialog box, click **OK**. To close the Stationery dialog box, click **Apply**, and then click **OK**. The next time you start a new message, your signature file automatically appears at the end of it.

In this lesson, you learned how to configure Outlook Express to contact your News server. In the next lesson, you will learn how to download a list of newsgroups and subscribe to the ones you want to read.

Subscribing to Newsgroups

In this lesson, you learn how to download a list of newsgroups and subscribe to the ones you want to read.

Getting a List of Newsgroups

After you configure Outlook Express, the next step is to retrieve a list of available newsgroups. Outlook Express has no default newsgroups, so you have to find those you want and select them yourself. You can read articles in newsgroups that you haven't subscribed to.

Follow these steps to find the newsgroups and see what's available:

1. With Outlook Express running, scroll through the list of folders and select the name of your news server, as shown in Figure 2.1. (Alternatively, you can open the **Go** menu and select **News**.) This enables you to automatically connect to your Internet service provider.

2. Once you're connected, Outlook Express asks you if you want to download the list of available newsgroups. Click **OK**, and a list of the newsgroups appears on your screen as your news server downloads it to your computer.

3. When all of the newsgroups have been downloaded and sorted, Outlook Express displays the Newsgroups window, shown in Figure 2.2. It lists all the newsgroups to which you have access.

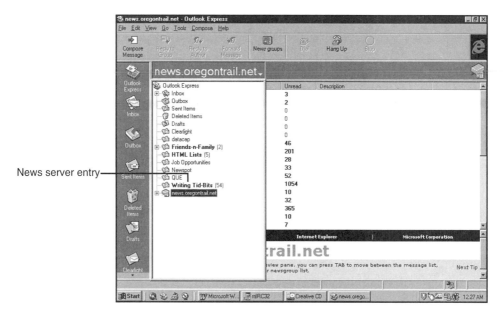

News server entry

Figure 2.1 The folder list showing your news server entries.

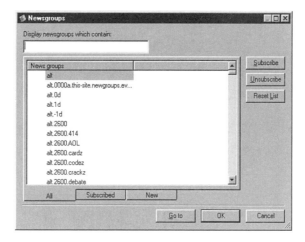

Figure 2.2 The list of newsgroups that are available from your service provider's news server.

This list originally shows you all of the newsgroups available from your news server. However, you can sort this list so that you see only groups you're interested in.

Sorting the Newsgroup List

If you had to browse through a list of more than 22,000 newsgroups, it might be impossible to find newsgroups that discuss topics you're interested in. To assist in this search, Outlook Express provides a sorting utility that looks for specific words and phrases in your list of newsgroup names. Here's how to sort the list:

1. With Outlook Express running, open the **Go** menu and select **News**.

2. Open the **Tools** menu and select **Newsgroups**, or click the **Newsgroups** button on the toolbar. The Newsgroups dialog box opens.

3. In the **Display Newsgroups Which Contain** field, type a topic that's of interest to you. For example, you could type **barefoot** to see a list of newsgroups related to bare feet (see Figure 2.3).

TIP   **Don't Press Enter**   You do not have to press Enter after typing a topic; as you type, the list of newsgroups is sorted automatically.

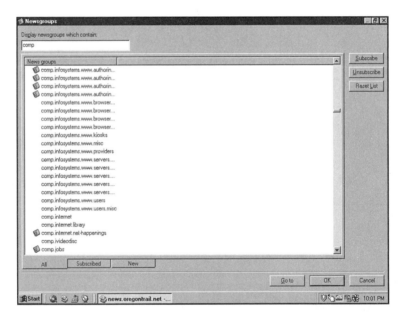

Figure 2.3   The list now displays only newsgroups discussing your specified topic.

Subscribing to Newsgroups

Once you subscribe to a newsgroup, the subject information for each article in that newsgroup is automatically downloaded every time you connect to your news server. You don't need to subscribe to a newsgroup in order to review its messages; however, subscribing does make it easier to find the newsgroup again later.

 Subscribe The process used to mark a list of favorite newsgroups that you read frequently. This lets you access your favorite newsgroups in a manner similar to that in which you access your favorite Web sites.

Follow these steps to subscribe to a newsgroup:

1. With Outlook Express running, select your news server from the folders drop-down list or the Outlook toolbar. (Or, open the **Go** menu and select **News**.)

2. Because you already have a list of newsgroups, open the **Tools** menu and select **Newsgroups**.

3. Read through the list of newsgroup names until you find one that interests you. Click to select the one you want.

 TIP **Reading Unsubscribed Newsgroups** To read the messages in a newsgroup you have not subscribed to, click the **Go To** button at the bottom of your Newsgroups dialog box.

4. With a group name selected, click **Subscribe**. You can repeat this process for as many newsgroups as you're interested in. In the newsgroup list, a newspaper icon appears to the left of each newsgroup to which you've subscribed.

5. To see the list of newsgroups you've subscribed to, click the **Subscribed** tab (see Figure 2.4).

251

Figure 2.4   The newsgroups you've subscribed to are listed in the Subscribed tab.

In this lesson, you learned how to download and update your list of newsgroups and subscribe to the newsgroups you're interested in. In the next lesson, you will learn how to retrieve the articles in your subscribed newsgroups.

Retrieving Articles

In this lesson, you learn how to download specific articles so you can read them at your leisure.

Downloading Article Headers

Outlook Express enables you to control how much of your time and hard drive space is going to be taken up by the articles you download from newsgroups. The first time you connect to a newsgroup, you have to download the message *headers*. The headers are the only part of the messages that are downloaded automatically.

 Message Header   The portion of the message containing information about the original author of the message, who the article was sent to, and the subject of the message.

The following steps show you how to download the new message headers for your subscribed newsgroups:

1. With Outlook Express running, scroll through the folders list and select the newsgroup you want to read. (Alternatively, you can open the **Go** menu, select **News**, and choose a newsgroup from the screen shown in Figure 3.1.)
2. Double-click the newsgroup you're interested in. Outlook Express automatically connects to your service provider, connects to your news server, and downloads the headers for the that newsgroup. Figure 3.2 shows a list of headers for a newsgroup.

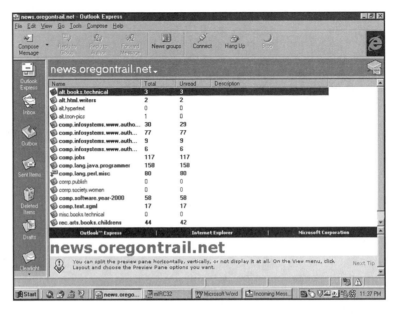

Figure 3.1   The main Outlook Express window, showing your available newsgroups.

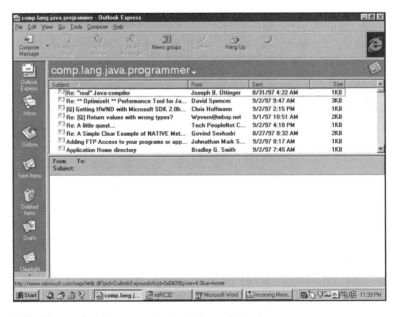

Figure 3.2   The available news articles in the selected newsgroup.

CAUTION   **Printing Messages**   You can print a message from the message window only (see the section "Printing Articles" in Part 4, Lesson 4). However, you can reply to the original author, reply to the newsgroup, or forward to another individual or group from the preview window.

TIP   **Downloading Headers**   Outlook Express does not have to automatically download each message when you select it. Instead, you'll want it to download all selected messages at one time to reduce your connect time (which leaves your phone line open for incoming calls and also keeps your Internet connection charges to a minimum). You can select all the messages you want to read while you're offline, connect for a few minutes to download them from the server, and then disconnect before reading them.

Tagging Articles

As you read through the message headers, you can find out what type of conversations are taking place and decide whether you want to participate in them. The bodies of messages take up large amounts of space on your hard drive. And if files are attached to the messages, they take up even more space. By taking advantage of the option of reading the message headers before downloading the entire message, you can conserve your online time and your hard drive space—two major considerations when using a computer on the Internet. When you find particular articles that you would like to read in their entirety, you *tag* them. To tag an article, perform the following steps:

1. Open **Outlook Express** but don't connect to the Internet.

2. Open your newsgroups list and select a newsgroup to read—one that you have already downloaded the headers for.

3. Select a message that you didn't view while online. The preview window tells you that the message is not cached and needs to be downloaded (see Figure 3.3).

4. To tag this article, right-click the article's header and select **Mark Message for Download** from the shortcut menu. Outlook Express displays a green arrow icon to the left of the article (see Figure 3.4). This icon identifies articles that will be downloaded the next time you connect to your service provider.

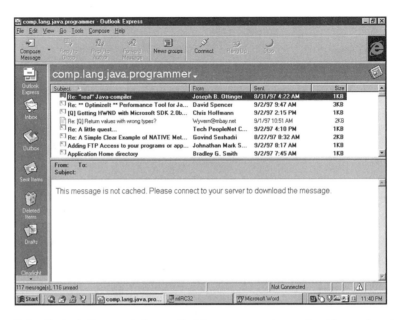

Figure 3.3   Outlook Express tells you that the message has not yet been downloaded.

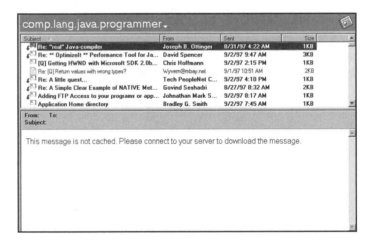

Figure 3.4   Messages with a green arrow have been tagged for downloading.

TIP   **Tagging Message Threads**   If you tag a message that has multiple replies, Outlook Express automatically downloads all of its replies, too.

Downloading Selected Messages

In the previous sections, you tagged some messages you wanted to read. Now you need to get those messages from the news server to your computer. To download all tagged messages, follow these steps:

1. Click the **Connect** button to connect to your service provider.

2. Open the **Tools** menu and select **Download All**. This starts the automatic retrieval process for all the articles that you have marked. The Post and Download window, shown in Figure 3.5, shows you the progress of your download.

3. When the articles are completely downloaded, double-click one to see the entire message.

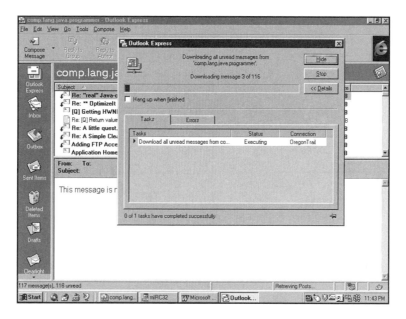

Figure 3.5   You can monitor the progress as Outlook Express downloads your articles.

In this lesson, you learned how to retrieve your article headers, tag articles for later retrieval, and download the body of your newsgroups articles. In the next lesson, you will learn how to open, print, read, and reply to articles you have retrieved.

Reading and Working with Articles

In this lesson, you learn how to read and reply to newsgroup articles that you have downloaded.

Opening Articles

Generally, you download messages so you can read them. Outlook Express provides you with a preview window so you can skim a message quickly, without waiting for a message to open all the way. You can use the preview window to read your messages and to perform any other message-specific action.

When you need to open an article in a true article window, double-click the message header. This opens the message in its own window (see Figure 4.1). If a message is a reply, greater than marks (>>) appear in front of the original message's text. As you can see, this message is a reply to a previously posted message that was also a reply.

Printing Articles

Once in a while, you might read a message and decide you want to print it (to keep on file or to pass along to a friend, for example). Printing an article is quite easy. Follow these steps:

1. Double-click a message's header to open the message in the message window.
2. Open the **File** menu and select **Print** (Ctrl+P).
3. In the Print dialog box, select the printer, number of copies, and print range. Click **OK**.

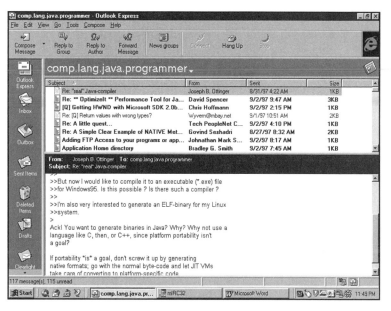

Figure 4.1 The article window showing a message sent to the newsgroup.

 TIP   **Quick Print**   With a message open, you can simply click the **Print** toolbar button to have the article sent to the currently selected printer.

Threading Articles

A *thread* is made up of the original message and all responses to that message chained together to create a flowing conversation. By following a message thread, you can read the original message and everyone's responses to it. Then you can read the responses to the responses until you have read the entire conversation.

In the Outlook Express window, a plus sign next to a message indicates that the message has a thread of responses. You click the plus sign to see the headers of all messages sent as responses to that original message. If any of those responses have generated responses, a plus sign appears next to the first response to show that the thread continues. Again, you click the plus sign to see the next level of responses. A minus sign appears next to a message when you have displayed all of its responses.

To follow a thread of articles, take these steps:

1. With Outlook Express open, scroll through the messages you downloaded. Search for one that has a plus sign in front of it. Click that symbol.

2. Scroll through the thread list to see all of the responses to the original message (see Figure 4.2). If you see more plus signs, you can click them to expand the thread further. By selecting each message in a thread, you can read through the entire conversation.

The plus sign [+] notes that the message is part of an expandable thread

The minus sign [-] shows that a message's thread has been completely expanded

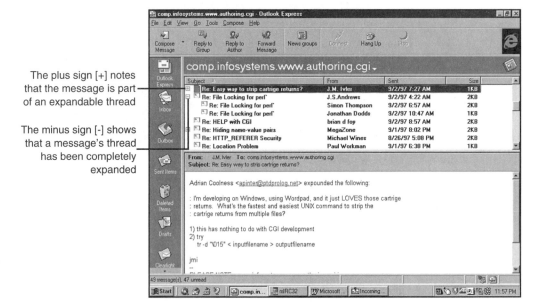

Figure 4.2 Plus and minus signs identify a thread: original messages and their responses.

Linking to Web Sites or Other Newsgroups

Some messages contain links to mail addresses, FTP sites, or Web sites. When Outlook Express reads an article, it converts every type of address it can recognize into a link. For example, if someone sends the address of his Web site to a newsgroup, Outlook Express converts it to a link. You can go directly to that Web site by clicking the link, just as if you were on a Web page to begin with.

The following steps should help you navigate through these types of links.

1. Open a message with an internal link similar to the one shown in Figure 4.3, or leave one open while you're scanning the articles that are available.

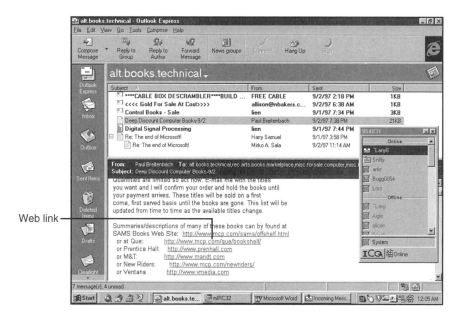

Figure 4.3 An internal link stored in a news article can take you to a Web site or let you send e-mail to another individual.

2. Scroll down to the Web or e-mail address and select it. If you select an e-mail address, Outlook Express automatically opens the mail client; if you select a Web address, it automatically opens Internet Explorer to that particular Web page.

Replying to an Article

If you're reading an actual newspaper and want to respond to something you read, you have to write a letter and mail it. And even though you go to that effort, you never know if anyone other than the editor will read it. When you're working in newsgroups, you have the opportunity to respond to any message at any time. And you don't have to worry about there not being enough room on a page to print it out. Your articles are always posted.

But there's one drawback to knowing that what you say will be seen by thousands of other people: Hotheaded remarks won't be moderated by an editor, and anyone who is irritated or offended by a harsh statement can write back to you either publicly or privately.

When you respond to an article in a newsgroup, you have the option of responding publicly so everyone in the newsgroup can see your response or responding privately so that only the author of the message can see it. The next two sections cover how to send responses.

Replying to a Newsgroup

When you want to respond to a news article with a public statement, you respond to the entire group. This enables everyone, including the casual observer, to read your message. Posting messages to an entire newsgroup is often the best way to get an answer to your question. To respond to an entire newsgroup, perform the following steps:

1. With Outlook Express open, select a message that you have read and would like to comment on. Click the **Reply to Group** button. The original message opens in the message window (see Figure 4.4).

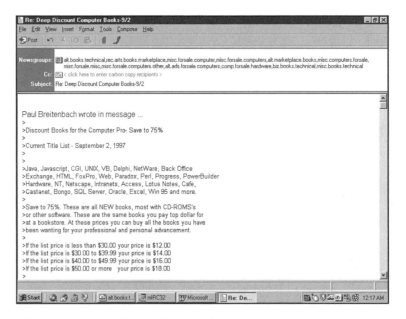

Figure 4.4 A response addressed to an entire newsgroup.

2. As you can see, the Newsgroups field automatically displays the original newsgroup's name. The Subject field contains the subject of the original message with the reply tag (Re:) added, and your cursor appears in the body of the message where you will enter your comments. Add all the comments you want.

3. When you finish your message, click the **Send** button. Outlook Express places a copy of your message in the Outbox to be posted to the newsgroup the next time you connect to your service provider.

Replying to the Original Author

Sometimes you read something that you want to talk to the author—and only the author—about. Maybe you want to clarify a point with them, or maybe you simply want to get to know that person better because you seem to have a shared interest. No matter the reason, replying to an individual is essentially the same as replying to a group, except that you use the Internet Mail client to send the information. Follow these steps:

1. With Outlook Express open, select a message that you would like to comment on. Click the **Reply to Author** button. The original message opens in a mail window, as shown in Figure 4.5.

2. The To field automatically displays the original newsgroup name. The Subject field contains the subject of the original message with the reply tag (Re:) added, and your cursor appears in the body of the message where you will enter your comments. Add any comments you want.

CAUTION

Legal E-Mail Because you're legally responsible for e-mail messages in the same way you're responsible for written messages, you need to make sure that your response isn't slanderous and that it contains no copyrighted information.

3. When you finish your reply, click the **Send** button. Outlook Express places a copy of your message in the Outbox of the Internet Mail client. The next time you connect to your service provider, the message is mailed to the selected recipients.

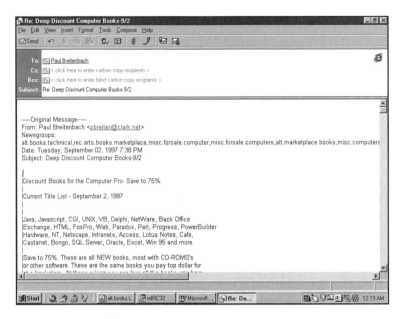

Figure 4.5   The e-mail message is addressed to the author of the newsgroup article to which you are responding.

In this lesson, you learned to download all or part of a news article, navigate through message threads, read articles, and send replies. In the next lesson, you will learn how to write articles to be posted to newsgroups.

Writing an Article

In this lesson, you learn how to write articles for newsgroups.

Sending Text

After you have familiarized yourself with the way posted articles read on your subscribed newsgroups, you may want to send a message yourself. Before you mail that message though, you should consider a few things. Most people who read newsgroups are *lurkers*: they don't post anything, they just read the information. This is perfectly acceptable. Also, it's frowned upon to post an article just for the sake of posting something. Make sure that the topic you are discussing is appropriate for the group. People who read the backpacking newsgroup don't want to hear about the great sailing trip you had last year.

Follow these steps to write an article to post:

1. With Outlook Express open, click the **Compose Message** button. A news window opens.

2. The Newsgroups field automatically contains the name of the currently selected newsgroup, the Subject field is blank, and your cursor is in the body of the message where you will enter your comments. Type the message you want to send.

> **TIP** **Posting to Unselected Groups** If you want to send this message to one or more other newsgroups, you can click the note card icon by the **Newsgroups** field and select other newsgroups from the list.

3. When you finish entering your message, click the **Post** button. Outlook Express places a copy of your message in the Outbox of the news client. The next time you connect to your service provider, the message is posted to the selected newsgroups.

265

Inserting Text

As you gain friends on the Internet, you may want to forward articles to large groups of people or organizations. But you're not limited to forwarding newsgroup articles only. You can easily insert the text from another document into your message using the following steps.

1. Open the **Insert** menu and select **Text from File**. The Insert Text File dialog box shown in Figure 5.1 appears.

Figure 5.1 Select a file to insert into your news article.

2. Select the text file that contains the information you want to add to your message.

3. Click the **Open** button. The message window opens, showing your inserted text.

 TIP **Alternative Insert** If want to insert text from a file you currently have open, use the Copy and Paste commands on the Edit menu to move the text from your document to your message.

Using HTML for Rich Text

Using HTML Rich Text with newsgroups may not be a very good idea. Because you're sending this article to a potentially gigantic number of readers, you will probably want to send your newsgroup articles in Plain Text. However, if you do want to send information in rich text format, the following steps will help you.

1. With Outlook Express open, click the **New Message** button on the toolbar, or open the **Compose** menu and select **New Message** (Ctrl+N).

2. Address your message to the intended recipient.

3. Place your cursor in the message body area and type your message. As you can see in Figure 5.2, the text originally appears on your stationery in the default font and font color.

Formatted text

Default text

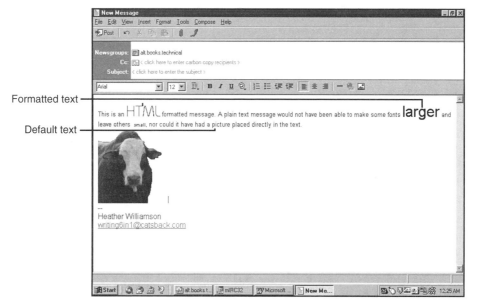

Figure 5.2   Creating a message using HTML is just as easy as formatting a standard text message.

4. Highlight the part of the text you want to change.

5. Use the controls on the formatting toolbar to make whatever changes you want. For example, to change the font size, open the font size drop-down list and select the size you want to use. To bold information, highlight it and click the **Bold** button (or press **Ctrl+B**).

CAUTION

Sending HTML Messages   Not all e-mail clients in use today can properly read HTML-formatted messages. If you send a formatted message to an individual whose mail reader doesn't support HTML, he or she will see all of your HTML codes in the body of the message, which makes reading a message quite difficult.

Inserting an Internet Link

Adding URLs to text in newsgroup messages is very important, and it's done much more often than adding URLs to e-mail messages. Newsgroup users are generally looking for specific information, and providing them with an URL for a site that contains that information is often faster than copying or summarizing the information for them.

1. With Outlook Express open to a message window, type the following Web address: **http:/www.mcp.com/**.

   As you enter this address, it automatically changes color and becomes underlined. You have just created an active link to the Macmillan Web site. Anyone you send this message to that's using an URL-aware browser will be able to click the link to go directly to that Web site.

2. Type your e-mail address, as you would in your signature file. As you type, your address turns into an active link. If you add your address to your signature file, people will be able to send you a message immediately by clicking the link.

In this lesson, you learned how to write articles, insert text and files, create rich text format articles, and link your messages to other Web sites or newsgroups. In the next lesson, you will learn how to post articles you have written.

Posting an Article

In this lesson, you learn how to post articles that you have written to a newsgroup or to multiple newsgroups.

Sending While Connected

When you're connected to your service provider through your phone line, you are "online." When you're not connected to another computer, you're "offline." These terms can refer to many different parts of the computing world, but in this case they refer to a state of connection between your computer and the service provider's computer. Working offline enables you to minimize your *connect time charges* (the costs associated with connecting to your Internet service provider are based solely on the amount of time you use their services). If you have an "unlimited" account, you do not have to worry about these charges. However, you may still want to keep your connect time to a minimum in order to free up your phone line for incoming calls.

The only way to get your messages onto the news server is to upload them with Outlook Express or a similar newsreader. When you upload a message, it is copied into a Sent Items folder on your computer and placed on your service provider's news server. This process is called *posting*: You post your article to the news server so other people can use it, and you can use it again later.

Follow these steps to post a message to a newsgroup:

1. With Outlook Express running, open the **Tools** menu and select **Send** to send mail to your news server. The Connect To: dialog box appears.
2. Click the **OK** button. You'll receive notice of a connection, and then the dialog box shown in Figure 6.1 appears so you can watch Outlook Express send and receive your messages.

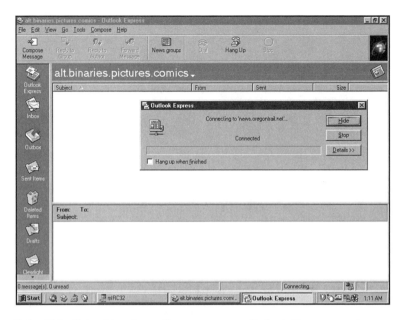

Figure 6.1   This dialog box shows the progress as Outlook Express exchanges your messages.

   3. When Outlook Express has retrieved all of your messages, click **Disconnect** on the main Outlook Express toolbar.

Scheduling Message Posting

If you leave your computer and mail client running for long periods of time, you might want to configure Outlook Express to exchange your messages automatically at specified intervals. To do so, follow these steps.

   1. With Outlook Express running, open the **Tools** menu and select **Options**.

   2. Click the **Send** tab.

   3. Check the **Send Messages Immediately** option.

   4. Click the **General** tab.

   5. Check the **Check for New Messages Every** *xx* **Minutes** check box. The default setting for this option is 30 minutes. You can change that to whatever is most appropriate for your situation. In most situations, every hour is sufficient.

   6. Click the **Dial Up** tab.

7. Check the **Hangup When Finished Sending, Receiving, or Downloading** check box.

8. Click **Apply**, and then click **OK** to activate and save your changes.

In this lesson, you learned how to post messages. In the next lesson, you will learn how to work the file attachments.

Working with Attached Files

In this lesson, you learn how to send and receive files through Usenet newsgroup articles.

Recognizing Attached Files

Sending files to others is one of the more common uses of Usenet newsgroups. With Usenet, you can share the pictures of your latest family vacation, the new software you just finished developing, or maybe a hot tune from a local jazz band. No matter what you want to share, if it can be digitized and stored, you can send it through a Usenet group.

When you're reading through a series of articles in a newsgroup, it might be hard to tell which messages contain files and which ones don't. There are a few quick ways (which are by no means 100 percent sure) for identifying those articles with files attached. Let's take a look at some of these signs.

- **The Subject Line.** In most messages, the subject line is used to explain the main topic of a message. When a file is attached to the message, the name of the file appears on the subject line. Many times, however, files are too large to attach to only one message. In that case, many news clients add both the file name and an order number so you know which messages go together to create a complete file. Figure 7.1 shows an example of this.

- **The Article Size.** Most news articles are generally under 300 lines, although some may be more even if they do not have files attached. Most articles with file attachments are between 800 and 1,000 lines.

TIP   News Article Sizes Many newsreaders won't post messages with more than 1,000 lines without breaking them up into multiple messages first. Because 1,000 lines is approximately three pages of solid text, you won't see many all-text messages larger than that.

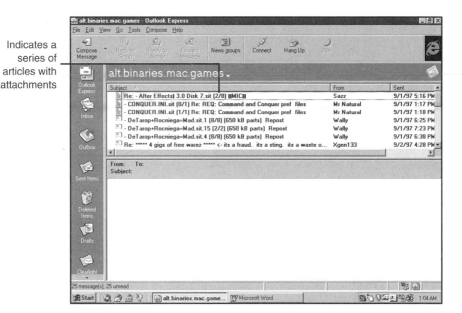

Indicates a series of articles with attachments

Figure 7.1 The detailed subject line lets you know which articles contain parts of the file.

- **Message Contents and the File Icon.** Outlook Express attaches a yellow paperclip icon to each article that has a file attached. You can see these icons in the preview window only.

Downloading and Opening Attached Files

After you have identified a message with an attached file, you need to download and unscramble the file to view it. To unscramble a file, perform the following steps.

1. Open the article with the file attachment you want to see. As you can see in Figure 7.2, the file appears at the bottom of the article window.

2. If you have configured Outlook Express to show attached images inline (the default), an icon appears in your message. Double-click that icon.

TIP **Showing Images Inline** If you want to show your image as part of the body of your message, open the **Tools** menu and select **Options**. Select the **Read** tab and check the **Automatically Show Picture Attachments in Message** check box.

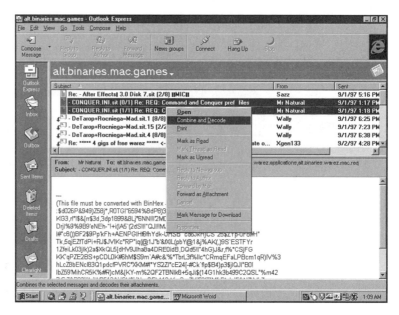

Figure 7.2 An article window with a file attachment.

3. If the file is a standard JPG or GIF image, Internet Explorer opens and displays that image for you automatically (see Figure 7.3). If it's some other type of file for which you have a viewing application, that application opens to display your file.

No Associated File Type   If you attempt to open a file for which there is not an associated application, you are given an opportunity to assign an application to that file. For more information on assigning file types and using **CAUTION** other applications to view files from the Internet, see Part 2, Lesson 1, "Using Add-Ons and Plug-Ins."

TIP   **View Images in Messages**   You can configure Outlook Express to display images within your articles automatically. To do so, open the **Tools** menu and select **Options**. Click the **Read** tab and check the **Automatically Show Picture Attachments in Messages** check box.

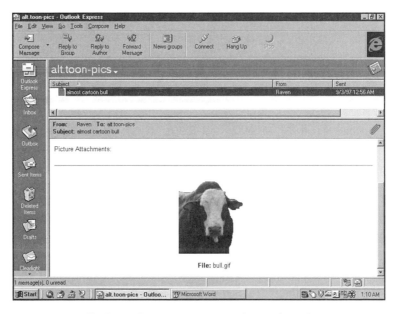

Figure 7.3 Internet Explorer displaying a cartoon image from the alt.binaries.pictures.cartoon newsgroup.

Uploading Files to a Newsgroup

As you familiarize yourself with Usenet newsgroups, you may want to interact with the people you meet. One way to do this is by sharing unique files and images with them. If you want to send a file to a Usenet group, follow these steps:

1. Click the **New Message** button on the Outlook Express toolbar, or open the **Compose** menu and select **New Message** (Ctrl+N).

2. In the New Message window, click the **File Attachment** icon, or open the **Insert** menu and select **File Attachment**.

3. In the Insert Attachment dialog box (see Figure 7.4), select the file you want to send to the newsgroup. Then click **OK**.

4. Place your cursor in the **Subject** field and type the name of the file you're sending. This is simply netiquette; it's not necessary for posting the file or your article.

Figure 7.4 In the Insert Attachment dialog box, select a file to add to a newsgroup article.

Netiquette Simple rules of etiquette that are followed on the Internet are commonly referred to as *netiquette*. By following these often unwritten rules, you can help keep the peace with all of your fellow Internet citizens.

5. Click the **Post** button, or open the **File** menu and select **Send Message** (Ctrl+S).

File Copyrights You need to be more careful about the contents of files sent to Usenet groups than you do files sent through e-mail or on paper. If you post a copyrighted image or program to a newsgroup, you are undoubtedly breaking the copyrights—unless you have written consent to publish the file in that forum.

In this lesson, you learned how to receive and send file attachments.

FrontPage
Express and
HTML

Starting and Navigating FrontPage Express

In this lesson, you learn about Web page basics and Microsoft's Web page editor,
FrontPage Express.

Although most Web pages appear to contain text and pictures, what they really contain are text and *HTML tags*. The text looks just like any text in a word-processing or desktop publishing program. The HTML (hypertext markup language) tags serve other functions, including controlling how the text appears; inserting pictures, sounds, and video clips; and linking the page to other pages. Figure 1.1 shows what a Web page looks like behind the scenes.

Not long ago, people were creating Web pages by typing all their text and HTML tags in a simple text editor, such as Windows Notepad. However, Internet Explorer comes with its own Web page editor, called FrontPage Express, which works as a word processing program for Web pages. Instead of typing complicated HTML tags, you simply enter text and insert graphics and other objects, as you would do in a word processing program. FrontPage Express inserts the necessary HTML tags for you.

HTML Tags   HTML tags are codes that are used to create and format Web pages. For example, a simple paired code for displaying bold text appears like this: **Bold Text**. However, with FrontPage Express, you rarely (if ever) have to deal with these codes.

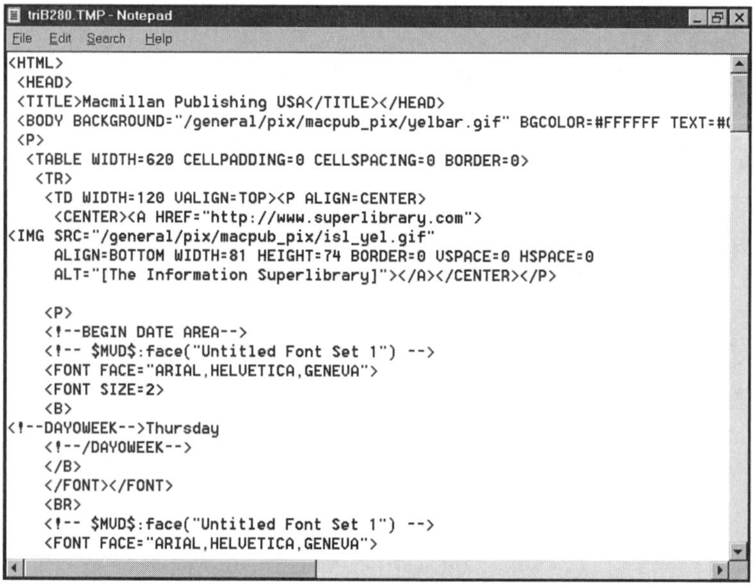

Figure 1.1   The HTML codes behind a typical Web page.

Running FrontPage Express

Before you can use FrontPage Express to create your own Web pages, you must run it. Take the following steps:

1. Open the **Start** menu and point to **Programs**. The Programs submenu appears.

2. Point to **Internet Explorer**, and select **FrontPage Express**. The FrontPage Express window appears and displays a blank page, as shown in Figure 1.2.

If you have a Web page and want to edit it, or you found a page on the Web that you want to modify and use as your own page, you can open the page in Internet Explorer, and then run FrontPage Express from Internet Explorer. Take the following steps:

1. Open your Web page in Internet Explorer. You can open the page from your hard drive or from the Web.

2. Open Internet Explorer's **Edit** menu, and select **Page**, or click the **Edit** button on the right end of the Standard Buttons toolbar. (If the Edit button is hidden, select **View**, **Toolbar**, **Text Labels** to hide the button labels.)

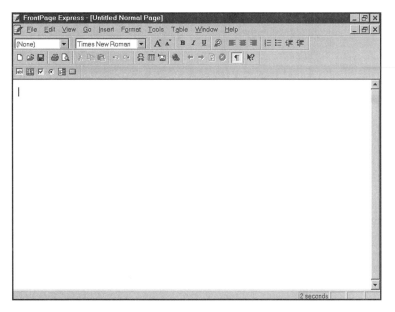

Figure 1.2 When you start FrontPage Express, it displays a blank page.

TIP **Open Pages from FrontPage Express** You can open a page directly from FrontPage Express without having to use Internet Explorer. Use FrontPage Express's **File**, **Open** command.

CAUTION **"Borrowing" Existing Pages** Although you can open pages from the Web and edit them in FrontPage Express, you should not use someone else's original creation as your own. If you want to modify someone else's page and use it as your Web page, obtain written permission from the person before you proceed. Many Web page authors have learned their trade by looking at other people's creations and are usually willing to grant permission.

Touring the FrontPage Express Window

Figure 1.3 shows FrontPage Express displaying a Web page. As you can see, FrontPage Express looks very similar to a low-end word processing application. The FrontPage Express window has several features you are probably already familiar with, as outlined in the following list:

- The *menu bar* (near the top of the window) gives you access to all available commands.

- The *Format toolbar* (just below the menu bar) contains buttons that enable you to bypass the Format menu for common formatting options, such as text size, enhancements (bold and italic), and alignment (left, center, and right). See Part 5, Lesson 4, "Formatting Text."

- The *Standard toolbar* (below the Format toolbar) gives you quick access to commands, such as New, Open, Save, and Print. It also contains buttons for inserting additional objects, such as images and links, and for navigating any open pages.

- The *Forms toolbar* provides the tools you need to create a fill-in-the-blank form. You can use these buttons to insert text boxes, check boxes, option buttons, drop-down menus, and command buttons to your Web page to create a form. See Part 5, Lesson 12, "Creating Forms."

- The *Status bar* (at the bottom of the window) displays messages that provide general information about the selected command or option.

- *Scroll bars* appear near the bottom and on the right side of the window when your page is too large to fit inside the window. Use the scroll bars to bring hidden portions of your Web page into view.

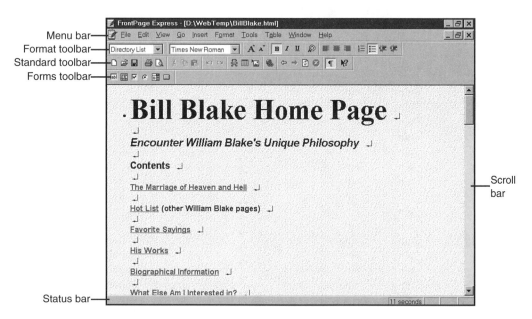

Figure 1.3 The FrontPage Express window contains a standard menu bar and several toolbars.

TIP **Total Toolbar Control** The View menu contains options for turning the toolbars on or off. You might want to turn toolbars off to provide more room for displaying your Web page.

In this lesson, you saw how HTML tags are used to create and format a Web page, and you learned how to run FrontPage Express. In the next lesson, you will learn how to quickly create a Web page using one of FrontPage Express's templates or wizards.

Creating a Web Page with a Template or Wizard

In this lesson, you learn how to create a simple Web page using the FrontPage Express templates and wizards.

FrontPage Express takes the work out of Web pages. With FrontPage Express, you can create your own Web page in a matter of minutes by using one of the templates or wizards included with FrontPage Express and then modifying the design and content to fit your needs.

Creating a Personal Home Page with the Wizard

You can use FrontPage Express's Web page templates and wizards to create your own personal home page or create forms for gathering data. To create your own personal home page using FrontPage Express's Personal Home Page Wizard, take the following steps:

1. Open FrontPage Express's **File** menu and select **New**. The New Page dialog box appears, as shown in Figure 2.1, displaying a list of the FrontPage templates and wizards.

2. Select **Personal Home Page Wizard**, and click **OK**. The first Personal Home Page Wizard dialog box appears, prompting you to select the contents of your home page.

3. Select each section you want to include on your home page, as shown in Figure 2.2. Each item you select appears as a heading on your page. Keep in mind that you can edit the headings later. If a heading doesn't exactly match what you had in mind, select it anyway, and edit it later.

Figure 2.1 FrontPage Express presents a list of templates and wizards.

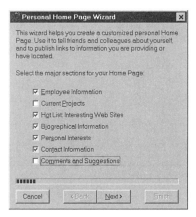

Figure 2.2 The wizard prompts you to specify the content of your page.

4. Click **Next**. You are now asked to name the page.

5. In the **Page URL** text box, type the name of the page (its file name). The name should have the file name extension .htm or .html. (Some service providers are picky about file names. Before you attempt to post your page, check your service provider's file name requirements.)

6. In the **Page Title** text box, type the name of the page as you want it to appear in the title bar when a visitor opens the page in his or her Web browser. Click **Next**.

7. The remaining dialog boxes vary, depending on the content you selected in step 3. For example, if you choose to include a list of links, the wizard asks if you want the list presented as a bulleted list, numbered list, or definition list. Follow the on-screen instructions to make your selections.

285

8. When the last dialog box appears, click **Finish**. The wizard creates your home page and displays it in FrontPage Express, as shown in Figure 2.3, where you can edit it.

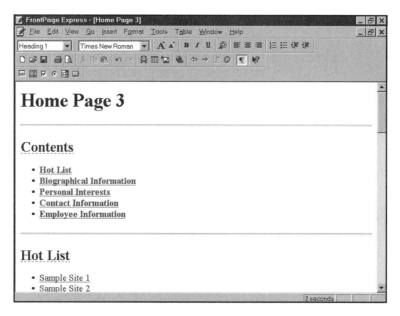

Figure 2.3   FrontPage Express displays your new personal Web page.

Saving Your Web Page to Your Hard Drive

The File, Save command works a little differently in FrontPage Express than in other applications. By default, FrontPage Express attempts to save your page to a Web server, which you learn how to do in Part 5, Lesson 13, "Publishing Your Web Page." For now, take the following steps to save your page as a file on your hard disk:

1. Open the **File** menu and select **Save**, or press **Ctrl+S**. The Save As dialog box appears, as shown in Figure 2.4, displaying the page's title and the address of the Web server where the page will be saved.

2. In the Page Title text box, type the title of your page. The title appears in the title bar of the visitor's Web browser window. (If you created your page with a wizard, the page already has a title, but you can change it now, if desired.)

Figure 2.4 FrontPage Express prompts you to enter a title for your page.

3. Click **As File**. The standard Save As File dialog box appears.

4. Select the drive and folder in which you want the page stored, and click **Save**. FrontPage Express saves the Web page file to your hard disk in the specified folder.

TIP **Think Ahead**   If you plan on publishing a single Web page, store it and any associated files (for example, graphics) in a separate folder, to prevent mixing them up with your other document files. By doing this, you can later save the entire contents of the folder to a Web server to place your page on the Web.

TERM **Publish**   Unlike other documents, which require you to print them in order to publish them, Web pages are *published* electronically. To publish a Web page, you save it and any graphics, video clips, audio clips, and other associated files to a directory (folder) on a Web server.

Making Pages with Templates

The Personal Home Page Wizard is the best tool for creating an opening Web page. The Confirmation Form and Survey Form templates (and the Form Page Wizard) help you create forms, as explained in Part 5, Lesson 12, "Creating Forms." The Normal Page template creates a blank page. The New Web View Folder template creates a page you can use as a Web background for folders you view in My Computer or Windows Explorer.

Most templates mentioned in the previous paragraph are covered in greater detail in later lessons. However, the following steps provide an overview of how easy it is to create a Web page from a template. Take the following steps to create a blank page using the Normal Page template:

287

1. Open FrontPage Express's **File** menu and select **New**. The New Page dialog box appears, as you saw in Figure 2.1, displaying a list of the FrontPage templates and wizards.

2. Click the name of the desired template. In this case, choose **Normal Page** to create a new, blank page.

3. Click **OK**. FrontPage Express immediately displays a blank page, which you can then add to and modify as explained in Lessons 3 through 12.

Opening a Web Page

If you close your Web page before finishing it or if you decide to modify it later, you must open it in FrontPage Express. Take the following steps to open an existing Web page from your hard disk:

1. Open the **File** menu and select **Open** (Ctrl+O) or click the **Open** button in the Standard toolbar. The Open File dialog box appears, as shown in Figure 2.5.

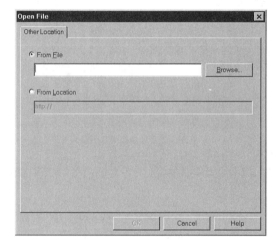

Figure 2.5   The Open File dialog box enables you to select a file from your hard drive or from the Web.

2. Make sure **From File** is selected and click the **Browse** button. The Open File dialog box appears, displaying the contents of the current disk.

3. Change to the disk and folder in which your Web page is stored and click the name of the Web page you want to open.

4. Click the **Open** button. FrontPage Express opens the file and displays your Web page.

 TIP   **Working with Multiple Pages**   If you're constructing a *web* (a collection of interconnected Web pages), you may want to open all related pages. To switch to an open Web page, select it from the Window menu.

In this lesson, you learned how to create simple Web pages using FrontPage Express's wizards and templates, and how to save and open your creations. In the next lesson, you will learn how to add headings and other text to your Web page.

Adding Headings and Other Text

In this lesson, you learn how to insert headings and add paragraphs to your Web page.

If you used the Personal Home Page Wizard to create your Web page, it already contains some headings and text that you can edit to customize the page for your own use. To create additional headings or paragraphs, you can simply copy what's already on the page and paste it where you need it. However, you may need more control over your headings and running text. This lesson explains the tools that provide this additional control.

Adding Headings to Introduce Sections

You already gave your Web page a title when you saved it (or created it with a wizard). However, this title appears only in the Web browser's title bar when you open the page (where nobody really looks). To add a title that appears at the top of the Web page, you must insert the title as a heading.

HTML standards support six heading levels, from Heading 1 to Heading 6. You typically use Heading 1 (the largest heading) to format the heading at the top of the page, and use the remaining headings to format section titles. To format your page title as a Heading 1, or format section titles, take the following steps:

1. Move the insertion point where you want the page title or section heading inserted. (Insert the heading on a line of its own.)

2. Type your title or heading.

3. Open the **Change Style** drop-down list, as shown in Figure 3.1, and select the desired heading level. FrontPage Express inserts the required HTML codes before and after the heading to format it. (You can view the codes by selecting **View**, **HTML**, but you really don't have to deal with them.)

4. If you created a page title, you probably want the title centered at the top of the page. Click the **Center** button in the Format toolbar.

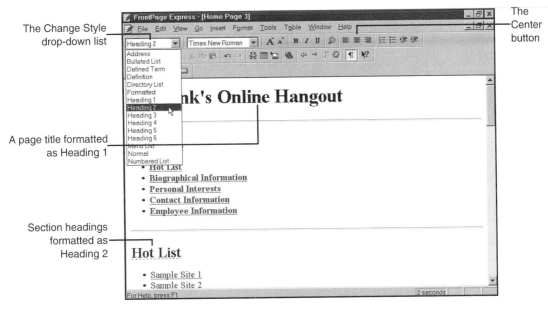

The Change Style drop-down list

A page title formatted as Heading 1

Section headings formatted as Heading 2

The Center button

Figure 3.1 You can use Heading styles to control the look of your page title and section headings.

Insert Normal Paragraphs

No matter how precise and descriptive your section titles are, you should add a paragraph or two after each heading to introduce the page and each section. To add text after a heading, take the following steps:

1. Move the insertion point to the end of the heading and press **Enter**. This creates a new paragraph styled as Normal text. If you centered the title or heading, the paragraph is centered, too.

2. To left-justify the paragraph, click the **Align Left** button in the Format toolbar, as shown in Figure 3.2.

3. To change the type size or add an enhancement, such as bold or italic, to your text, first drag over the text to select it.

4. To change the type size, click the **Increase Text Size** or **Decrease Text Size** button in the Format toolbar.

5. To add an enhancement, click the **Bold**, **Italic**, or **Underline** button.

291

6. To change the text color, click the **Text Color** button, select the desired color, and click **OK**. (For additional formatting options, see Part 5, Lesson 4, "Formatting Text.")

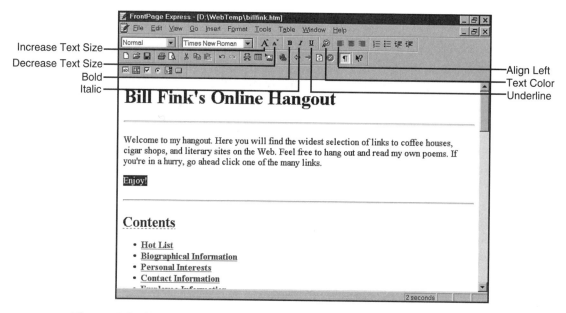

Figure 3.2   You can add normal text, and then change its size and color and add enhancements.

 TIP   **Text Sizes**   HTML tags provide general instructions on how to display text. The visitor's Web browser interprets the tags to determine the actual size it displays. Because of this, FrontPage Express uses the Increase and Decrease Text Size controls rather than enabling you to enter an absolute setting.

In this lesson, you learned how to divide your page into sections with headings, and how to insert normal text. In the next lesson, you will learn how to use additional formatting options to control the appearance and position of text.

Formatting Text

In this lesson, you learn how to change the size, color, alignment, and other attributes of your text.

In the previous lesson, you learned how to add headings and paragraphs to your Web page and how to apply some basic text formatting. However, the Format toolbar and the Format menu offer additional options that have not yet been discussed. This lesson introduces you to these options.

Selecting Text

Before you can format text, you must select (highlight) it. As mentioned in the previous lesson, you can select text by dragging over it with the mouse pointer. You also can use the following mouse shortcuts to select text:

- To select a word, double-click it.
- To select a line, move the mouse pointer to the left of the line until it appears as an arrow and then click the left mouse button (see Figure 4.1).
- To select a paragraph, move the mouse pointer to the left of the paragraph and then double-click the left mouse button.

TIP **Edit, Select All** To select all the text in the document, open the **Edit** menu and choose **Select All** or press **Ctrl+A**.

Table 4.1 lists additional ways you can select text using the keyboard.

When the mouse
pointer points up and
to the right, you can
select text

Drag down to extend
the highlight over
additional text

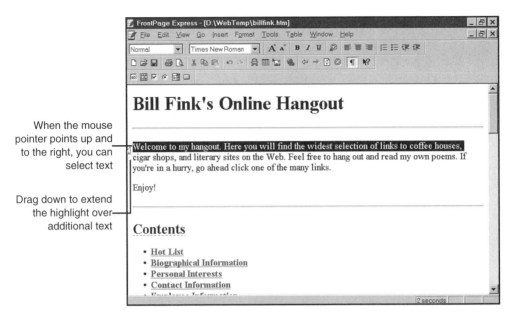

Figure 4.1   To the left of the text is a blank area where the mouse takes on a different role.

Table 4.1   Text Selection Shortcuts

Press	To
Shift+Arrow	Extend the highlight from the insertion point in the direction of the arrow.
Ctrl+Shift+Arrow	Extend the highlight from the insertion point in the direction of the arrow one word at a time.
Shift+End	Extend the highlight from the insertion point to the end of the line.
Shift+Home	Extend the highlight from the insertion point to the beginning of the line.
Ctrl+Shift+End	Extend the highlight from the insertion point to the end of the document.
Ctrl+Shift+Home	Extend the highlight from the insertion point to the beginning of the document.
Ctrl+A	Select all text on the page. (This is the same as choosing Edit, Select All.)

Easy Formatting with the Format Toolbar

You can do a pretty good job of formatting your Web page without ever opening the Format menu. Simply select your formatting options from the Format toolbar, shown in Figure 4.2.

Figure 4.2 Use the Format toolbar for the most common character and paragraph formats.

Table 4.2 explains the purpose of each format button. The Format toolbar offers the following two types of formatting tools:

- The character formatting tools change the type style, size, and color of text, and apply enhancements—bold, italic, and underline. To apply a character format to existing text, you must first drag over the text to select it, or choose the desired formats and then start typing.

- The paragraph formatting tools enable you to choose a paragraph style, indent paragraphs, change their alignment, or transform paragraphs into bulleted or numbered lists. To apply a paragraph format, you must move the insertion point somewhere in the paragraph; you don't have to select text unless you want to format more than one paragraph.

Table 4.2 FrontPage Express's Format Toolbar Buttons

Button	Name	Description
Normal ▼	Change Style	Applies a general style to the entire paragraph. For example, you can click in a paragraph and select Heading 1 to transform the text into a top-level heading.
Times New Roman ▼	Change Font	Changes the type style.
A	Increase Text Size	Increases the text size (eight sizes are available).
A	Decrease Text Size	Decreases the text size.

continues

Table 4.2 Continued

Button	Name	Description
B	Bold	Makes text thick and dark.
I	Italic	Makes text slanted.
U	Underline	Underlines text.
	Text Color	Displays a dialog box with several color options.
	Align Left	Places all lines of the paragraph against the left margin.
	Center	Centers the paragraph between the margins.
	Align Right	Butts all lines of the paragraph against the right margin.
	Numbered List	Transforms selected paragraphs into a numbered list.
	Bulleted List	Transforms selected paragraphs into a bulleted list.
	Decrease Indent	Moves paragraph to the left.
	Increase Indent	Moves paragraph to the right.

You can apply formatting before or after you type your text. To apply formatting before typing, move the insertion point where you want the text to appear, use the Format toolbar to enter your preferences, and then start typing. To format existing text, select the text and then use the buttons on the Format toolbar to specify your preferences.

Applying Paragraph Styles

You already worked with some paragraph styles in the previous lesson when you created headings. Paragraph styles contain format settings that take care of all the details for you. For example, if you apply the Defined Term style to a paragraph, FrontPage Express left-aligns the term and makes it bold. The Definition style indents the term's definition directly below the term and uses normal (non-bold) text.

Table 4.3 describes the paragraph styles on the Change Style drop-down list. Remember, to apply a style to a paragraph, you must first position the insertion point in the paragraph.

Table 4.3 Paragraph Styles

Style Name	What It Does
Address	Displays text in italics, which is useful for adding an e-mail address to your Web page.
Bulleted List	Formats paragraphs as a bulleted list. See Part 5, Lesson 5, "Creating Lists."
Defined Term	Makes a term or phrase bold. If you use the Defined Term style and you press Enter to create a new paragraph, the next paragraph is automatically formatted using the Definition style.
Definition	Indents the entire left side of the paragraph. This is typically used along with the Defined Term style.
Directory List	Similar to a bulleted list, the Directory List provides a tool to help visitors access additional resources at your Web site.
Formatted	Formats text in a fixed-width font, so all characters and spaces are allotted the same amount of space. This is useful for arranging text in columns and rows.
Heading 1-6	Formats up to six heading levels to help you organize your page and divide it into logical sections.
Menu List	Similar to a bulleted list. In a menu list, a blank line is inserted between each paragraph in the list.
Normal	Displays text without any additional enhancements, such as bold or italic, and uses the default font style and size.
Numbered List	Formats paragraphs as a numbered list.

TIP **Adding an E-Mail Address to Your Page** It's good practice to add your e-mail address to your Web page so that a visitor can contact you if your page has an error. This feedback is useful in helping you perfect your page. In Part 5, Lesson 8, "Linking Your Page to Other Pages," you learn how to add a link that a user can click to automatically send you an e-mail message. Addresses typically appear at the bottom of a page.

Applying Character Formatting

With character formatting, you can change the type style, size, and color of text and add enhancements, such as bold and italic. To apply character formatting to existing text, take the following steps:

1. Select the text you want to format.

2. Open the **Change Font** drop-down list, and select the desired type style.

3. Click the **Increase Text Size** or **Decrease Text Size** button to cycle through the eight standard text sizes. (You can click either button more than one time.)

4. Click the button for any text enhancement you want to add: **Bold**, **Italic**, or **Underline**. You can use more than one text enhancement. To remove an enhancement, click the button again.

5. To change the color of the text, click the **Text Color** button, select the desired color, and click **OK**.

Controlling Text Alignment and Indents

FrontPage Express's Format toolbar contains buttons for controlling the position of a paragraph in relation to the left and right margins and for indenting paragraphs from the left margin. To change the text alignment or indent paragraphs, take the following steps:

1. Move the insertion point to any position inside the paragraph you want to align or indent.

2. To change the position of the paragraph in relation to the left and right margin, click one of the following buttons: **Align Left**, **Center**, or **Align Right**.

3. To indent a paragraph from the left margin, click the **Increase Indent** button. (You can click the button more than once to increase the indent.)

4. To move an indented paragraph back toward the left margin, click the **Decrease Indent** button. (You can click the button more than once to move the paragraph closer to the left margin.)

Applying Formats Using the Format Menu

Although the Format toolbar provides buttons for most of the paragraph and text formatting you need to apply, you can access additional options by opening the **Format** menu and selecting **Font** or **Paragraph**. The following sections provide instructions on how to apply formatting using these options.

Adding Character Formatting

To change the appearance of selected text, you can apply character formatting. Take the following steps to format existing text:

1. Select the text you want to format.

2. Open the **Format** menu and select **Font**. The Font dialog box appears, offering many of the same character formatting options that are available in the Format toolbar.

3. Choose the desired font, text style, size, and other effects for the selected text. The preview area displays the text as it will appear in the selected format.

4. Click the **Special Styles** tab for additional formatting options, as shown in Figure 4.3. The bracketed text next to each option represents the HTML tag that the option will insert.

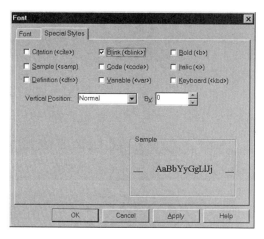

Figure 4.3 The Font dialog box provides additional character formatting options.

5. Click any of the desired special styles you want to use for your text. When you click a style, a check mark appears in its box (you can click the style again to remove the check mark).

6. To view the effects of your format changes on the text, click the **Apply** button. The format settings are put into effect for the selected text.

7. To create a subscript or superscript, select the desired option from the **Vertical Position** list, and enter the number of points you want the bottom of the text positioned above or below the line. (A point is approximately 1/72 of an inch.)

8. When you're satisfied with your format settings, click **OK**.

CAUTION

Blink Text Doesn't Blink   If you turned on the Blink option on the Special Styles tab, a teal box appears around the text, but it doesn't blink. Save the page, as explained in Part 5, Lesson 2, "Creating a Web Page with a Template or Wizard," and then open it in Internet Explorer to see your text blink. FrontPage Express is incapable of displaying several Web page features that Internet Explorer can display.

Entering Paragraph Settings

The Format toolbar offers more paragraph formatting options than are available via the Format, Paragraph command. However, the Format, Menu command does enable you to select a paragraph style and alignment at the same time. Take the following steps to enter paragraph settings:

1. Move the insertion point anywhere in the paragraph you want to format. To apply formatting to more than one paragraph, you must select a portion of each paragraph.

2. Open the **Format** menu and select **Paragraph**. The Paragraph Properties dialog box appears, as shown in Figure 4.4.

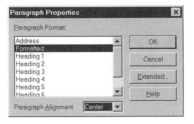

Figure 4.4   The Paragraph Properties dialog box enables you to select a style and alignment at the same time.

3. From the **Paragraph Format** list, select the desired paragraph style: **Address, Formatted, Heading 1-6**, or **Normal**.

4. Open the Paragraph Alignment drop-down list, and select the desired alignment: **Left, Center**, or **Right**.

5. Click **OK**.

 What Is the Extended Button? The Extended button in the Paragraph Properties dialog box appears in many FrontPage Express dialog boxes. It enables you to type additional HTML tags for controlling the format of selected text, graphics, and other objects. To use this button effectively, you should have a good knowledge of HTML tags.

Setting Margins

FrontPage Express sets the left and right page margins so that your text fits inside most Web browser windows. If desired, you can increase the top or left margin to give your page a unique layout. Take the following steps to set the margins:

1. Open the **File** menu and select **Page Properties**. The Page Properties dialog box appears.

2. Click the **Margins** tab to see the options shown in Figure 4.5.

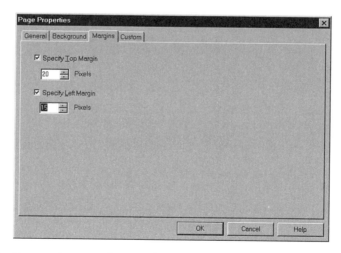

Figure 4.5 You can increase the margins.

3. Click **Specify Top Margin** or **Specify Left Margin** (or both) to place a check mark in the box(es).

4. Use the **Pixels** spin box to set the top or left margin. (One pixel is equivalent to a dot on the screen).

5. Click **OK**. Your new margin settings are applied to your page.

In this lesson, you learned how to format text and change margins for your Web page. In the next lesson, you will learn how to create and modify lists.

Creating Lists

In this lesson, you learn how to insert bulleted and numbered lists and other types of lists.

Lists are the staple of any successful Web page. You use lists to break down complex material into steps, present items that would get lost in normal paragraphs, define terms, and arrange links to simplify navigation. You can create a list from scratch or by transforming existing paragraphs into a list. The following sections show you how to create bulleted, numbered, and definition lists.

Creating a Bulleted List

The most common type of list is the bulleted list. Bulleted lists are excellent tools for breaking down long paragraphs into easily digestible chunks of information.

If you have already typed the paragraphs that you want to use as your bulleted list, select the paragraphs, and then click the **Bulleted List** button in the Format toolbar.

If you haven't yet typed the paragraphs, take the following steps to create a bulleted list from scratch:

1. Move the insertion point to a blank line. (You can do this by moving the insertion point to the end of a paragraph and pressing **Enter**.)
2. Click the **Bulleted List** button in the Format toolbar. An indented bullet appears.
3. (Optional) To give the bullets a different look, open the **Format** menu and select **Bullets and Numbering**. The List Properties dialog box appears, as shown in Figure 5.1, with the Bulleted tab in front.
4. Click the desired bullet style, and click **OK**.

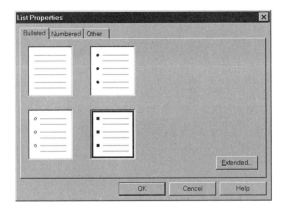

Figure 5.1 Select the bullet design you want to use.

5. Type the first item you want to appear in your list. If the item is two lines or longer, FrontPage Express automatically wraps the text, creating a hanging indent, with the bullet to the left of all the text.

6. Press **Enter** to start a new paragraph. FrontPage Express automatically formats the paragraph as a bulleted list item.

7. Keep typing and pressing **Enter** until your list is complete. Press **Enter** at the end of your list to create a new paragraph.

8. To return to typing normal paragraphs, click the **Bulleted List** button again. Figure 5.2 shows a sample bulleted list.

TIP **Reformatting a Bulleted List** You can change the appearance of bullets in an existing list. First, select all the items in the list. Then, use the Format, Bullets and Numbering Command to change the properties of the list. You can even convert a bulleted list into a numbered list, or vice versa.

Creating a Numbered List

You can quickly create a numbered list from scratch by clicking the **Numbered List** button in the Format toolbar and typing your list. FrontPage Express automatically inserts the numbers for you, in order, as you create new paragraphs. To convert existing paragraphs into a numbered list, select the paragraphs, then click the **Numbered List** button.

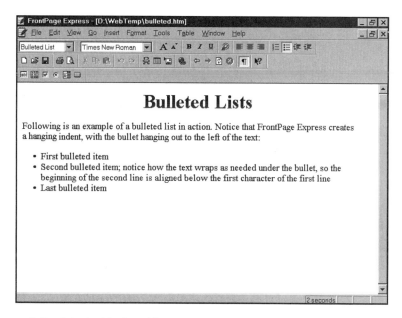

Figure 5.2   A typical bulleted list.

When you create a numbered list, FrontPage Express inserts Arabic numerals (1, 2, 3…) starting with the number 1. To use Roman Numerals (I, II, III…) or letters (A, B, C…) or to start with a number other than 1, follow these steps:

1. Position the insertion point on a blank line by pressing **Enter** at the end of a paragraph.

2. Open the **Format** menu and select **Bullets and Numbering**. The List Properties dialog box appears, with the Bulleted tab in front.

3. Click the **Numbered** tab, as shown in Figure 5.3.

4. Select the desired numbering format.

5. To start with a number other than 1, I, i, A, or a, use the **Start At** spin box to set the desired starting number.

6. Click **OK**.

7. Type your list, using the **Enter** key to create new items in the list. When you press Enter, FrontPage Express inserts the next number in the series.

8. At the end of the list, press **Enter** to create a new paragraph, then click the **Numbered List** button in the Format toolbar to turn off numbering for this paragraph. Figure 5.4 shows a typical numbered list.

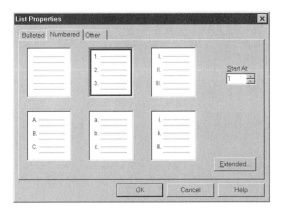

Figure 5.3 FrontPage Express offers several formats for creating numbered lists.

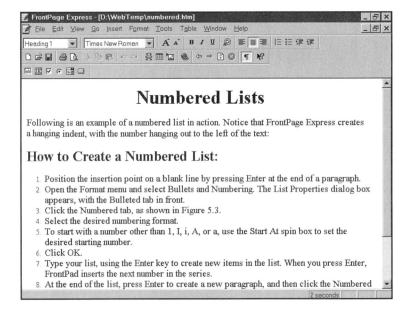

Numbered Lists

Following is an example of a numbered list in action. Notice that FrontPage Express creates a hanging indent, with the number hanging out to the left of the text:

How to Create a Numbered List:

1. Position the insertion point on a blank line by pressing Enter at the end of a paragraph.
2. Open the Format menu and select Bullets and Numbering. The List Properties dialog box appears, with the Bulleted tab in front.
3. Click the Numbered tab, as shown in Figure 5.3.
4. Select the desired numbering format.
5. To start with a number other than 1, I, i, A, or a, use the Start At spin box to set the desired starting number.
6. Click OK.
7. Type your list, using the Enter key to create new items in the list. When you press Enter, FrontPad inserts the next number in the series.
8. At the end of the list, press Enter to create a new paragraph, and then click the Numbered

Figure 5.4 A typical numbered list in action.

 TIP **Additional Formatting** Keep in mind that you can use other formatting options for your lists. For example, you can change the font, text size, and color, and add bold and italic.

306

Creating a Definition List

Definition lists are useful for creating online glossaries for your documents. The term you define is positioned flush left, and the definition is indented directly below the term. To create a definition list, take the following steps:

1. Position the insertion point on a blank line where you want the list to start.

2. Open the **Change Style** drop-down list in the Format toolbar, and then select **Defined Term**.

3. Type the term you want to define. The term appears flush left.

4. Press **Enter**. FrontPage Express automatically formats the new paragraph as a definition. The insertion point is positioned directly below the term and is indented.

5. Type the term's definition. All lines of the definition appear indented.

6. Press **Enter**. FrontPage Express automatically formats the new paragraph using the Defined Term style. Repeat steps 3 through 5 to type additional terms and definitions.

7. When you're done, press **Enter** to create a blank paragraph, and then select the desired style from the **Change Style** drop-down list. Figure 5.5 shows a sample definition list.

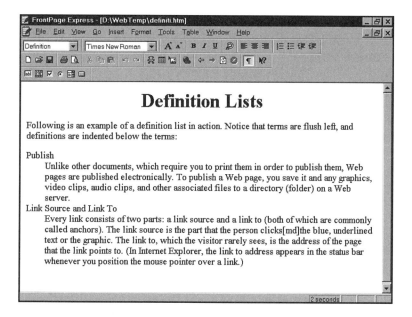

Figure 5.5 A sample definition list.

TIP **Indenting the List** If the definition list has normal text above it, you may want to indent the list. Select all terms and definitions in the list, and then click the **Increase Indent** button in the Format toolbar.

In this lesson, you learned how to create and format lists. In the next lesson, you will learn how to arrange text in rows or columns using tables.

Inserting Tables

In this lesson, you learn how to arrange text in rows and columns using tables.

Tables are useful for arranging text in columns and rows. With FrontPage Express, you can specify the number of rows and columns you want the table to have, and FrontPage Express creates it. All you have to do is type entries into each cell.

 Cell The box formed by the intersection of a row and column. Each cell can contain text or graphic images.

Creating a Basic Table

To create a table in FrontPage Express, you simply specify the number of rows and columns you want in the table. FrontPage Express creates the table for you, and you can start typing.

 TIP **Organize Your Entire Page** You can use a table to organize your entire Web page. Simply insert the table on a blank page.

To create a table, take the following steps:

1. Move the insertion point to a blank line where you want the table inserted.
2. Click the **Insert Table** button in the Format toolbar, and drag down and to the right to select the number of columns and rows you want the table to have (see Figure 6.1).

3. Release the mouse button. FrontPage Express inserts the table on your page. The table appears as wide as the page, and is divided into the specified number of columns, each of equal width.

Click the Insert
Table button

Drag over the
desired number of
rows and columns

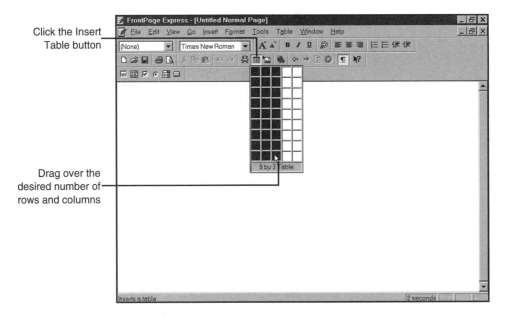

Figure 6.1   You can quickly insert a table in your Web page.

CAUTION

Dinky Table?   If you get a small table whose cells expand as you type your entries, right-click the table, select **Table Properties**, click the **Specify Width** check box, and click **OK**. You'll learn more about table properties in the section "Redesigning Your Table," later in this lesson.

Typing Entries into Cells

Once you have created the table layout, you can start typing entries into the cells. Take the following steps:

1. Click in the cell or use the Tab key or the arrow keys to move from cell to cell.

2. When the insertion point is in the desired cell, start typing. As you type entries into the cells, the text automatically wraps inside the cell as needed (see Figure 6.2).

You also can insert links or graphics into cells; the size of the cell automatically adjusts to accommodate whatever object you insert. See Part 5, Lesson 7, "Inserting Images and Horizontal Lines," and Part 5, Lesson 8, "Linking Your Page to Other Pages."

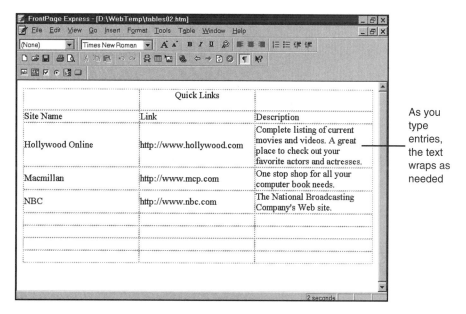

Figure 6.2 A table automatically arranges your text in rows and columns.

Selecting Cells, Columns, and Rows

When you start to work with your table, you will find that selecting cells is a little difficult. You can drag over cells in a row, but if you try to drag over columns, you'll end up selecting all the columns in the table. To select cells, columns, or rows, take one of the following steps:

- To select a single cell, hold down the **Alt** key and click the cell.
- To select a row, move the mouse pointer to the left of the row until a right-pointing arrow appears, and then click. Drag to select additional rows.
- To select a column, move the mouse pointer to the top of the column until a down-pointing arrow appears, and then click. Drag to select additional columns.

- To select a cell, row, or column, first move the insertion point into the cell or into any cell in the row or column you want to select. Open the **Table** menu and choose **Select Cell**, **Select Row**, or **Select Column**.

Redesigning Your Table

The table you created in the previous section is pretty generic. All the columns are the same width, and the rows are the same height. If this works for you, fine, but if you need something special, you can change the properties of the entire table or of selected cells, and you can add a caption to introduce the table. To change the table properties, take the following steps:

1. Click in the table.
2. Open the **Table** menu, and select **Table Properties** (or right-click the table, and select **Table Properties**). The Table Properties dialog box appears, as shown in Figure 6.3, allowing you to enter your preferences. Table 6.1 provides descriptions of the table properties.

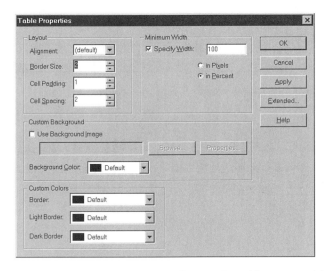

Figure 6.3   You can change the properties of the entire table to control its appearance.

3. Click **OK** to save your settings. FrontPage Express reformats the table according to your specifications.

Table 6.1 Table Properties

Property	Function
Layout	Changes the alignment of the table (left, center, or right). You also can specify the width of the borders that separate the cells, the cell spacing (space between cells), and the cell padding (the space between the text inside each cell and the cell's borders. All measurements are in pixels (a dot on the screen).
Minimum Width	Minimum width is the skinniest the table can possibly be. If you leave Specify Width unchecked, you get a narrow table whose cells expand as you type. To prevent this from happening, make sure Specify Width is checked, and then specify the minimum width as a percentage of the page width or as an absolute measurement in pixels.
Custom Background	Sets a background color or image to use as the table's background. If you don't select anything here, your page background (if you use one) acts as the table's background.
Custom Colors	Specifies colors for the border lines that define the cells (assuming you entered a border width under Layout). The Border Color controls the color only if you don't specify a Light Border and Dark Border color. If you choose a Light Border and Dark Border color, FrontPage Express uses the two colors to create a drop-shading effect for the cells.

Changing Cell Properties

In addition to changing the properties of the entire table, you can change the properties of individual cells. This can come in handy if you need a cell that spans several rows or columns, or if you want to shade cells using a different color. To change cell properties, click in a cell, or drag over the cells you want your changes to affect. Open the **Table** menu and select **Cell Properties**. You can then change the properties listed in Table 6.2.

Table 6.2 Cell Properties

Cell Property	Function
Layout	Controls the properties for the text inside the cells. You can change the vertical and horizontal alignment of the text, turn on Header Cell (to make the text bold), and turn on No Wrap (so text doesn't wrap inside the cells).
Minimum Width	Specifies the minimum width of cells as a percentage of the table width or as an absolute measurement (in pixels). Enter settings here if you want columns that aren't uniformly wide.
Custom Background	Specifies a background image or color for the selected cells.
Custom Colors	Control the colors only of the cell borders. See "Custom Colors" in Table 6.1 for details.
Cell Span	Makes the selected cell span two or more columns or rows. To have a cell span two or more columns, enter the desired number of rows or columns you want the cell to span. For example, if you have a three-column table, and you want a cell at the top that spans all three columns, type **3** in the **Number of Columns Spanned** text box.

If you choose to make a cell span two or more columns or rows, FrontPage Express doesn't merge the selected cell with the other cells in that row or column, so you must delete those cells. If the cells contain entries, use the **Cut** and **Paste** buttons to move the entries to other cells. Then, drag over the cell that spans the columns or rows and the extraneous cells. Open the **Table** menu and select **Merge Cells**.

 TIP **Add a Caption**   You can insert a caption that appears centered above the table. With the insertion point anywhere inside the table, open the **Table** menu and select **Insert Caption**. The insertion point appears above the table, where you can type your caption.

Editing Cells

When you first create a table, you rarely know how many rows and columns you need. You make your best guess and then you add or delete columns and rows as needed. You can easily add or delete rows, columns, and cells in FrontPage Express.

To insert a row or column, take the following steps:

1. Select any cell in the row or column where you want the new row or column added.
2. Open the **Table** menu, and select **Insert Rows or Columns**. The Insert Rows or Columns dialog box appears, as shown in Figure 6.4.
3. Click **Rows** or **Columns**.
4. Use the spin box to set the desired number of rows or columns.
5. Select the position of the new row or column. For example, if you're inserting rows, you can insert them above or below the current row.
6. Click **OK**.

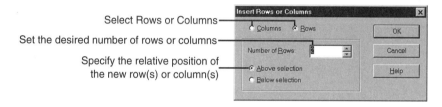

Select Rows or Columns

Set the desired number of rows or columns

Specify the relative position of
the new row(s) or column(s)

Figure 6.4 You can insert rows or columns.

You also can insert one or more cells by taking one of the following steps:

- To insert cells, select the cell where you want the new cell added. The new cell will be inserted to the right of the selected cell. Open the **Table** menu and select **Insert Cell**.
- Right-click a cell, point to **Insert**, and select the item you want to insert: **Row**, **Column**, or **Cell**. (If you choose Cell, the new cell will be inserted to the right of the selected cell.)

To delete rows, columns, or cells, select the row, column, or cell you want to delete and press the **Delete** key.

In this lesson, you learned how to take control of text layout with tables. In the next lesson, you will learn how to spruce up your document with images and horizontal lines.

Inserting Images and Horizontal Lines

In this lesson, you learn how to accessorize your Web page with graphic images and horizontal lines.

No Web page is complete without a few horizontal lines to divide sections and graphics to accentuate its appearance. In this lesson, you learn all you need to know about inserting, moving, and resizing images and horizontal lines.

Inserting Images

Studies have shown that users spend more time on a page that has images than they do on text-only pages. So if you want to appeal to the masses, you will want to insert at least a couple of images on your page.

Understanding Graphic Formats

Before you add graphics and video clips to your pages, you should know a few things about file formats and file size. First, most Web browsers can display graphics stored as GIF or JPG (JPEG) files. It's a good idea to use only these two graphic file formats in your Web pages. Also, graphic files are relatively large, adding to the time it takes to download your page, so use graphics sparingly.

 TIP **Downloading Images from the Web** If you don't have any graphics to insert, you can download sample graphics off the Web. However, if you plan to borrow original artwork, be sure you get permission from the person who created the Web page.

Inserting a Graphic Image

Inserting an image on your Web page is fairly simple. Take the following steps:

1. Position the insertion point where you want the image inserted.

2. Open the **Insert** menu, and select **Image**. (To save a step for inserting a graphic, click the **Insert Image** button in the Standard Buttons toolbar.) The Image dialog box appears, prompting you to select a file.

3. Take one of the following steps:

   To use a file that's on your hard drive, make sure **From File** is selected, click the **Browse** button, and select the graphic or file you want to use.

   To use a file that's stored on a Web server, click **From Location**, and type the file's address and name in the text box (for example, **http://www.mcp.com/include/resc_mpu.gif**).

4. Click **OK**. The selected image is inserted, as shown in Figure 7.1.

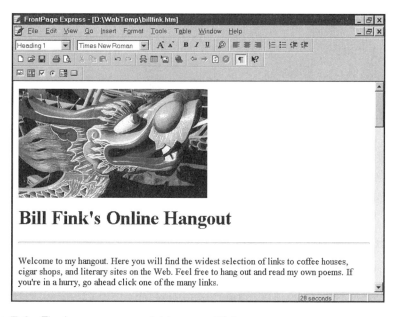

Figure 7.1 The image appears right on your Web page.

Online Images If you insert an image that's stored on a Web server, you should be connected to the Internet so that FrontPage Express can download the image and insert it in your Web page.

CAUTION

317

Moving and Resizing Images

To move or resize an image, first click the image to select it. Then take one of the following steps:

- To move the image, position the mouse pointer over it, hold down the left mouse button, and drag the image to the desired position on your page.

- To resize the image, position the mouse pointer over one of its handles (the squares that surround the image), hold down the mouse button, and drag the handle. Use a corner handle to resize the image proportionally (so its relative height and width remain constant). Use a top or side handle to change only the height *or* width (for a Silly Putty effect). See Figure 7.2.

Figure 7.2 shows the mouse pointer as a two-headed arrow, which it becomes when it's over a handle.

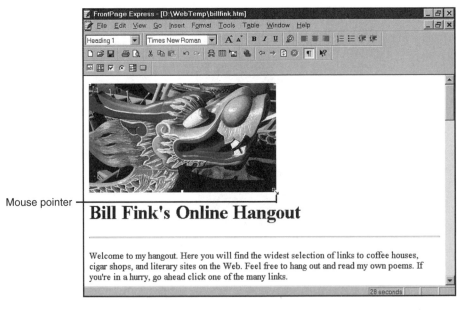

Mouse pointer

Bill Fink's Online Hangout

Welcome to my hangout. Here you will find the widest selection of links to coffee houses, cigar shops, and literary sites on the Web. Feel free to hang out and read my own poems. If you're in a hurry, go ahead click one of the many links.

Figure 7.2   Drag a corner handle to resize both the height and width of the image.

TIP   **Image Properties**   To change the properties of an image (for example, its location or quality), right-click the image and select **Image Properties**, or select the image and press **Alt+Enter**.

Dividing Sections with Horizontal Lines

If you have a long page, consider using horizontal lines to divide the page. To insert a horizontal line, take the following steps:

1. Move the insertion point to the end of the paragraph below which you want the line inserted.

2. Open the **Insert** menu and select **Horizontal Line**. FrontPage Express inserts the line below the current paragraph.

To select the line, click it. You can move the line by dragging it. To change the width, thickness, alignment, or color of the line, take the following steps:

1. Right-click the line and select **Horizontal Line Properties**, or select the line and click **Alt+Enter**. The Horizontal Line Properties dialog box appears, as shown in Figure 7.3.

2. To change the width of the line (actually its length), select **Percent of Window** (to set the width as a percentage of the window width) or **Pixels** (to specify an absolute measurement in pixels). Use the spin box to set the desired percentage or number of pixels.

3. To change the height of the line (actually its width), use the **Height** spin box to enter the desired height in pixels.

4. By default, the line is centered and extends the entire width of the window. If you made the line shorter, you may wish to change its alignment. Select the desired alignment: **Left**, **Center**, or **Right**.

5. To change the color of the line, open the **Color** drop-down list and select the desired color.

6. To use a solid (not shaded) line, click **Solid Line (No Shading)** to place a check mark in the box.

7. Click **OK** to save your changes.

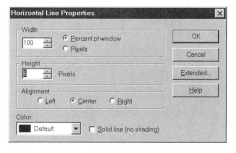

Figure 7.3 You can change the line width, thickness, alignment, and color.

TIP   **Graphic Lines**   In your Web wanderings, you may have noticed that some pages have fancy horizontal dividers. These are actually graphic images (typically stored as .GIF or .JPG files). If you have a graphic image that will work as a horizontal line, you can use it instead of the standard lines. However, as graphics, they take up more storage space and take more time to download.

Drag-and-Drop Web Page Creation

One of the easiest ways to create a Web page is to copy text, graphics, links, and other objects from an existing page and paste them into your page. Of course, you need permission from the person who created the original page before you can legally (or ethically) copy and use the person's material.

To copy and paste items from one page to another, take the following steps:

1. Open the page you want to copy from in Internet Explorer.

2. Open the page you want to copy to in FrontPage Express.

3. Select and drag the desired object (image, link, or text) from the page in Internet Explorer to the page displayed in FrontPage Express as shown in Figure 7.4.

Drag an image to your page

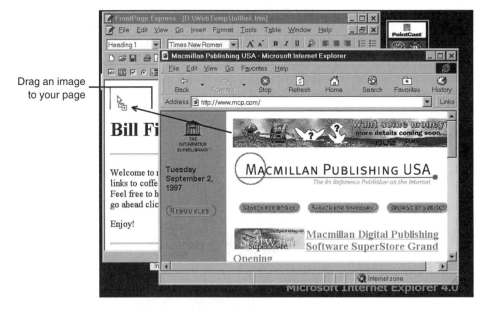

Figure 7.4   You can drag images, links, or text from a page displayed in Internet Explorer to your page.

You also can drag files and shortcuts from your Windows desktop and from folders on your hard drive. Use My Computer or Windows Explorer to display the icon for the file or shortcut you want to place on your page. Then, drag the icon from the My Computer or Windows Explorer window to the desired location on your page.

In this lesson, you learned how to enhance your page with graphic images and horizontal lines. In the next lesson, you will learn how to insert links that point to other pages on the Web.

Linking Your Page to Other Pages

In this lesson, you learn how to insert links that point to other Web pages and to other sections in the same page.

Links are the threads that stitch together the pages, documents, and files that comprise the Web. Without links, you couldn't wander the Web. Each page would be a dead end. You would have to type the specific address of each Web page you wanted to visit. In this lesson, you learn how to add links to your own Web page.

Creating a Text Link

You have used links to skip from one page to another on the Web. Links typically appear as blue, underlined text that changes color after you select it. To create a simple text link on your Web page, take the following steps:

1. Type the text you want to use as the link, and select it.
2. Click the **Create or Edit Hyperlink** button in the Standard toolbar (or press **Ctrl+K**). The Create Hyperlink dialog box opens, with the World Wide Web tab displayed, as shown in Figure 8.1.
3. Open the **Hyperlink Type** drop-down list and select the Internet resource type. In most cases, you select **http:** to point to a Web page. However, you can choose to point to a file on your hard drive, an FTP server, e-mail address (mailto:), or other Internet resource.
4. In the **URL** text box, type the address of the page or other resource you want the link to point to. For example, you might type **http://www.hollywood.com**.
5. Click **OK**. FrontPage Express converts the selected text into a link and displays the text as blue and underlined.

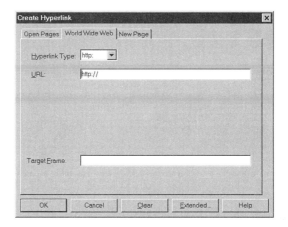

Figure 8.1 Enter the address of the page that the link points to.

The other tabs in the Create Hyperlink dialog box, Open Pages and New Pages, enable you to create links that point to pages you have created or will create. For details on how to link your page to other pages stored on your Web server, see "Linking Your Page to Other Pages at Your Site," later in this lesson.

 TERM **Link Source and Link To** Every link consists of two parts: a *link source* and a *link to* (both of which are commonly called *anchors*). The link source is the part that the person clicks—the blue, underlined text or the graphic. The link to, which the visitor rarely sees, is the address of the page that the link points to. (In Internet Explorer, the link to address appears in the status bar whenever you position the mouse pointer over a link.)

Editing and Removing Links

If you transform text into a link and then decide later that you don't want the text acting as a link, you can quickly remove the link property from the object. Take the following steps:

1. Click the link.
2. Open the **Edit** menu and select **Unlink**.

In most cases, you don't want to remove the link entirely. You just want to change the address of the page or object to which the link points. To change a link's address, take the following steps:

1. Right-click the link, and click **Hyperlink Properties**. The Edit Hyperlink dialog box appears.

323

2. In the **URL** text box, type the new address.

3. Click **OK**.

Understanding Absolute and Relative Links

As you work with links, you should be aware that there are two types of links: *absolute* and *relative*:

- The code behind an *absolute* link includes a complete path that describes the exact location of the page or file. For example, a link such as **http:// www.iquest.com/~smith/resume.html** tells the name of the server, the directory where the file is stored, and the file's name.

- A *relative* link describes the location of the page or file in relation to the folder or directory in which the page containing the link is stored. For example, a link such as resume.html tells only the file name; for the link to work, the file resume.html must be in the same directory as the Web page that contains the link to resume.html. If you store the file on the same server, but in a different directory, the relative link should also specify the path to the directory where the file is stored—for example, **/~smith/ resume.html**. It need not specify the domain name of the server.

Relative links are usually shorter and easier to edit than absolute links. However, when you transfer your page to a Web server, to publish it, you must make sure that you place any files that the relative links point to in the same relative locations on the Web server as those files are stored on your hard drive. The easiest way to do this is to store your Web page and all files it points to in the same folder on your hard drive. When you publish the page, place all the files in a single directory on the Web server.

Linking Your Page to Other Pages at Your Site

If you're creating a personal home page that's not very long, chances are that you will publish a single page. However, if you have a business or work for a company that has several Web pages, you can create links to your other Web pages.

You can create links to existing pages or create a new page on-the-fly and link to it. To link to a page that you have already created, take the following steps:

1. In FrontPage Express, Open the page in which you want to insert the link, and open the page you want the link to point to.

2. Type the text you want to use as the link, and then select it.

3. Click the **Create or Edit Hyperlink** button (or press **Ctrl+K**). The Create Hyperlink dialog box opens, with the World Wide Web tab showing.

4. Click the **Open Pages** tab. A list of all the Web pages opened in FrontPage Express appears (see Figure 8.2).

5. Select the page you want to link to, and click **OK**. (The Bookmark option enables you to link to a specific location on the page, which you will learn how to do later in this lesson.)

The Open Pages tab —

A list of pages that are open in FrontPage Express

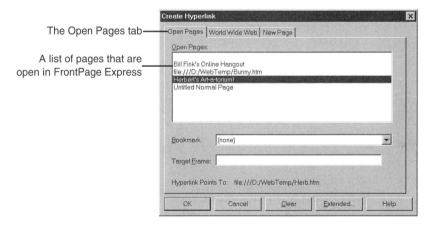

Figure 8.2   You can link to another one of your Web pages simply by selecting it from a list of open pages.

TIP   **Link to a New Page**   To link to a page that you haven't yet created, click the **New Page** tab, and type the title and file name you want to use for the new page. When you click **OK**, the New Page dialog box appears, as explained in Part 5, Lesson 2, "Creating a Web Page with a Template or Wizard," prompting you to create the new page. Follow the on-screen instructions to create the page.

Linking to a Specific Place on a Page

If you have a long Web page, you might want to place a table of contents at the top of the page that provides links to various places on the page. This enables the visitor to quickly navigate your Web page without wearing out the scroll bar.

Inserting a Bookmark

To create a link that points to a specific part of a page, you must first mark the destination point as a *bookmark*. You can then create a link that points to the bookmark instead of to an URL. (I usually insert all my bookmarks first.) To insert a bookmark, take the following steps:

1. Click where you want the bookmark placed, or select the text you want to use as a bookmark. If you select text to use as the bookmark, FrontPage Express uses that text as the target name, saving you some keystrokes. If you don't select text, you must type a name for the bookmark; FrontPage Express inserts a flag to mark the location.

2. Open the **Edit** menu and select **Bookmark**. The Bookmark dialog box appears, as shown in Figure 8.3, prompting you to type a name for your bookmark.

Type a name for the bookmark ──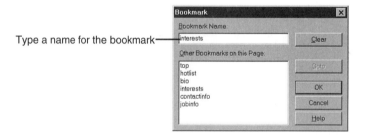

Figure 8.3 Insert your bookmarks first so you will have something to link to.

3. Type a brief but descriptive name for the bookmark. When you create a link to the bookmark, you must select the bookmark from a list of marked bookmarks; be sure you type a name you'll remember. (The bookmark name doesn't appear on the page.)

4. Click **OK**. If you selected text in step 1, FrontPage Express displays a dashed underline below the text. If you didn't select text, a flag symbol appears; it won't be seen by visitors who view the page.

Repeat the preceding steps to mark any additional places on the page as book-marks. You can quickly edit a bookmark by right-clicking the bookmark text or icon and selecting **Bookmark Properties**.

Linking to a Bookmark

Once you have inserted at least one bookmark on the page, you can create a link that points to it. Take the following steps:

1. If necessary, type the text that you want to act as the link. Drag over the text to select it.

2. Click the **Create or Edit Hyperlink** button (or press **Ctrl+K**). The Create Hyperlink dialog appears.

3. Click the **Open Pages** tab, and select the page that contains the bookmark. (You can link to a bookmark on the same page or on another page you have created.)

4. Open the **Bookmark** drop-down list, and select the desired bookmark you want the link to point to. The Bookmark list displays all the bookmarks on the page you selected in step 3 (see Figure 8.4).

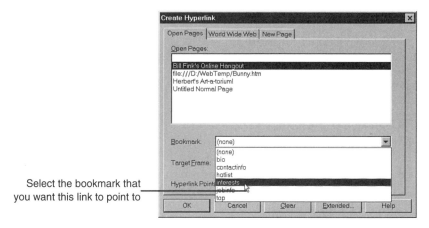

Select the bookmark that you want this link to point to

Figure 8.4   FrontPage Express lists all the bookmarks on the current page.

5. Click **OK** to accept this link.

6. Click the **Save** button.

7. Repeat these steps to link to other bookmarks on the page.

TIP   **Good Form**   If you have a long Web page consisting of several sections, insert a link at the bottom of each section that points to a bookmark at the top of the page. This enables the user to quickly return to where she started. If you have a Web document consisting of several pages, insert links on the other pages that point back to the home page.

Inserting a Link for Your E-Mail Address

If you want people to be able to contact you after reading your Web page, you can insert a link at the bottom of the page that points to your e-mail address. If the user has an e-mail program that's set up properly, he or she can then click the link to send you a message. The person's e-mail program runs automatically and addresses a new message to you. All the person has to do is type the message and send it.

To insert a link to your e-mail address, take the following steps:

1. Type the text you want to use as the link text (for example, **I Need Mail!**, **E-Mail me**, or your e-mail address).

2. Select the text, and click the **Create or Edit Hyperlink** button (or press **Ctrl+K**).

3. Click the **World Wide Web** tab.

4. Open the **Hyperlink Type** drop-down list, and select **mailto:**.

5. In the **URL** text box, type **mailto:** followed by your e-mail address (for example, **mailto:bfink@internet.com**). Click **OK**.

Drag and Drop Links

One of the coolest aspects of FrontPage Express is that you can drag and drop objects onto a Web page you're creating in FrontPage Express. If you have a shortcut on the Windows desktop that points to a Web page, simply drag it into the FrontPage Express window and drop it on the page.

If you open a Web page in Internet Explorer that contains links you want to include on your own Web page, simply drag the link from the Internet Explorer window onto your Web page displayed in FrontPage Express (see Figure 8.5).

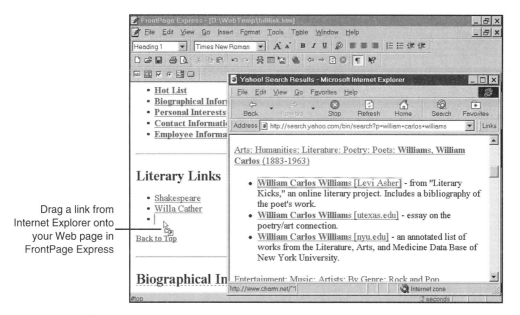

Drag a link from
Internet Explorer onto
your Web page in
FrontPage Express

Figure 8.5 You can drag links from a Web page to your page displayed in FrontPage Express.

Testing Your Links

Before you place your page on the Web, and after you place it on the Web, you should test your links to make sure they work properly. The easiest way to check your links is to open your page in Internet Explorer, and then start clicking. If you receive an error message, re-open the page in FrontPage Express, fix the error, and check the page again.

You also can check links directly from FrontPage Express by taking the following steps:

1. Right-click the link you want to test and select **Follow Hyperlink**. FrontPage Express opens the page.

2. You can click the **Close** (X) button for this page (not the Close button for the Internet Explorer window) to return to your page. Or, select your page from the **Window** menu.

CAUTION

No Frames FrontPage Express doesn't support frames (a Web page feature that divides the browser window into two or more frames). If you click a link that points to a frames-based page, FrontPage Express may display an error message or open an alternative (non-frames) page (assuming the site has an alternative page). Don't worry, your link will work in Internet Explorer. (Frames support is included in Microsoft's full-featured FrontPage product.)

In this lesson, you learned how to add links to your Web page to help users navigate the page and open other pages on the Web. In the next lesson, you will learn how to add a page background and select a color scheme.

Changing the Background and Color Scheme

In this lesson, you learn how to give your page a colorful background and change the overall colors for text, links, and other objects.

People seem to like pages with colorful backgrounds that play soothing music when you open them. If done tastefully, background graphics and muted colors can add a nice touch to a Web site. If you want to add a page background or background audio clip to your Web page or change the color scheme for text and links, this lesson can help.

Adding a Background Color or Graphic

You have probably visited at least one Web page that has a colorful background or uses a graphic image as its background. You can add such a background to your own page.

CAUTION

Text/Background Clash   Be careful when selecting a background color to ensure that your text stands out against the background. If you choose a dark background with black text, people will have trouble reading your page or highlighting text to copy it.

Take the following steps to add a page background to your page:

1. Open the **Format** menu and select **Background**. The Page Properties dialog box appears, as shown in Figure 9.1.
2. (Optional) To use a background image, click **Background Image**, click the **Browse** button, and select the image you want to use. If the image isn't

large enough to cover the entire viewing area, the browser tiles it (displays several copies of the image side by side).

You can use a GIF or
JPEG image as your page
background

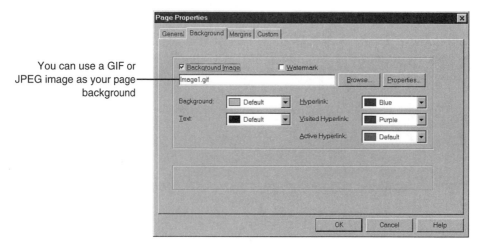

Figure 9.1   The Page Properties dialog box enables you to add a background color or image.

3. If you selected a background image, you can select **Watermark** to have the image appear as a transparent overlay.

4. To change the background color, open the **Background** drop-down list and select the desired color.

5. Click **OK** to save your background settings.

6. To preview your changes, save your page, and open it in Internet Explorer.

Color Overrides   As you know from customizing Internet Explorer, users can choose to have their Web browsers display a different background color. Their color settings may override any colors you add to your Web page.

CAUTION

Changing the Color Scheme

In addition to changing the background color or adding a background image, you can change the color of text, unvisited links, and visited links. Take the following steps to change the colors of these items:

1. Open the **File** menu and select **Page Properties**. The Page Properties dialog box appears.

2. Click the **Background** tab. The Background options appear, as shown in Figure 9.2.

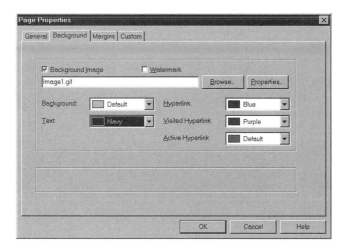

Figure 9.2 You can change the overall text and link colors.

3. To change the default text color, click and hold the arrow button to the right of the **Text** drop-down list, drag over the desired color, and release the mouse button. This changes the color of all text on the page (and the color of any bullets or numbers), but doesn't affect the color of links.

4. To change the color for hyperlinks, click and hold the arrow button to the right of the **Hyperlink** drop-down list, drag over the desired color, and release the mouse button.

5. To change the color of links that the user has already clicked, click and hold the arrow button to the right of the **Visited Hyperlink** drop-down list, drag over the desired color, and release the mouse button.

6. To have the link turn a specific color right when the user clicks it, click and hold the arrow button to the right of the **Active Hyperlink** drop-down list, drag over the desired color, and release the mouse button.

7. Click **OK** to save your color settings.

Adding Background Audio

If you have a sound card with speakers, you may have encountered Web pages that start to play music or some other sound when you open them. If you have an audio clip that's saved as a WAV, AIF, AU, or MID file type, you can use it to add background audio to your page. Take the following steps:

1. Open the **File** menu and select **Page Properties**. The Page Properties dialog box appears with the General tab in front (see Figure 9.3).

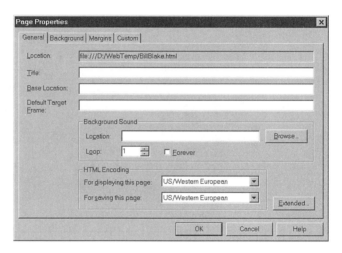

Figure 9.3 You can choose an audio file to play in the background.

2. Under Background Sound, click the **Browse** button. The Background Sound dialog box appears, prompting you to specify the location of the audio clip.

3. Take one of the following steps:
   - To use a file that's on your hard drive, make sure **From File** is selected, click the **Browse** button, select the audio file you want to use, and click **Open**.
   - To use a file that's stored on a Web server, click **From Location**, and type the file's address and name in the text box (for example, **http://www.mcp.com/include/resc_mpu.au**).

4. Click **OK**. The location and name of the selected file is inserted in the **Location** text box.

5. Use the **Loop** spin box to set the number of times you want the clip to play.

6. Click **OK** to save your changes.

To test the audio clip, first save your Web page and then open it in Internet Explorer. The clip should start to play and should replay the number of times specified.

CAUTION

Easy on the Looping Audio clips can become annoying if they play over and over again. When entering a Loop setting, keep the setting low. Whatever you do, don't select **Forever**.

In this lesson, you learned how to change the background and color scheme for your Web page and add a background sound. In the next lesson, you will learn how to add audio and video clips.

Adding Audio and Video Clips

In this lesson, you learn how to insert audio and video clips that play automatically or when a visitor clicks a link.

Up to this point, you have been working mostly with text and graphics, creating pages that are similar to pages that you create with a word processing or desktop publishing program. However, because Web pages are electronic, they give your publications another dimension: multimedia. By adding audio and video clips to your Web pages, you can take advantage of this third dimension.

File Size and Format Considerations

Text-only pages take up relatively little space on a Web server and are downloaded fairly quickly by visiting Web browsers. When you start adding graphics and audio and video clips, the size of the Web page quickly increases. For example, a high-quality, 15-second video clip can be over 4 megabytes.

To reduce the size of your Web page, use these large files sparingly. For large, high-quality audio, video, or graphic files, insert a link that points to the file instead of inserting the file as an inline image or video clip that downloads automatically with the page. The link should describe the file and specify its size, so the visitor can make the decision of whether or not to download the file.

In addition, you should try to stick with standard file formats, so most browsers will be able to play your files. The most common multimedia file formats are listed in Table 10.1.

Table 10.1 Common Multimedia File Formats

File Type	Format
Graphics	GIF and JPG (or JPEG)
Audio	AU, AIF, WAV, RAM, and MID
Video	MPG (or MPEG), AVI, and MOV

Inline Graphics and Video Inline graphics and video clips download and play when the user opens the page. The user has no choice in the matter. If the user doesn't have the required browser, plug-in, or ActiveX control for playing the file type, an error message appears, or the browser simply doesn't play the file.

Inserting Audio Clips

In the previous lesson, you learned how to add background audio to your Web page. However, you may have additional audio clips that you want visitors to be able to play by clicking a link. To insert an audio clip as a link, take the following steps:

1. Type the text or insert the image you want to use as the link, and select it.

2. Click the **Create or Edit Hyperlink** button in the Standard toolbar (or press **Ctrl+K**). The Create Hyperlink dialog box opens, with the World Wide Web tab displayed, as shown in Figure 10.1.

3. In the **URL** text box, type the name of the audio clip that should play when the user clicks this link. For example, you might type **cool.wav**.

4. Click **OK**. FrontPage Express converts the selected text or image into a link.

File Locations Step 3 assumes that you will store a copy of the sound file on the same Web server and in the same directory in which you store your Web page. If this isn't the case, you must include a complete path to specify the location of the file. If the sound file is already stored on a Web server, you can enter the file's address (for example, **http://www.mcp.com/sounds/cool.wav**). Then you don't need to store the sound file on your server.

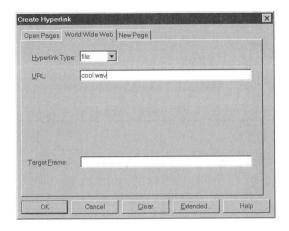

Figure 10.1   Type the name of the sound file.

Inserting Inline Video Clips

Some Web browsers, including Internet Explorer and Netscape Navigator, support inline video, allowing video clips to play right on a Web page. To include an inline video clip on your page, take the following steps:

1. Position the insertion point where you want the video clip inserted.

2. Open the **Insert** menu and select **Video**. The Video dialog box appears, as shown in Figure 10.2, prompting you to select a file. You can specify the location and name of a file on the Web or on your hard drive.

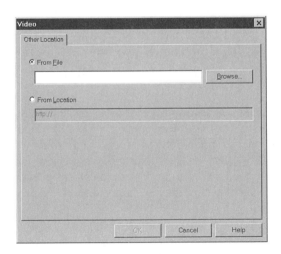

Figure 10.2   FrontPage Express prompts you to specify the location of the video file.

3. Take one of the following steps:

- To use a file that's on your hard drive, make sure **From File** is selected, click the **Browse** button, and select the video file you want to use.

- To use a file that's stored on a Web server, click **From Location**, and type the file's address and name in the text box.

4. Click **OK**. FrontPage Express is incapable of displaying the video clip, so it inserts a placeholder, as shown in Figure 10.3. To view the clip, save your Web page and open it in Internet Explorer.

Placeholder for inline video clip

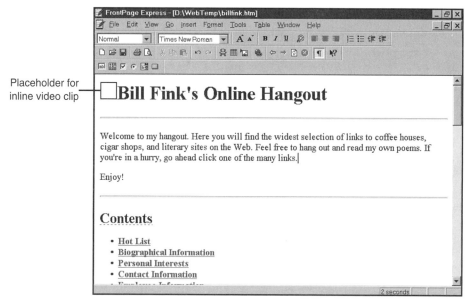

Figure 10.3 FrontPage Express displays a placeholder to show the location of the clip.

Using Audio or Video Clips Stored on the Web

If an audio or video clip is stored on a Web server, you can have the clip pulled into your Web page to save storage space on your Web server. However, finding out where the file is stored is a little tough. Take the following steps:

1. In Internet Explorer, open the page that contains the audio or video clip.

2. Open the **View** menu and select **Source**.

3. Look for the HTML tag that points to the file—for example, HREF="/video/hi_res.mov." In this example, only the directory and file name are specified, so the file is stored on the same Web server as the Web page.

To use the file, perform the steps in the previous section, "Inserting Inline Video Clips." In step 3, click **From Location**, and type the file's address and name in the text box. If no domain name is specified for the server (for instance **http://www.mcp.com**), as shown in the example, then type the domain name of the current page, and type the directory path and file name after it. In this example, you would type the following to specify the location of the video file:

http://www.mcp.com/video/hi_res.mov

 TIP **Other File Types** In addition to inserting common file types for graphics, audio, and video, you can insert special files, such as animated GIFs and Shockwave presentations. Use the **Insert**, **File** command.

In this lesson, you learned how to give your Web page an added dimension with audio and video clips. In the next lesson, you will learn how to insert additional active elements into your Web pages.

Inserting ActiveX Controls and WebBots

In this lesson, you learn how to insert additional components on your Web page to automate and enhance it.

Internet Explorer comes with several tools that you can use to make your Web page more active. ActiveX controls enable you to add objects, such as animated text, form controls, calendars, and other interactive objects, without knowing much about the programming behind these objects. FrontPage Express also includes its own WebBots, which enable you to add scripts. Scripts automatically perform certain tasks, such as inserting the date when you last modified your Web page. In this lesson, you learn the basics of inserting these objects on your Web page.

 TERM **Script** A program listing that contains commands telling the Web browser how to carry out a task. If you have some knowledge of programming, you can open your Web page in a text editor, such as Notepad, and write your own scripts. If you know little about programming, you can use prepackaged codes by inserting ActiveX controls and WebBots, as explained in this lesson.

Inserting WebBot Components

FrontPage Express comes with the following pre-scripted objects, called WebBots, that you can add to your pages without knowing anything about the complexities of scripting:

- **Include** automatically loads a resource from your Web server where you insert the WebBot. While the resource is loading, the WebBot displays "Getting *pageaddress* from server…"

- **Search** displays a search form that the visitor can use to search for pages on your server.
- **Timestamp** automatically inserts the current date whenever you edit your page, so visitors can quickly determine when the page was last updated. This is one of the most useful WebBots of the bunch.

To insert a WebBot, take the following steps:

1. Position the insertion point where you want the WebBot to appear.

2. Open the **Insert** menu and select **WebBot Component**, or click the **Insert WebBot Component** button in the Standard toolbar. The Insert WebBot Component dialog box appears, as shown in Figure 11.1.

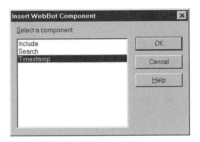

Figure 11.1 Select the desired WebBot component.

3. Click the desired WebBot, and click **OK**. A dialog box appears, prompting you to enter settings for the WebBot. The settings vary depending on the component you selected. Figure 11.2 shows the WebBot Timestamp Component Properties dialog box.

4. Enter the desired settings, and click **OK**.

You can choose to display the date when the page was last edited or when it was automatically updated

Choose the desired date and time format

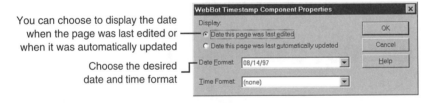

Figure 11.2 The WebBot Timestamp Component Properties dialog box.

TIP   **More WebBots**   Although you get FrontPage Express for free, it's a scaled-down version of Microsoft's full featured Web page editor, FrontPage. FrontPage includes additional WebBots, including Hit Counter, which shows you the number of people that have visited your site.

Inserting ActiveX Components

In addition to inserting WebBots, you can insert other active components into your Web pages, including Java applets, ActiveX components, and files that require plug-ins. The process consists of telling FrontPage Express the type of component you want to add, and then setting the component's properties, such as its size, the file that includes the active content, and what to do if the user's browser doesn't support the component.

Adding an ActiveX Component to Your Page

The procedure for adding ActiveX components to your Web page is fairly complicated and varies depending on the type of component you want to add. The following steps provide an overview by showing you how to insert the ActiveX movie object in your Web page:

1. First, you need to download a MOV, AVI, or MPG video clip from the Web. Save it to your Windows desktop so you can find it easily.

2. In FrontPage Express, position the insertion point where you want the component inserted.

3. Open the **Insert** menu, point to **Other Components**, and click **ActiveX Control**. The ActiveX Control Properties dialog box appears, as shown in Figure 11.3.

4. Open the **Pick a Control** drop-down list and select **ActiveMovieControl Object**. You can ignore the Name text box; the name doesn't appear on your page.

5. (Optional) Under **Layout**, specify the width, height, and border properties for the control. These settings control the appearance of the component on your page.

6. (Optional) Under **Alternative Representation**, you can type the address of a Web page that opens if the visitor's Web browser cannot play the movie clip.

343

Select the control that
will play the video clip

Specify the location and file
name of the video clip

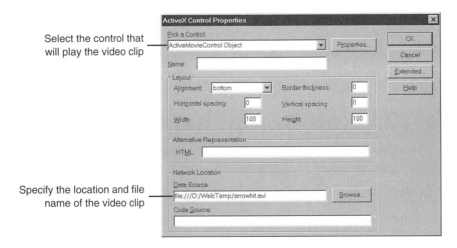

Figure 11.3 The ActiveX Control Properties dialog box.

7. Under **Network Location**, click in the **Data Source** text box, click the **Browse** button, and select the video clip you downloaded in step 1. This tells the ActiveX movie player which clip to play.

8. Ignore the **Code Source** text box for now. The next section explains this text box.

9. Click **OK**. FrontPage Express inserts the control on your page as an icon.

10. To view your video clip, save your page and open it in Internet Explorer. When you open the page, Internet Explorer runs the ActiveX movie player and starts playing the clip.

Specifying a Code Source

You could ignore the entry in the Code Source text box because you have the ActiveX Movie control installed on your system (it was installed when you installed Internet Explorer). However, if someone who doesn't have the ActiveX Movie control installed opens your page, he or she sees only a box with a red X in it. The Code Source entry indicates the location of the control needed to play the component.

ActiveX controls are stored in files that have the .ocx, .dll, or .exe file name extension. The ActiveX movie control is named amovie.ocx and is stored in your Windows\System folder. The easiest way to make the player available to your visitor is to place a copy of amovie.ocx in the same directory on your server where you store your Web page. You can then specify the location of the player by entering **amovie.ocx** in the Code Source text box.

More Information About ActiveX ActiveX makes it easy for users to play active content, but is a little complicated when you're authoring a page. If you're serious about adding ActiveX components to your Web pages, read Que's *Special Edition Using ActiveX*. This book shows you how to use Microsoft's ActiveX control pad to add controls and scripts to your Web pages.

CAUTION

Adding a Scrolling Marquee

A good, relatively easy way to animate your page is to add a scrolling marquee. The marquee appears in its own text box, typically at the top of the page, and scrolls whatever text you enter across the visitor's screen. To insert a scrolling marquee, take the following steps:

1. Position the insertion point where you want the marquee inserted.

2. Open the **Insert** menu and select **Marquee**. The Marquee Properties dialog box appears, as shown in Figure 11.4.

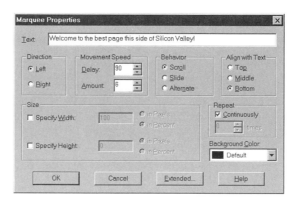

Figure 11.4 You can add text that scrolls across the screen.

3. In the **Text** text box, type the text that you want to scroll across the screen.

4. Use the remaining options in the dialog box to set the width and height of the marquee, the speed and direction in which the text scrolls, the background color, and any other marquee properties.

5. Click **OK**. FrontPage Express displays the text you typed, but the marquee doesn't scroll.

6. To view the marquee in action, save your page and open it in Internet Explorer.

In this lesson, you learned how to animate and activate your Web pages with WebBots, ActiveX controls, and scrolling marquees. In the next lesson, you will learn how to create forms for gathering information from your visitors.

Creating Forms

In this lesson, you learn how to create fill-in-the-blank forms for gathering information.

Forms enable you to interact with Web pages. You use forms to enter search instructions, register software, order products, and provide feedback to the person who authored the Web page. Some Web sites even use forms to enable you to chat with other people.

FrontPage Express offers a complete set of form controls and page templates that you can use to create your own online forms. In the following sections, you learn how to use these tools.

Creating a Form with a Wizard or Template

In Part 5, Lesson 2, "Creating a Web Page with a Template or Wizard," you learned how to create a simple Web page using FrontPage Express's Personal Web Page Wizard. You can perform similar steps to create a form using the Form Page Wizard. The steps required vary depending on the information and fields (blanks) you want to include on your form. The following steps provide instructions on how to run the Form Page Wizard and start your form:

1. Open the **File** menu and select **New**. The New Page dialog box appears.

2. Select **Form Page Wizard**, and click **OK**. The first Form Page Wizard dialog box appears, displaying general information about the wizard.

3. Click **Next**. You are now asked to name the page.

4. In the **Page URL** text box, type the name of the page (its file name). The name must have the file name extension .htm or .html.

5. In the **Page Title** text box, type the name of the page as you want it to appear in the title bar when a visitor opens the page in his Web browser.

6. Click **Next**. The next dialog box displays an empty list of questions you want the form to ask; you will add questions to the list.

7. Click **Add**. You are prompted to select the type of information you want to use the form to gather.

8. In the **Select the Type of Input to Collect for This Question** list, click the desired data you want the form to collect (for instance, Ordering Information or Personal Information). You can select only one item at this time. See Figure 12.1.

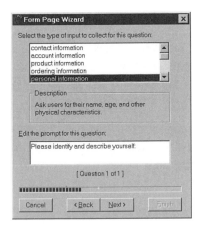

Figure 12.1 You must specify the type of data you want the form to collect.

9. In the **Edit the Prompt for This Question** text area, type the text that you want to introduce this area on the form. For example, if you selected Personal Information, you might type **We like to know our customers personally. Please use this form to enter information about yourself.**

10. Click **Next**. The next dialog box varies, depending on the input type you selected in step 6. Figure 12.2 shows the dialog box for gathering personal information.

11. Complete the dialog box to specify the specific data entries you want the form to request. Click **Next**. You are now returned to the dialog box that you saw at the end of step 4.

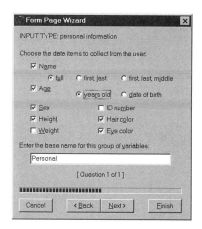

Figure 12.2 If you chose to prompt the user to enter personal information, specify the information you want.

12. To insert additional questions on your form, repeat steps 7 through 11. When you're done adding questions, click **Next**. You are then asked to specify how you want the questions presented (see Figure 12.3).

It's a good idea to organize the field entries on your form with tables

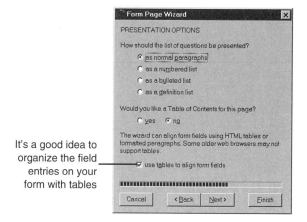

Figure 12.3 Select options to structure your form.

13. Select the desired options to specify the structure of your form. By default, FrontPage Express arranges the fields on your form using paragraphs and tables.

14. Click **Next**. You are asked where you want output from the form stored. You can store the user's entries as an HTML Web page, in a text file, or process them with a CGI script. See the section "Collecting Feedback from a Form," later in this lesson.

TERM   **CGI**   Short for Common Gateway Interface, CGI creates a link between the form and your database. A CGI script sends the data that the user enters on your form to a CGI application, which processes the data and passes it along to a database on your server. This gets pretty complicated, so get help from your local Internet database expert.

15. Specify where you want the user's input sent (to a Web page, text file, or CGI script), and enter the file's name. Click **Next**. The last wizard dialog box appears.

16. Click **Finish**. The wizard creates a forms-based Web page and displays it in FrontPage Express, as shown in Figure 12.4. You can format the form, as explained in Lesson 4, "Formatting Text." To insert additional form controls, move on to the next section.

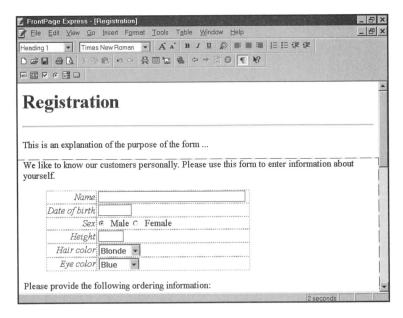

Figure 12.4   A completed form displayed in FrontPage Express.

> TIP **Form Within a Web Page**   To include your form as part of an existing Web page, instead of as its own Web page, copy the form and paste it into the desired Web page. Or, create the rest of your Web page around the form by adding headings, lists, graphics, links, and other objects.

Inserting Form Controls

Although the Form Page Wizard inserts most of the form controls you need for commonly used forms, the form it creates may not have all the fields you need. For example, if you're creating an order form, you may need fields that enable your customers to enter their preferences.

> TERM **Field**   A text box, option button, check box, or any other item on a form that returns a specific entry to your database.

You can insert additional controls by selecting them from the Insert, Form Field menu or by clicking a button for the form control in the Form Controls toolbar. Table 12.1 describes the available form controls.

Table 12.1 Form Controls

Icon	Control Name	Purpose
	One-Line Text Box	Prompts the user to type a simple entry, such as a name, address, or date.
	Scrolling Text Box	Enables the user to type a longer entry. You might use the scrolling text box to allow the user to enter additional comments or other text that doesn't fit into a one-line text box.
	Check Box	Allows the user to select more than one option in a group of options. For example, on a T-shirt order form, you might use check boxes to allow the user to select iron-ons for the shirt.
	Radio Button	Prompts the user to select only one item in a group of items. Going back to the T-shirt example, you might use radio buttons (also called option buttons) to allow the user to specify the shirt size.

continues

Table 12.1 Continued

Icon	Control Name	Purpose
	**Drop-Down Menu**	Inserts a scrolling text box with an up and down button. The user clicks the up or down arrow to scroll through a list of items, and then can click the desired item in the list.
	**Push Button**	Is generally used to submit the form.
N/A	Image	Available only on the Insert, Form Field menu, Image enables you to use a graphic image instead of the standard gray push button.

To insert a form control, take the following steps:

1. Move the insertion point where you want the control inserted.

2. Click the button for the desired control, or open the **Insert** menu, point to **Form Field**, and click the control. FrontPage Express inserts the selected control, and handles appear around the control.

3. You can drag the control to move it or drag a handle to resize it, as shown in Figure 12.5. You also can add text (usually to the left of the control) to describe it.

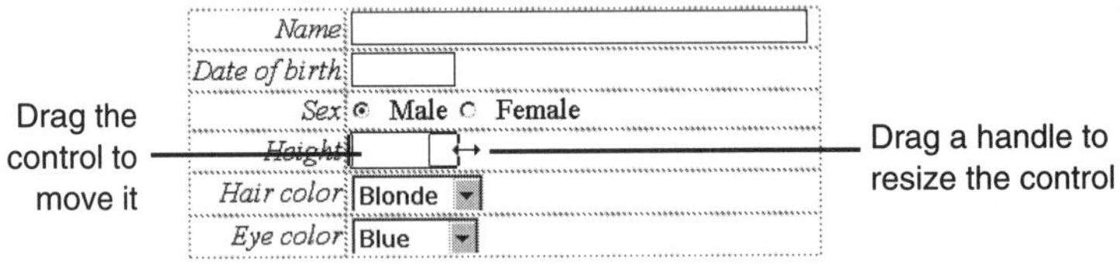

Drag the control to move it ———

Drag a handle to resize the control

Figure 12.5 You can move or resize the control just as you move or resize images.

Changing a Control's Properties

After inserting a control, you must set the control's properties. For example, if you insert a drop-down menu, you must enter the names of the items you want on the menu. If you insert a check box or radio button, you must enter the value that you want the check box or radio button to return when selected. To change a control's properties, take the following steps:

1. Double-click the control. The Properties dialog box that appears varies depending on the control. Figure 12.6 shows the Drop-Down Menu Properties dialog box.

2. Enter the desired properties. For example, in the Drop-Down Menu Properties dialog box, you can add items to the menu, rearrange menu items, specify the height of the menu (number of items displayed), and specify whether the menu allows multiple selections.

3. Click **OK** to save your settings.

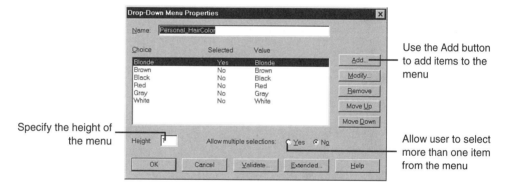

Figure 12.6 The Properties dialog box enables you to control the size and behavior of the control.

 TIP **Bona Fide Drop-Down Menu** By default, the drop-down menu displays two items and looks more like a spin box than a menu. To display it as a menu, set its height to 1 and make sure **Allow Multiple Selections** is set to **No**.

Collecting Feedback from a Form

The entire purpose of a form is to collect feedback from people and store it somewhere, usually in a database. Before you take on the monumental task of preparing your form to send data to a database, you should consult your network or Web administrator. The process consists of adding a script to your Web page and creating a CGI application that processes the incoming data and sends it to the database. The process varies depending on the type of server you're using on the database.

However, you can take an easier approach that saves data to a text file or Web Page using FrontPage Express's WebBot Save Results Component. You can enter additional settings for the WebBot Save Results Component, to specify how you want the results saved and to send a page back to the user to confirm that the data was received.

To return a confirmation page to the user, you must first create the page. FrontPage Express has a simple confirmation page template you can use to create the page. Select **File**, **New**, **Confirmation Form**, and click **OK**. Edit the page as desired and save it.

Take the following steps to enter settings for the WebBot Save Results Component:

1. Double-click the **Submit** button on your form to display the Push Button Properties dialog box.

2. Click the **Form** button to display the Form Properties dialog box, shown in Figure 12.7.

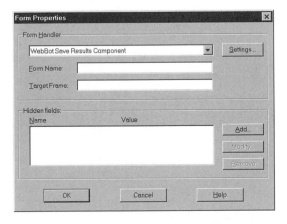

Figure 12.7   You can control the way the WebBot Save Results Component saves data that the user submits.

3. Click the **Settings** button. The Settings dialog box enables you to specify the location, name, and file type in which you want the user's input saved.

4. In the **File for Results** text box, type the name of the file in which you want the input saved, including a directory path specifying where the file is stored.

5. Open the **File Format** drop-down list, and select the desired file format. For example, you can choose to save the results in an HTML file or in a text file that uses tabs to separate field entries. To save field names along with field entries, make sure **Include Field Names in Output** is checked.

6. Under **Additional Information to Save**, select each item you want to save when the user clicks the **Submit** button.

7. If you created a confirmation page to send back to the user when she has successfully submitted data, click the **Confirm** tab and specify the location and name of the confirmation page.

8. Click **OK** to save your changes. Click **OK** to exit the other dialog boxes and save any settings you have entered.

In this lesson, you learned how to create fill-in-the-blank forms for gathering information. In the next lesson, you will learn how to place your page on the Web.

Publishing Your
Web Page

In this lesson, you learn how to place your page, its associated images, and other files on a Web server.

Once you have completed your Web page, you must place it on a Web server, where other people can open and view it with their Web browsers. In the past, the only way to place a page on a Web server was to use a separate FTP (File Transfer Protocol) program. However, FrontPage Express comes with its own file transfer program, called WebPost, that you can access simply by entering the File, Save As command.

Dealing with the Preliminaries

Unless you've been working directly on a *Web server* (a computer that stores Web sites where people browsing the Web can see them), you have to take the additional step of *publishing* your Web pages.

Before you start, you need to make sure you have somewhere to store your Web page. The best place to start is with your Internet service provider. Most providers make some space available on their Web servers for subscribers to store personal Web pages. Call your service provider and find out the following information:

- Does your service provider make Web space available to subscribers? If not, maybe you should change providers.
- How much disk space do you get, and how much does it cost (if anything)? Some providers give you a limited amount of disk space, which is usually plenty for one or two Web pages, assuming you don't include large audio or video clips.

- Can you save your files directly to the Web server or do you have to upload files to an FTP server?

- What is the URL of the server you must connect to in order to upload your files? Write it down.

- What username and password do you need to enter to gain access to the server? (This is typically the same username and password you use to connect to the service.)

- In which directory must you place your files? Write it down.

- What name must you give your Web page? In many cases, the service lets you post a single Web page, and you must call it **index.html** or **default.html**.

- Are there any other specific instructions you must follow to post your Web page?

- After posting your page, what will its address (URL) be? You'll want to open it in Internet Explorer as soon as you post it.

If you're using a commercial online service, such as America Online or CompuServe, you may have to use its commands to upload your Web page and associated files. For example, CompuServe has its own Web page publishing wizard. In similar cases, you should use the tools the online service provides instead of trying to wrestle with FrontPage Express.

If your service provider doesn't offer Web page service, fire up Internet Explorer, connect to your favorite search page, and search for places that enable you to post your Web page for free. These services vary greatly. Some services require you to fill out a form, and then the service creates a generic Web page for you (you can't use the page you created in FrontPage Express). At others, you can copy the HTML coded document (in Notepad or WordPad) and paste it in a text box at the site. A couple of other places let you send your HTML file and associated files. Find out what's involved.

TIP **Preparing a Folder** You can save yourself some time and trouble by placing your Web page, all its graphic files, and any other associated files in a single folder separate from other files. The Web Publishing Wizard can then transfer all the required files as a batch to your Web server. Make sure you use the correct filename for your Web page file, as specified by your service provider.

Saving Your Page to a Web Server

If you work on an intranet or use a service provider that enables you to save your Web page directly to its Web server, take the following steps to publish your Web page:

1. Open the page you want to place on the Web.

2. Open the **File** menu and select **Save As**. The Save As dialog box appears, displaying the name and location of your Web page file.

3. Click **OK**. If you used any images or other files in your Web page, a dialog box appears, as shown in Figure 13.1, asking if you want to save these files to the Web server.

Figure 13.1 Be sure to save all associated files to the Web server.

4. Click **Yes to All**. The Enter Network Password dialog box appears, prompting you to enter your username and password.

5. Type your username in the **Username** text box, tab to the **Password** text box, and type your password. Click **OK**. (FrontPage Express is set up to save your password, so you won't need to enter it the next time you publish a Web page.)

6. The Web Publishing Wizard appears, displaying an explanation of what you are about to do. Click **Next**. The wizard prompts you to type a name for your Web server.

7. Type a brief, descriptive name (you don't need to type the server's domain name at this point). Click **Next**. The wizard prompts you to type the URL of your Web page.

8. Type the address of your Web page, as specified by your service provider (for example, **http://www.internet.com/~bfink**). You may be prompted to enter your username and password again.

9. Click **Next**. The wizard prompts you to select your service provider, as shown in Figure 13.2. If you're unsure, select **HTTP Post** to place your files directly on a Web server, or select **Automatically Select Service Provider**. Click **Next**. You are now prompted to enter information about the server.

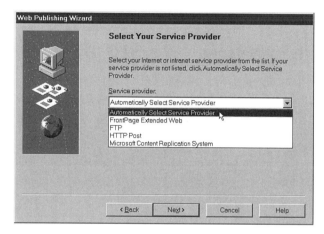

Figure 13.2 Select your service provider, or choose Automatically Select Service Provider.

10. Enter the server's name and any special command you need to upload your page to the Web server. Your service provider should have supplied this information.

11. Click **Next**. The final dialog box appears, indicating that the wizard is ready to publish your Web page.

12. Click **Finish**. The wizard dials into your service provider, if you aren't yet connected, and uploads your Web page and all associated files to the Web server. Dialog boxes appear, showing the progress.

CAUTION

Unable to Publish Files If you receive an error message indicating that the wizard was unable to publish the files, you may have entered the wrong username or password, typed the wrong Web server address, or selected the wrong service provider. Check with your service provider to ensure that you have the correct information, and then repeat the steps.

TIP   **Web Publishing Wizard**   You also can run the Web Publishing Wizard by selecting **Start**, **Programs**, **Internet Explorer**, **Web Publishing Wizard**. When you run it this way, the steps are a little different. For example, the wizard enables you to upload an entire folder and all of its subfolders to the server. If you have a complex collection of Web pages, this can save you some time.

Uploading Files to an FTP Server

Many service providers require that you upload your Web page and associated files to an FTP server. When you open your account, the service provider creates a separate directory on the FTP server that only you can access using your username and password. You rarely deal with this directory, so you may not know its path. Ask your service provider to specify the path to your directory.

Once you have the information you need, take the following steps to use the Web Publishing Wizard to upload files to your directory on the FTP server:

1. Open the page you want to place on the Web.

2. Open the **File** menu and select **Save As**. The Save As dialog box appears, displaying the name and location of your Web page file.

3. Click **OK**. If you used any images or other files in your Web page, a dialog box appears, asking if you want to save these files to the Web server.

4. Click **Yes to All**. The Enter Network Password dialog box appears, prompting you to enter your username and password.

5. Type your username in the **Username** text box, tab to the **Password** text box, and type your password. Click **OK**. (FrontPage Express is set up to save your password, so you won't need to enter it the next time you publish a Web page.)

6. The Web Publishing Wizard appears, displaying an explanation of what you're about to do. Click **Next**. The wizard prompts you to type a name for your Web server.

7. Type a brief, descriptive name (you don't need to type the server's domain name at this point). Click **Next**. You may be prompted to enter your username and password again.

8. Type the address of your Web page, as specified by your service provider (for example, **http://www.internet.com/~bfink**). You may be prompted to enter your username and password again.

9. Click **Next**. The wizard prompts you to select your service provider.

10. Open the **Service Provider** drop-down list and select **FTP**, as shown in Figure 13.3. Click **Next**. You are then prompted to enter information about the server.

Figure 13.3 Select FTP as your service provider.

11. Enter the server's domain name (for example, **ftp.internet.com**) in the **FTP Server Name** text box.

12. Tab to the **Subfolder Containing Your Web Pages** text box, and type the path to the directory in which you must store your Web pages, such as **/users/bf/bfink** (see Figure 13.4). Your service provider should have supplied this information.

13. Click **Next**. The final dialog box appears, indicating that the wizard is ready to publish your Web page.

14. Click **Finish**. The wizard dials into your service provider, if you aren't yet connected, and uploads your Web page and all associated files to the Web server. Dialog boxes appear showing the progress.

TIP **The Good News** The good news is that you won't have to go through this 14-step process the next time you need to upload your Web page. Simply select the **File**, **Save** command, and FrontPage Express automatically uploads your Web page and associated files to the FTP server.

361

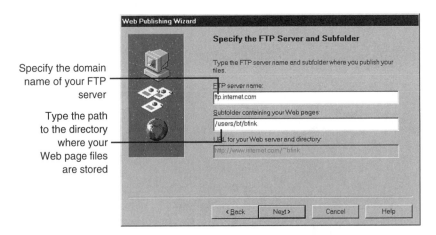

Specify the domain name of your FTP server

Type the path to the directory where your Web page files are stored

Figure 13.4 The wizard needs to know where to store your files.

In this lesson, you learned how to place your page on the Web. In the next lesson, you will learn how to register your page with search sites and announce your page to the online community.

Publicizing Your Web Page

14

In this lesson, you learn how to register your Web page with various search sites so people can find it.

Placing your page on the Web doesn't ensure that someone will open it. Unless you specifically tell people your Web page address, they may not be able to find your page. In addition, although some search engines frequently scour the Web for new pages, they often overlook personal Web pages. You must specifically request that your page be registered with these search sites. The following sections explain various ways to register your site and announce it.

TIP **Before You Go Public** Make sure you check your page thoroughly once you have placed it on the Web to make sure it looks right and that your links work properly. Don't announce your page to the Web community until it's ready for public showing.

Trading Links

Chances are that pages similar to yours in content already exist on the Web. If you can create a link from those sites to yours, you have a good chance of drawing in people who are surfing that link. So, consider swapping links with the authors of those related pages. You place a link to her Web page on your Web page, and she places a link on her page that points to your page.

To swap links, contact the author of the related page via e-mail. You might include the URL of your page in your e-mail message, along with a suggested name for the link. Then the other author can cut and paste that information instead of typing it. Be sure to offer the author the courtesy of adding a link to your page that points to her page. Better yet, inform the other author that you have already inserted a link to her page, and invite her to visit your page to check it out.

Registering Your Page with Search Engines

There are dozens of different search engines and World Wide Web directories designed to help people find what they're looking for on the Web and the rest of the Internet. These systems can help steer interested people toward your site— but only if the systems know about your site. A search engine or directory finds out about a Web site in either or both of two ways.

- You *register* your site by supplying the URL, the topic of your site, and other relevant pieces of information.
- The system finds your site by means of its *Web crawler program*. A Web crawler program runs unmanned, searching the Web and following whatever links it finds; as it does, it looks for new Web pages it hasn't seen before and grabs the information from them.

If you want to register with a directory, go to that directory's Web site. (Try looking up *search engines* using your favorite Web search tool, and you should find links to more Web directories.) If the directory accepts registrations, there should be a clearly marked link to a registration form. You might also try searching for "publicize web page" or "announce web page."

The following steps show you how to register your page with Yahoo!:

1. Use Internet Explorer to connect to Yahoo!'s Home Page at **http://www.yahoo.com**.
2. Click links to change to the category in which you want your page listed. For example, you might click **People**, and then click **Personal Web Pages**.
3. Click the **Add URL** icon at the top of the screen, as shown in Figure 14.1. This opens a page providing instructions and a form for registering your site.
4. Scroll down to the form, as shown in Figure 14.2. As you can see, the Category entry is already listed. The form varies depending on the category you selected.
5. Click in the **URL** text box and type the address of your page. This is the most important entry on the form.

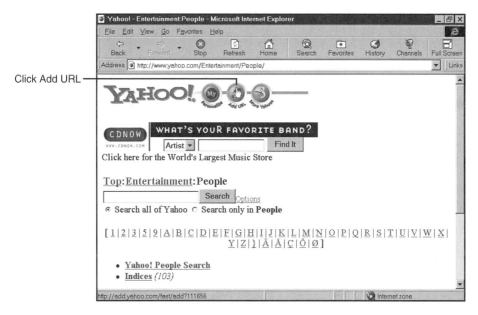

Click Add URL

Figure 14.1 You can add your page to any category at Yahoo!.

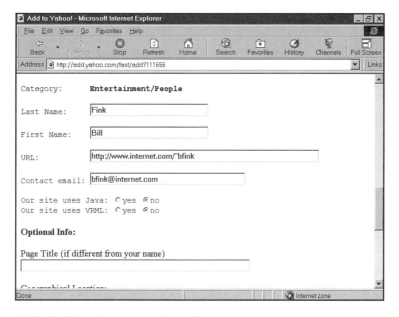

Figure 14.2 At Yahoo!, you complete a form to register your site.

6. Click in the **Title** text box and type your page's title.

7. Click in the One or Two Sentences About Your Page text area and type a description of your page. This description appears in the list of links that appear when someone performs a search that lists your page.

8. Enter any additional information as desired. The more information you enter, the more likely it is that your page will be listed when somebody performs a search.

9. Click the **Submit** button.

TIP **More Search Sites**   At the bottom of the Yahoo! registration form is a link that you can click to register your page with additional search sites.

Making Your Page More Noticeable

You can do a number of things to increase the chances that a Web crawler program will find your site. The following tips help your page stand out on the Web:

- Use a descriptive, attention-grabbing page title. Some search engines search only for page titles.

- Make sure that the first few lines of text on your page contain appropriate keywords that someone might use in a search for such a page.

TIP **Spamdexing**   You have probably heard of "spamming," the practice of sending unsolicited advertisements via e-mail or in newsgroups. Spamdexing is a more sinister marketing tactic, in which a company repeats a key word hundreds of times in its page description so the page is more likely to turn up when users search for that term.

In this lesson, you learned how to announce your Web page to the online community. In the next part, you will learn how to master the new Active Desktop.

The Active Desktop

Integrating the Web and the PC

In this lesson, you learn how to install the Web Integrated Desktop and you learn about what it brings to your computer.

The biggest news in Internet Explorer 4.0 is the capability to integrate the Web and your PC desktop. In the new Web Integrated Desktop, your desktop looks and works like a Web page. All of your folder names are underlined like links in a Web page, and they open with a single click instead of a double-click. You can display Web content directly on your desktop, customize folder windows to look and work like Web pages, and use the same toolbars and menu bars in both folder and browser windows. For a total immersion experience on the Web, you can use Full Screen view in the browser window so that everything but the Web page itself is hidden.

 TIP **One Restriction** The Web Integrated Desktop is available only if you performed a Standard or Full installation of Internet Explorer 4.0. If you performed a Minimum (or browser-only) installation, the Active Desktop features discussed throughout this part are not available. However, the next section, "Installing the Web Integrated Desktop," tells you how you can go back and install the Web Integrated Desktop if you didn't already.

With the Web Integrated Desktop installed, you can browse the Web from anywhere on your computer: the Start menu, your Favorites menu, toolbars, the taskbar, and icons on your desktop. A single click launches your browser and heads for the Web site. You use the same window and navigation tools to browse your hard drive, the company network, and the Internet.

 Shell Integration Shell Integration is computerese for the theory behind the installed feature of the Web Integrated Desktop; it refers to the integration of your computer desktop and the Internet into one seamless and cohesive unit, or *shell*, that looks and acts like a Web page.

Installing the Web Integrated Desktop

The Web Integrated Desktop brings the Internet to your computer. You may have already installed the Web Integrated Desktop when you installed Internet Explorer 4.0; if not, follow these steps to install the Web Integrated Desktop:

1. Click the **Start** button.
2. Point to **Settings**, then click **Control Panel**.
3. Double-click **Add/Remove Programs**.
4. Click **Microsoft Internet Explorer 4.0**, then click **Add/Remove**.
5. Click the **Add the Windows Desktop Update Component from Web Site** option button, then click **OK**. If you don't see the option, then the Web Integrated Desktop is already installed, and you can click the **Cancel** button in each dialog box to back out of the installation process.
6. Internet Explorer 4.0 goes online to retrieve the files it needs, and then installs them. Follow the steps in the online wizard.

TIP   **Is It Installed Already?**   If you right-click the desktop and see the Active Desktop command on the shortcut menu, the Web Integrated Desktop is already installed. If the Active Desktop command is not on the shortcut menu, follow the preceding steps to add the Web Integrated Desktop.

If you want to remove the Web Integrated Desktop and use Internet Explorer 4.0 as a simple browser, follow these steps:

1. Click the **Start** button.
2. Point to **Settings**, then click **Control Panel**.
3. Double-click **Add/Remove Programs**.
4. Click **Microsoft Internet Explorer 4.0**, then click **Add/Remove**.
5. Click the **Remove the Windows Desktop Update Component, But Keep the Internet Explorer 4.0 Browser** option button.
6. Click **OK**.

You can install the Web Integrated Desktop again later if you leave the Internet Explorer 4.0 setup files on your hard drive.

Elements of the Web Integrated Desktop

The Web Integrated Desktop contains a slew of new elements designed to make it easier to integrate the Internet into your desktop. Among the new elements are a common Standard toolbar at the top of every folder and browser window, a taskbar with expanded features, a pumped-up new Start menu, Explorer bars for every folder and browser window, and the new Active Desktop, which puts live Web content on your computer screen.

The Common Standard Toolbar

The new Standard toolbar provides you with consistent navigation methods, whether you're browsing your computer's hard drive, the company intranet, or the Internet. The new Standard toolbar is called a *smart* toolbar because it changes to give you just the buttons you need for the type of information you're looking at. As you can see in Figure 1.1, if you're looking at a folder on your hard drive, the toolbar has buttons to Cut, Copy, and Paste files and folders; but if you're looking at a Web page (see Figure 1.2), the toolbar replaces those buttons with Stop, Refresh, and Home buttons.

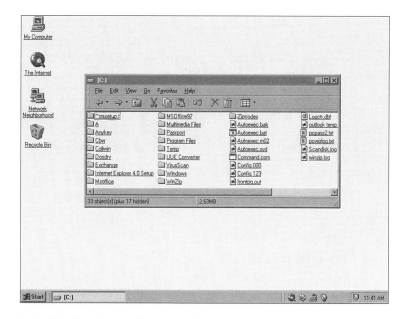

Figure 1.1   The Standard toolbar in a folder window.

371

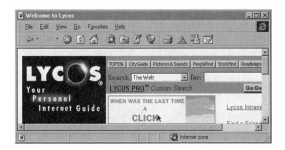

Figure 1.2 The Standard toolbar in a browser window.

There are other buttons that switch, too, and you can learn more about the Standard toolbar and other smart toolbars in Part 6, Lesson 2, "Using Smart Toolbars."

The New Taskbar

The new taskbar is much more useful than the old taskbar. It has its own set of toolbars, all of which are shown in Figure 1.3, and those toolbars can be resized, rearranged, and dragged away from the taskbar to float on the desktop. Another new feature is the toggle capability for open windows: As before, each open window has a button on the taskbar, but now you can minimize a window and then open it again just by clicking its button on the taskbar.

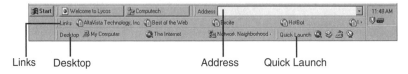

Figure 1.3 The new taskbar, with all of its toolbars displayed.

You can learn more about the taskbar in Part 6, Lesson 3, "The New Taskbar."

The New Start Menu

The new Start menu works just like the old Start menu, but now it does more. It has your list of Favorites, so you can launch your browser and go to a favorite Web site directly from the Start menu. In addition, you can customize it: You can rearrange your list of Favorites or Programs by dragging an icon to a new location on the list (which means you don't have to keep them in alphabetical order), and you can add a shortcut to a folder by dragging it onto the Start button. There are more improvements, too; to learn more about the Start menu, check out Part 6, Lesson 7, "Using the New Start Menu."

The Explorer Bars

The Explorer bars are specialized toolbars that sit vertically on the left side of the browser window. Figure 1.4 shows one of the four Explorer bars; the other three Explorer bars are the Search bar, the Favorites bar, and the Channels bar.

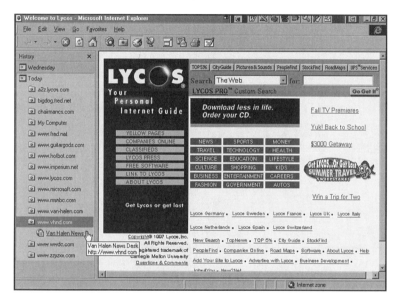

Figure 1.4   The History bar is an Explorer bar that keeps a history of Web sites you've visited.

To learn more about the Explorer bars, see Part 6, Lesson 4, "The Active Desktop and Your PC."

The Active Desktop

The Active Desktop is the part of the Web Integrated Desktop that brings live Web content, such as a stock-market ticker display like the one shown in Figure 1.5, to your computer. It also enables you to customize your desktop so it behaves like a Web page, with single-click access to folders and files and desktop shortcuts to Web sites.

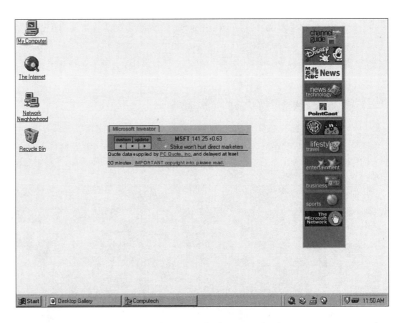

Figure 1.5 This stock ticker and Channel Guide are desktop components that reside on your Active Desktop.

Web pages that are regularly updated with current information, called Desktop Components, can reside on your Active Desktop where they're instantly available, and you have an Internet full of choices for your desktop background. To learn more about the Active Desktop, see Part 6, Lesson 4, "The Active Desktop and Your PC."

 TIP **An Internet Full of Choices for Desktop Background** You can use any graphic you find on the Internet as a background. Open the Web page, right-click the graphic you want to use, and click **Set As Wallpaper**.

In this lesson, you learned about installing the Web Integrated Desktop and what you'll find on your new desktop. In the next lesson, you will learn about Internet Explorer 4.0's new Smart Toolbars.

Using Smart Toolbars

In this lesson, you learn how to use and customize Internet Explorer 4.0's new "smart" toolbars.

Using the Standard Toolbar

All your computer's folder windows and the Internet Explorer 4.0 browser window share the same Standard toolbar at the top of the window. The new Standard toolbar is called *smart* because it knows whether you're looking at folders on your hard drive or links on a Web page, and displays buttons that are appropriate to the contents of the window.

If you're looking at a list of files on your hard drive, the Standard toolbar has Cut and Paste buttons; for an HTML page, the Standard toolbar has Stop, Refresh, and Home buttons instead. Regardless of the contents of the window, the Standard toolbar always has Back and Forward navigation buttons (see Figure 2.1 and Figure 2.2). You can navigate backward and forward using the same buttons, whether you're navigating pages on the Web or files on your hard drive.

 TIP **You Can Get There Faster** To return to a Web page or folder that's several pages away, click the down arrow or the **Back** or **Forward** button, and then click the folder or page you want on the list of previously visited pages.

Figure 2.1 The Standard toolbar for a folder on the hard drive.

Figure 2.2 The Standard toolbar for an HTML page.

Table 2.1 explains the function of each button in the folder window.

Table 2.1 Standard Toolbar Buttons in a Folder Window

Button	Name	Description
	Back	Opens the last folder you visited.
	Forward	Opens the next folder you visited, if you already backed up to a preceding folder.
	Up	Navigates up your file tree toward your hard drive, one folder at a time.
	Cut	Cuts selected files or folders to the Windows Clipboard.
	Copy	Copies selected files or folders to the Windows Clipboard.
	Paste	Pastes selected files or folders to a new folder.
	Undo	Reverses last action.
	Delete	Sends selected files or folders to the Recycle Bin.
	Properties	Displays properties information for a selected file or folder.
	Views	Cycles through window display options (click the down arrow to select a view instead of cycling through views).

Table 2.2 explains the function of each button in the browser window.

Table 2.2 Standard Toolbar Buttons in a Browser Window

Button	Name	Description
	Back	Opens the last Web page you visited.
	Forward	Opens the next Web page you visited, if you already backed up to a preceding Web page.
	Stop	Stops the current page from loading.
	Refresh	Reloads the current page.
	Home	Opens your browser's default Home page.
	Search	Displays Search Explorer bar.
	Favorites	Displays Favorites Explorer bar.
	History	Displays History Explorer bar.
	Channels	Displays Channels Explorer bar.
	Print	Prints the current page.
	Font	Reduces or magnifies the text in the current page for easier reading, or changes the default text font (doesn't affect graphics).
	Mail	Starts your mail program so you can read or send mail; creates messages containing the current Web page or a link to the current Web page.
	Edit	Opens FrontPage Express and displays the current page in HTML format.

Displaying and Using a Toolbar

Other new toolbars include the Quick Launch toolbar, the Links toolbar, the Address toolbar, and the Desktop toolbar. The Links and Address toolbars are available both at the top of your folder/browser window and on the taskbar; the Quick Launch and Desktop toolbars are available only on the taskbar.

To display a toolbar on the taskbar, right-click the taskbar, point to **Toolbars**, and then click the name of the toolbar you want.

To display a toolbar at the top of the folder/browser window, right-click the menu bar, and then click the name of the toolbar you want.

To hide a toolbar, follow the same procedure you used to display it.

Showing and Hiding Descriptions

Whether you're new to Windows programs or just to Internet Explorer 4.0, all those nameless Standard toolbar buttons are mysterious and confusing. Internet Explorer 4.0 gives you an easy way to make them less confusing: display their labels to identify them, as shown in Figure 2.3.

Figure 2.3 Text labels identify the Standard toolbar buttons.

To display the button labels, right-click anywhere on the Standard toolbar and click **Text Labels**. Follow the same procedure when you no longer need the labels and you want to make that half-inch of screen display available again.

TIP **Which Button Is Which?** If the button labels are turned off and you forget which button does what, point the mouse pointer at a button to see a ToolTip description.

Changing the Size of Toolbar Buttons

On the taskbar, the buttons on the toolbars are quite small. You can double their size by viewing them as large icons, as shown in Figure 2.4.

Larger size

Figure 2.4 The Quick Launch buttons might be easier to see as large icons.

To change the size of the toolbar buttons, use the following steps:

1. Right-click the toolbar you want to change. Click the toolbar name or an empty space on the toolbar, not on a button.

2. Point to **View**, then click **Large**. The buttons double in size.

To change large buttons back to small, repeat the preceding steps, and then drag the top of the taskbar downward to shorten it.

Floating a Toolbar on the Desktop

Some toolbars have so many buttons that they cannot be fully displayed on the taskbar, as you can see in Figure 2.5. Unfortunately you cannot make the buttons narrower to save space.

Click here to see more buttons

Figure 2.5 The taskbar cannot display all the buttons on the Desktop toolbar.

The buttons on a long toolbar are easier to see and use if you drag them away from the taskbar and let them float on the desktop, as shown in Figure 2.6.

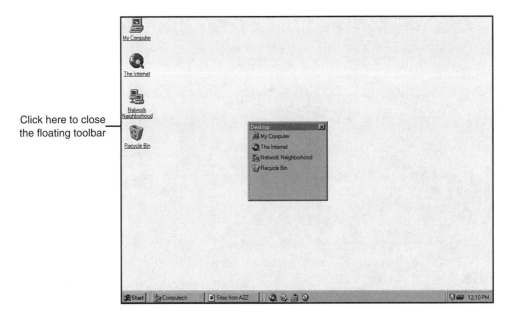

Click here to close
the floating toolbar

Figure 2.6   A floating Desktop toolbar.

Follow these steps to float a toolbar:

1. Point to the vertical bar at the left end of the toolbar. You'll see a two-headed arrow when the mouse pointer is in the right place.

2. Press the left mouse button and drag the toolbar away from the taskbar onto the desktop. Then release the mouse button to drop the toolbar on the desktop.

3. Point to the lower-right corner of the floating toolbar, and then drag the corner with the two-headed arrow to resize the toolbar to a convenient size.

4. Move the toolbar to a new location by dragging its title bar.

When you want to remove the floating toolbar from your desktop, click the **Close (X)** box in its upper-right corner.

Using the Quick Launch Toolbar

The Quick Launch toolbar resides on the taskbar. Its buttons give you quick access to the Internet Explorer 4.0 browser, your desktop, channels in Full Screen view, and any other Internet Explorer 4.0 features you may have installed. Table 2.3 explains each button's purpose.

Table 2.3   The Quick Launch Toolbar Buttons

Button	Name	Purpose
	Launch Internet Explorer Browser	Launches a new browser window and goes to your default home page.
	Show Desktop	Minimizes all open windows so that only the desktop is displayed.
	View Channels	Launches a new browser window in Full Screen view, with the Channel bar displayed.
	Launch Mail	Launches Outlook Express to send and pick up e-mail.

TIP   **Which Toolbar Is Which?**   To display the names of the taskbar toolbars, click one of the toolbars with the right mouse button, then click **Show Title**. Follow the same procedure to turn the toolbar names off.

Using the Links Toolbar

You can display the Links toolbar on the taskbar and at the top of the folder/ browser window, and you can drag it away from the taskbar to float on the Desktop. It contains a number of buttons that are primarily Microsoft self-promotion, but that's okay because you may want to use those buttons to get to information at the Microsoft site. You can add your own links as new buttons on the Links toolbar, and when you no longer want direct links to Microsoft sites, you can delete those buttons.

To go to a Links button site, click the button. Internet Explorer 4.0 launches the browser and navigates to the button site automatically.

You can create new buttons on the Links toolbar by dragging Web page links, Web page graphics, and the Address toolbar icon onto the Links toolbar. Follow these steps to create new buttons on the Links toolbar:

1. Browse to a site you want to add to the Links toolbar, and then display the **Links** toolbar. (The easiest way to do this is to display the Links toolbar floating on the desktop and reduce the browser window's size so you can see both.)

2. Drag the link you want to save onto the Links toolbar, and drop it in any location (as shown in Figure 2.7).

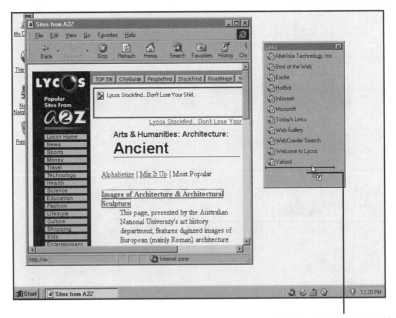

The new button appears here

Figure 2.7   Create a new button on the Links toolbar by dragging a Web link to the toolbar.

To add a URL from your browser's Address toolbar to the Links toolbar, follow these steps:

1. Type the URL into the Address toolbar, or navigate to the site so that the complete URL is displayed in the Address toolbar.

2. Drag the small **Web** icon (to the left of the URL) onto the Links toolbar.

Eventually your Links toolbar can get unmanageably full of link buttons. To remove buttons, follow these steps:

1. Right-click the button you want to remove.

2. Click **Delete**. A message box appears, asking whether you're sure you want to send the link to the Recycle Bin. Click **Yes**.

If you change your mind and regret deleting the link, you'll find it in the Recycle Bin.

Using the Address Toolbar

The Address toolbar can be found on both the folder/browser window and the taskbar, and you can float it on your desktop. This is another of Internet Explorer 4.0's smart toolbars—it knows the difference between folder addresses on your computer or network, and Web site addresses on the Internet. For example, if you type **www.microsoft.com** (see Figure 2.8), the Address toolbar launches the browser and navigates to the Microsoft Web page.

Figure 2.8   The Address toolbar adds the http:// and Web page icon for you.

If you type **c:\windows\personal** (see Figure 2.9), the Address toolbar opens your Personal folder.

Figure 2.9   Type the path to the folder you want to open.

It also maintains a list of your recently visited sites, so you can select one of them and open it directly. To use the Address toolbar to go to a Web site, follow these steps:

1. Click in the **Address** bar, and then type the URL of the Web site. You don't need to type the http:// part, but you do need to type the entire Internet address.

2. Press **Enter**.

To use the Address toolbar to go to a folder or file on your hard drive or network, follow these steps:

1. Click in the **Address** toolbar, and then type the path to the folder or file, beginning with the drive letter. (For example, the path to your Personal folder might be **c:\windows\personal**.)

2. Press **Enter**.

To use the Address toolbar to return to a recently visited site, click the down arrow on the right side of the Address box, and click the site you want in the list of recently visited sites.

TIP   **Search for It**   To run an Internet search with the Address toolbar, type **go** or **find** or **?**, followed by the word or words you want to search for, and press **Enter**. Your browser launches, and the search begins.

Another smart feature is AutoComplete. If you begin to type an address, AutoComplete looks for a match in its recently visited sites list. To use AutoComplete to return to a site, follow these steps:

1. Click in the **Address** toolbar, and then type the first few letters of the folder name or Web site. (If it's a Web site, type **www.** first, then the first letter of the site.) AutoComplete looks for a match and fills in the rest of the address for you.

2. If the address AutoComplete finds is not the one you want, right-click the highlighted address, then point to **Completions** (see Figure 2.10).

3. In the Completions list, click the address you want and press **Enter**. Your browser launches and navigates to the Web site.

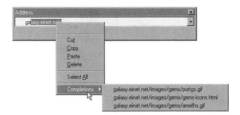

Figure 2.10   If AutoComplete makes a wrong match, choose another from the Completions list.

If you find AutoComplete annoying, you can turn it off. In the browser window, click the **View** menu, then click **Options**; on the Advanced tab, under *Browsing*, uncheck the **Use AutoComplete** check box.

Using the Desktop Toolbar

The Desktop toolbar contains buttons for all the icons and shortcuts on your desktop, which keeps them within easy reach when you're working in a maximized program or browser window.

To display the Desktop toolbar, right-click the taskbar, point to **Toolbars**, and click **Desktop**.

In this lesson, you learned about the new Smart toolbars—what they can do for you and how to get the most from them. In the next lesson, you will learn about the new features that Internet Explorer 4.0 adds to the taskbar.

The New Taskbar

In this lesson, you learn about using the taskbar features in Internet Explorer 4.0.

Launching a Task

You can open any number of programs and windows at the same time, and the ensuing desktop confusion can be difficult to handle; the taskbar gives you a convenient, unobtrusive central control point for managing your desktop. Using the taskbar, you can display several different toolbars for launching programs and control which open programs and windows are displayed (see Figure 3.1).

The taskbar's built-in toolbars include the Quick Launch, Address, Desktop, and Links toolbars.

The Address toolbar launches a browser or folder window, depending on the type of address you enter. It also keeps a list of Web sites and folders you visited recently, so you can select a site and launch the browser without re-entering the address (see Part 6, Lesson 2, "Using Smart Toolbars," to learn more about the Address toolbar).

The Desktop toolbar holds buttons for all the icons and shortcuts on your desktop, which enables you to launch a program from the taskbar instead of uncovering the icons buried beneath the open windows on your desktop.

The Links toolbar holds buttons for Web site links, and you can add and remove any buttons you want (see Part 6, Lesson 2, to learn more about the Links toolbar). When you click a button on the Links toolbar, your browser launches and opens the linked Web site.

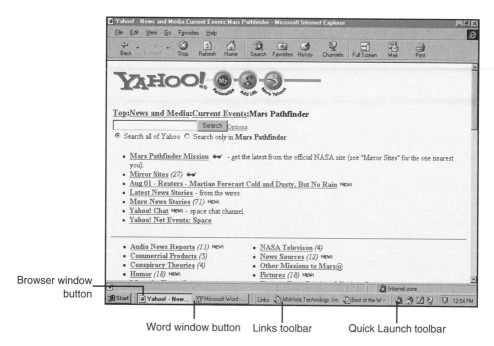

Browser window
button

Word window button   Links toolbar   Quick Launch toolbar

Figure 3.1 This taskbar displays two toolbars and buttons to control two open windows.

The Quick Launch toolbar holds buttons that launch your browser and any other Internet Explorer 4.0 programs you have installed, and a Show Desktop button that minimizes all the open windows on your desktop.

To launch a program from the taskbar, follow these steps:

1. Display the toolbar that holds a button for the program.

2. Click the program's button.

To display a specific open window on top of all the other open windows on your desktop, click its button on the taskbar.

TIP   **Toggle Your Tasks** Each open program or window on your desktop has a button on the taskbar; you can toggle a window between open and minimized by clicking its button. You can also use the old Alt+Tab method of toggling between tasks: Hold down the **Alt** key and press **Tab** repeatedly to cycle through open windows.

387

Displaying the Toolbars

To display any of the taskbar's toolbars, follow these steps:

1. Right-click the taskbar.

2. Point to **Toolbars**, and then click the name of the toolbar you want.

To close a toolbar, repeat the preceding steps.

Controlling Window Displays

Sometimes you need to see two (or three, or more) open windows at the same time so you can move or copy items between the windows more easily. The taskbar makes it easy to arrange your open windows in different displays, including Cascaded (as in Figure 3.2), Tiled Vertically (see Figure 3.3), and Tiled Horizontally (like Figure 3.4), and it's just as easy to undo the window display when you're finished with it.

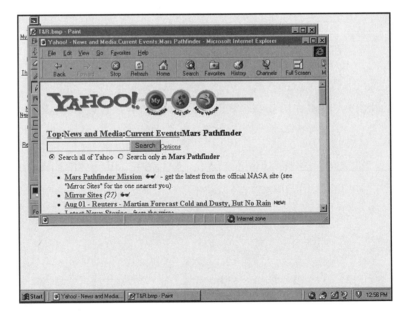

Figure 3.2 Cascaded windows.

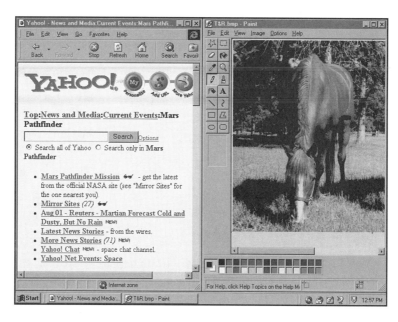

Figure 3.3 Windows tiled vertically.

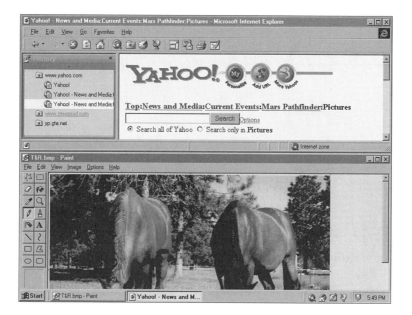

Figure 3.4 Windows tiled horizontally.

To change your window display, follow these steps:

1. Right-click the taskbar.

2. Click a display: **Cascade Windows**, or **Tile Windows Horizontally**, or **Tile Windows Vertically**.

To undo the cascaded or tiled window display, follow these steps:

1. Right-click the taskbar.

2. Click the **Undo** command. (The command is Undo Tile or Undo Cascade, depending on what display you originally selected.)

The Desktop Button

Your icons and Active Desktop Components are buried beneath the open windows you're working in, but it's easy to take a quick glance at the stock ticker on your Active Desktop and then return to work.

To clear your desktop and get to those items instantly, click the **Show Desktop** button (on the Quick Launch toolbar). All open windows and programs are minimized.

To replace your workspace after minimizing everything, click the **Show Desktop** button again.

 TIP   **Without the Toolbar...**   If your Quick Launch toolbar isn't displayed, you can clear your desktop and then replace your workspace with a shortcut menu command. To do so, right-click the taskbar and click **Minimize All Windows**. To replace your workspace, right-click the taskbar and click **Undo Minimize All**.

Using AutoHide

Even in a big monitor screen, you might want more screen real estate than you have. You can give yourself a bit more screen space by using AutoHide to hide the taskbar when you aren't actually clicking a button on it.

AutoHide hides the taskbar when you're not using it, and displays it when you need it. Follow these steps to turn on AutoHide:

1. Right-click the taskbar and click **Properties**. The Taskbar Properties dialog box appears.
2. On the Taskbar Options tab, click the **Auto hide** check box.
3. Click **OK**.

The taskbar disappears. When you need it, point at the bottom edge of your screen. The taskbar reappears so you can click a button, and then hides again when you move the mouse away.

If you get tired of chasing the taskbar or toolbars and you want them to stay in view, repeat the preceding steps to turn off AutoHide.

Customizing the Taskbar

When you add enough toolbars, your taskbar gets to be like the hall closet—so full that you can't find anything in it, like the one in Figure 3.5. One solution is to close toolbars, and another solution is to resize or move the taskbar.

Figure 3.5 The taskbar floweth over.

 TIP **What Button Is This?** If you can't read the truncated titles on your taskbar buttons, point to a button. After a moment, a ToolTip appears with the entire button title.

If your taskbar begins to look like the one shown in Figure 3.5, you can move it and resize it to make it more useful (possibly at the expense of some screen space).

To resize the taskbar, follow these steps:

1. Point to the border of the taskbar, until you see a two-headed arrow.
2. Drag the border toward the center of the screen to make the taskbar larger (as shown in Figure 3.6).

391

Figure 3.6   You can resize the taskbar to be as big as you want.

TIP   **Can I Hide That Clock?**   Yes. Right-click the taskbar and click **Properties**. On the Taskbar Options tab, click the **Show Clock** check box to clear it, and click **OK**. Follow the same procedure to return the clock to the taskbar.

You also can move the taskbar to the top or side of your screen, as shown in Figure 3.7. To move the taskbar, point at an empty spot on the taskbar (not on a toolbar or the Start button), and drag it towards another edge of the screen. (Sometimes it takes a few tries to find the right spot to drag from—dragging the clock usually works.)

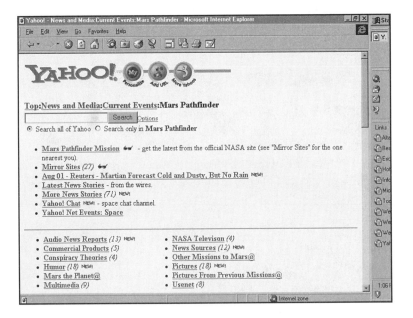

Figure 3.7   Move the taskbar to the side edge to make more screen space bottom-to-top.

TIP   **My Buttons Are Monsters!** If you move your taskbar and find that your toolbar buttons are suddenly huge, right-click the toolbar name, point to **View**, and click **Small** to resize them.

Creating a Custom Toolbar

You can create a custom toolbar out of any folder on your hard drive, and the toolbar will have buttons for all the files and subfolders in the folder. You can display the custom toolbar on the taskbar, or you can float it on your desktop.

To create a custom toolbar, follow these steps:

1. Right-click the taskbar, point to **Toolbars**, and click **New Toolbar**. The New Toolbar dialog box appears, displaying your hard drive's file tree.

2. Browse through the file tree for the folder you want on the toolbar.

3. Click the name of the folder, and click **OK**. A new toolbar, named with the folder name, appears on your taskbar.

When you close this toolbar, it will be gone, and you'll have to recreate it to use it again.

Watch Those Buttons   Don't delete buttons from custom toolbars. Although you can delete the buttons, you'll be deleting those files from your hard drive and sending them to the Recycle Bin.

CAUTION

In this lesson, you learned about features of the new taskbar. In the next lesson, you will learn about Internet Explorer 4.0's Active Desktop.

The Active Desktop and Your PC

In this lesson, you learn how to use and customize Internet Explorer 4.0's Active Desktop.

About the Active Desktop

The Active Desktop is a combination of your normal desktop (the icon layer) and a layer of active Web content that lays on top (the HTML layer). You can turn the Active Desktop on or off, which adds or removes the layer of active Web content.

To turn the Active Desktop off (or back on again), follow these steps:

1. Right-click an empty spot on the desktop background.
2. Point to **Active Desktop**, and click **View As Web Page**. If the View as Web Page command has a check mark next to it, the Active Desktop is turned on.

Underneath everything on the Active Desktop is the background, which can be wallpapered with a picture, an HTML page on your hard drive, or a graphic that you pick up from the Web. To use an HTML page on your hard drive as a background, follow these steps:

1. Right-click an empty spot on the desktop, and click **Properties**.
2. On the Background tab, click **Browse**.
3. Browse through your hard drive to an HTML page you want, then select the file name and click **Open**. The HTML page appears in the preview window in the Display Properties dialog box.
4. Click **OK**. Any links in the HTML page background will be active.

Is It On?   The Active Desktop must be turned on to use an HTML page as desktop wallpaper.

CAUTION

To use a picture on your hard drive as a background (like the one shown in Figure 4.1), follow these steps:

1. Right-click an empty spot on the desktop, and click **Properties**.
2. On the Background tab, click **Browse**.
3. Browse through your hard drive to the graphic file you want, then select the file name and click **Open**. The picture appears in the preview window in the Display Properties dialog box.
4. In the Display box, select **Center** or **Tile**, and then click **OK**.

Figure 4.1   A scanned photo set as a background.

To use a graphic you find on the Internet as a background (like the one shown in Figure 4.2), follow these steps:

1. Launch your browser and go find a graphic you like on the Internet (perhaps a company logo, or a photograph of your favorite celebrity).

2. Right-click the graphic, and click **Set As Wallpaper**. The graphic appears on your desktop, centered. If that's what you want, you're done; if you want to tile or stretch the graphic, continue to step 3.

3. Right-click an empty spot on the desktop, and click **Properties**.

4. On the Background tab, in the Display box, select **Center** or **Tile**, and, then click **OK**.

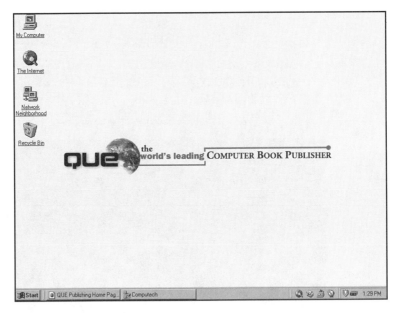

Figure 4.2   This background is a centered Web site graphic.

The Icon Layer

The icon layer is your normal desktop, with your icons and taskbar and wallpaper. If you turn off the Active Desktop, what remains is the icon layer.

The HTML Layer

The HTML layer is a transparent layer on top of the icon layer. It holds Desktop Components like the Channel Guide, Web pages you subscribe to and get updated regularly, and other items like a stock-market ticker or weather map that you can download from Microsoft (see Part 6, Lesson 5, "Using Desktop Components," to learn more about adding live items to the HTML layer).

Using Shortcut Icons on the Desktop

Whether the Active Desktop is turned on or off, you can add shortcut icons to your desktop so you can get to work more quickly. You can place shortcut icons on your desktop to launch a program, or to open a specific file, and you can arrange the icons to be as neat or as messy as you want. You can create shortcut icons to anything: programs, files, folder windows, and Web pages.

Launching Programs and Opening Files

How easy is it to launch programs and open files with shortcut icons? All you have to do is click the icon. You've probably already done it, by opening the My Computer window (even though the My Computer icon isn't a shortcut, it works exactly the same way).

If your desktop is in Internet Explorer 4.0's Web style of single-click mode, one click launches the program or file. If your desktop is in the classic Windows 95 double-click mode, one click selects the icon, and a double-click launches the file or program.

Adding Icons to the Desktop

Adding shortcut icons to your desktop is almost as fast as using them. To add a shortcut icon for a file or folder, follow these steps:

1. Open the **My Computer** window and browse to find the folder or file you want.

2. Press and hold the right mouse button and drag the file or folder you want from the window onto the desktop.

3. On the shortcut menu that appears, click **Create Shortcut(s) Here**.

To add a shortcut icon for a program, follow these steps:

1. Open the **My Computer** window and browse to find the program file you want. It will probably be in a program folder and have the program-specific icon next to it, and the file name will end in .exe.

2. Press and hold the right mouse button and drag the file from the window onto the desktop.

3. On the shortcut menu that appears, click **Create Shortcut(s) Here**.

To add a shortcut icon for a Web link, first browse to the site. Then resize the browser window so it's not maximized (you want to be able to drag from the browser window to your desktop). To create a shortcut to the page you're looking at, drag the icon from the Address toolbar in the browser window onto your desktop. To create a shortcut to a link on the page you're looking at, drag the link from the page onto your desktop.

Now that you've added lots of shortcut icons to your desktop, it might be getting a bit disorderly. You have a few options for arranging icons on your desktop:

- Right-click an empty spot on your desktop, point to **Arrange Icons**, and click **AutoArrange**. All of your icons are lined up in columns on the left side of your desktop. If you move an icon, it will be sucked back into line.

- If AutoArrange is too much like your third-grade teacher, turn it off: Right-click an empty spot on your desktop, point to **Arrange Icons**, and click AutoArrange to remove the check mark.

- Right-click an empty spot on your desktop, then click **Line Up Icons**. Your icons are aligned in a grid formation on your desktop. Each one is near where you left it, but in an orderly manner with no overlapping.

Removing Icons from the Desktop

Some of the icons on your desktop, such as My Computer or Recycle Bin, aren't shortcuts—they're the actual folder or file (and any file or folder that you save in your Desktop folder has an icon on the desktop). If you move or delete these icons, you move or delete the actual folder or file.

Shortcut icons have a little curving arrow in the lower-left corner. You can move or delete shortcut icons as much as you want to, because they're only shortcuts and you won't be moving or deleting the actual file.

To delete a shortcut icon, drag it onto the Recycle Bin.

Single-Click Mode versus Double-Click Mode

The Active Desktop can make your desktop work like a Web page, which includes turning your desktop icons into underlined, single-click links. To switch to single-click mode, follow these steps:

1. Click **Start**, then point to **Settings**.
2. Click **Folders & Icons**.

3. On the **General** tab, click the **Web Style** option button.

4. Click **OK**.

One drawback to the new single-click mode is that you can no longer rename an icon by clicking its title and typing a new name. If you miss that feature, you can change your Active Desktop settings back to pre-Internet Explorer 4.0 behavior (called Classic style). To switch back to double-click mode, follow these steps:

1. Click **Start**, then point to **Settings**.

2. Click **Folders & Icons**.

3. On the **General** tab, click the **Classic Style** option button. This option changes your settings to the default Windows 95 settings: double-click mode and multiple windows.

4. Click **OK**.

You have options other than the new Web style and the Classic style. To mix and match the settings you want, follow these steps:

1. Click **Start**, then point to **Settings**.

2. Click **Folders & Icons**.

3. On the **General** tab, click the **Custom, Based on Settings You Choose** option button, and then click the **Settings** button.

4. On the Custom Settings dialog box (see Figure 4.3), click option buttons for the settings you want.

5. Click **OK**, and then click **OK** again.

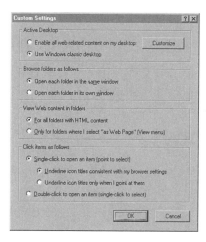

Figure 4.3   Customize your window behavior in the Custom Settings dialog box.

About the Explorer Bars

Explorer bars are a new feature Internet Explorer 4.0 has added to your browser and folder windows. The four Explorer bars—Search, Favorites, History, and Channels—are a quick means of getting to the Web sites you use the most.

The Explorer bars appear on the left side of the folder or browser window. They AutoHide when you move your mouse away from them, and reappear when you point at the left side of the window.

To open an Explorer bar in a browser window, click one of the Explorer buttons on the Standard toolbar (see Figure 4.4).

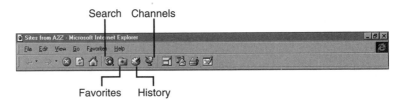

Figure 4.4   In a browser window, use the buttons to display Explorer bars.

To open an Explorer bar in a folder window, click **View**, then point to **Explorer Bar** and click the name of the bar you want. Click **None** to hide them all.

Using the History Bar

The History bar (see Figure 4.5) keeps track of all the Web sites you've visited each day in the recent past.

To open a Web page you visited recently, follow these steps:

1. Click a day. A list of the Web pages you visited that day unrolls. To roll up the list, click the day again.
2. Click the Web page you want.

To clear the History bar, follow these steps:

1. In a browser window, click **View**, then click **Internet Options**.
2. On the **General** tab, click the **Clear History** button, then click **OK**.

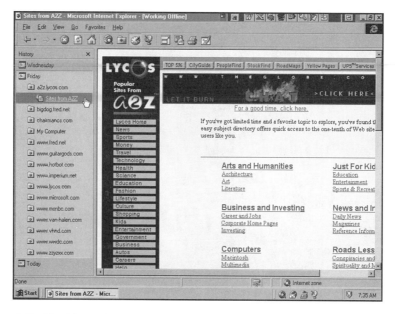

Figure 4.5 The History bar.

To change the number of days saved in the History bar, follow these steps:

1. In a browser window, click **View**, then click **Internet Options**.

2. On the **General** tab, under History, change the number in the **Days to Keep Pages in History** box, and then click **OK**.

Using the Favorites Bar

The Favorites bar (see Figure 4.6) displays a list of your Favorites Web sites. To go to a Web site on your Favorites list, click the name of the site. Click the tiny arrow bar at the bottom or top of the Favorites bar to scroll through a long list.

Using the Channels Bar

The Channels bar (see Figure 4.7) displays the available channels so you can subscribe to them or look at what's been downloaded on the channels you've subscribed to. Internet Explorer 4.0's channels are like television channels, but on the Internet. You can learn more about channels in Part 6, Lesson 9, "Managing Channels."

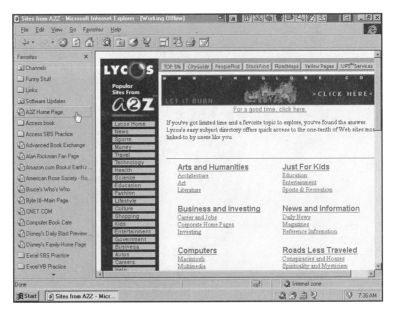

Figure 4.6   The Favorites bar.

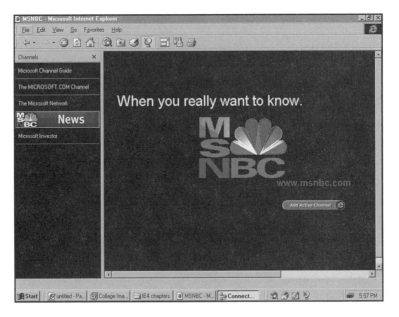

Figure 4.7   The Channels bar.

Using the Search Bar

The Search bar (see Figure 4.8) is for conducting searches for information in the Internet, and it connects to one of the search engines at the Microsoft home page. Unfortunately, you cannot set a default search engine (a randomly selected search engine appears each time you use the search bar), but if you don't want to use the search engine that's selected when you open the Search bar, you can select a different search engine from the list box at the top of the Search bar. You can learn more about searching the Internet for information in Part 6, Lesson 10, "Performing Searches."

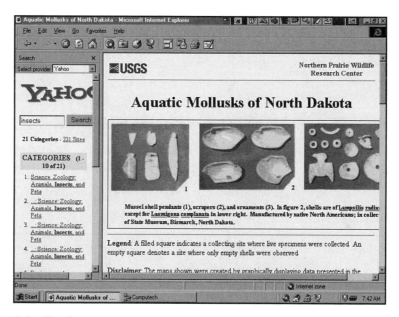

Figure 4.8   The Search bar.

In this lesson, you learned how to use and customize the Active Desktop. In the next lesson, you will learn about Desktop Components, items that reside in the HTML layer of your Active Desktop.

Using Desktop Components

In this lesson, you learn about what Desktop Components are and how to get them onto your desktop, schedule them, update them, and customize them.

Viewing Desktop Components

Desktop Components are ActiveX and Java objects that bring live Web content to your Active Desktop. Currently they include items like a stock-market investment ticker, a national weather map, a 3-D clock, and your Channel Guide (see Figure 5.1). As time goes by, more Desktop Components will become available.

Desktop Components reside in the HTML layer of your Active Desktop. You can view them and hide them by turning your Active Desktop on or off.

 TIP **Channel Guide** When you first install Internet Explorer 4.0, the only Desktop Component you'll have is the Channel Guide.

To turn your Active Desktop on (and see your Desktop Components), follow these steps:

1. Right-click an empty spot on your desktop, then point to **Active Desktop**.
2. Click **View As Web Page**. If the Active Desktop is turned on, the View As Web Page command has a check mark next to it.

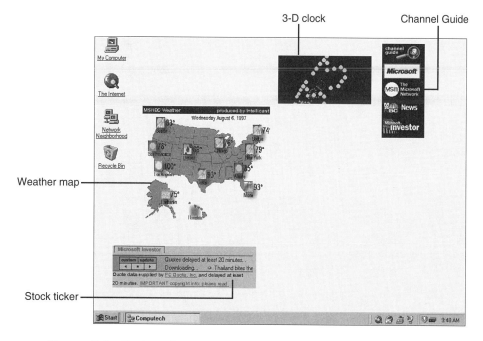

Figure 5.1 Desktop Components on the Active Desktop.

To turn the Active Desktop off (and hide all your Desktop Components), repeat the preceding steps.

Adding a Desktop Component

How do you get one of these Desktop Components onto your Active Desktop? Follow these steps:

1. Right-click an empty spot on your desktop, then point to **Active Desktop**.
2. Click **Customize My Desktop**.
3. On the Web tab (see Figure 5.2), click the **New** button.
4. The New Active Desktop Item message box asks if you'd like to visit Microsoft's Active Desktop gallery. Click **Yes**. (If you want to add a Desktop Component from someplace other than Microsoft's Gallery, click **No**, then type the path to the new item, or browse to locate it, in the New Active Desktop Item dialog box.)

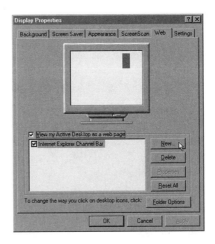

Figure 5.2   Find and add Desktop Components on the Web tab.

5. Your browser goes online to the Microsoft Active Desktop gallery. Click an item you want to add to your desktop.

6. Your browser opens a Web page that describes the item you clicked. To add the item to your desktop, click the **Add to My Desktop** button. A Security Alert message box asks you to confirm that you want to add a Desktop item. Click **Yes**.

7. In the Create a New Desktop Item dialog box that appears, you can customize the update schedule for the new Desktop Component by clicking the **Customize Subscription** button, or you can accept the default schedule and click **OK**. Your new Desktop Component is downloaded.

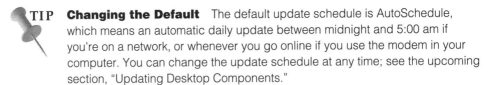

TIP   **Changing the Default**   The default update schedule is AutoSchedule, which means an automatic daily update between midnight and 5:00 am if you're on a network, or whenever you go online if you use the modem in your computer. You can change the update schedule at any time; see the upcoming section, "Updating Desktop Components."

8. Your browser returns to the item's Web page. From here you can add more Desktop Components or return to your desktop and look at the new item.

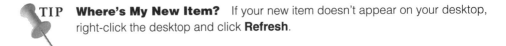

TIP   **Where's My New Item?**   If your new item doesn't appear on your desktop, right-click the desktop and click **Refresh**.

The Desktop Component Gallery The Desktop Component Gallery is a collection of ActiveX and Java objects that Microsoft has assembled for you to freely download. By the time you read this, there will probably be several more items than you see pictured here; the best way to see what's available is to follow the preceding steps to add a new item and then read the Microsoft Active Gallery Web page to find out what's there.

You aren't limited to the items in Microsoft's Desktop Component Gallery; any ActiveX or Java object with live Web content can be displayed on your Active Desktop.

Customizing a Desktop Component

Once you get a new Desktop Component onto your Active Desktop, you can resize it and move it for more convenient viewing, and for some components you can select which information is downloaded (for example, you may want to download quotes for specific stocks in the stock ticker, or download weather information for a different country).

To resize a Desktop Component, follow these steps:

1. Point to an edge of the item; a border appears, and the pointer becomes a two-headed arrow.
2. Drag the border of the item to the size you want.

To move a Desktop Component, follow these steps:

1. Point to the top edge of the item. A title bar appears (see Figure 5.3).
2. Drag the title bar to relocate the item.

Selecting what information to download is a little different for each Desktop Component, so you need to experiment a bit with different components. In general, to customize the information that's downloaded, follow these steps:

1. Right-click the component.
2. Click **Custom**. If there isn't a Custom command, try clicking the item itself (for example, in the Weather Map this takes you online for weather all over the world).
3. Fill out the Properties dialog box that appears. (The dialog box is different for each item; Figure 5.4 shows the Properties dialog box for the Microsoft Investor Stock Ticker.)

407

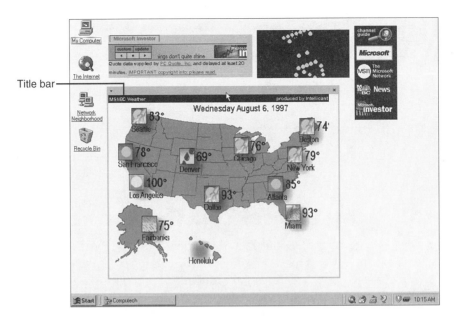

Title bar

Figure 5.3 To move a Desktop Component, drag its title bar.

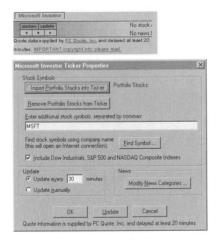

Figure 5.4 Select the information you want to download in the item's Properties dialog box.

Updating Desktop Components

The magic of Desktop Components is that they're updated with current information on a regular basis. How often they are updated is up to you. You can set a regular, automatic schedule for updating, or you can update only when you decide to update. Each item has its own update schedule, so you have great flexibility.

Keep in mind that updating often means your computer will be going online often to download updated information, which can be disruptive to your normal work.

To set an update schedule, follow these steps:

1. Right-click an empty spot on the desktop.

2. Point to **Active Desktop**, then click **Customize My Desktop**.

3. On the Web tab, select the item you want to schedule, then click **Properties**.

4. On the Schedule tab, select a scheduling option.

The AutoSchedule option only works for computers on a corporate-type network that connect to the Internet through a network server, and the item is updated whenever the item's publisher decides to update.

If you're not on a network and you connect directly from your modem, you can select the **Custom Schedule** option or the **Update Now** option. The Custom Schedule option enables you to set a regular schedule for your modem to go online and download new information; the Update Now option enables you to update information only when you decide to update.

5. Click **OK**.

If you scheduled automatic updates, there's nothing else you have to do (except leave your computer on during the time when the update is scheduled so your modem can go online and download the information).

If you set an Update Now schedule, you get updated information when you decide to update. To update your desktop items, follow these steps:

1. Right-click an empty spot on the desktop.

2. Point to **Active Desktop**, then click **Update Now**.

Hiding a Desktop Component

You may not want to see all your items all the time. You can hide them, which keeps them available for viewing, but only when you want them.

To hide a Desktop Component, follow these steps:

1. Point to the top edge of the item, until the title bar appears.
2. Click the **Close** (X) button at the right end of the title bar. The item disappears from your desktop.

To display a hidden item, follow these steps:

1. Right-click an empty spot on your desktop, then point to **Active Desktop**.
2. Click **Customize My Desktop**.
3. On the Web tab, in the Items on the Active Desktop section, click to place a check mark in the box next to the item you want to display.
4. Click **OK**.

Removing a Desktop Component

To remove a Desktop Component, follow these steps:

1. Right-click an empty spot on your desktop.
2. Point to **Active Desktop**, then click **Customize My Desktop**.
3. On the Web tab, in the section Items on the Active Desktop, click the item you want to remove. Then click the **Delete** button.
4. A message box asks if you're sure you want to delete the item and its subscription. Click **Yes**.
5. Click **OK** to close the Display Properties dialog box.

 TERM **Subscriptions** Subscriptions are what keep the information in each item updated; see Part 6, Lesson 8, "Managing Subscriptions," to learn more about them.

In this lesson, you learned about Desktop Components—what they are, how to get more of them, and how to customize them. In the next lesson, you will learn about the WebView window, Internet Explorer 4.0's new feature for finding and viewing information on your computer screen.

Exploring a WebView Window

In this lesson, you learn how to use and customize the new WebView window.

The Menu Bar

The menu bar in the WebView window is expanded to include more menus and commands, and is a *smart* menu bar: The available commands change depending on whether you're looking at a folder or a Web page (see Figure 6.1). For example, if you're looking at a folder, the File menu has a New command so you can create new folders, shortcuts, or files, while the File menu in a browser window has Page Setup and Print commands so you can print a Web page.

The menu bar in both folder and browser windows has a new menu for Favorites, which lists all the files, folders, and links in your Favorites folder. This enables you to jump from a Web page to a folder on your hard drive in the same window by clicking an item on the Favorites menu.

 TIP **I Can't See All My Favorites** The Favorites menu can get pretty long, and Internet Explorer 4.0 has made it easier to get to the end of the list. Click the narrow arrow bar at the bottom of the menu to scroll to the end (and click the narrow arrow bar at the top of the menu to scroll back to the top).

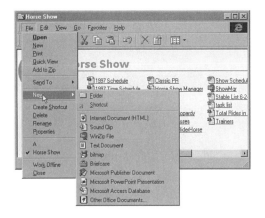

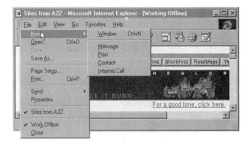

Figure 6.1   The menus carry commands that are appropriate to the kind of information you're looking at.

The Toolbars

The three toolbars in the WebView window are the Standard, Address, and Links toolbars. All three can be displayed, hidden, moved, and resized. You can learn more about the individual toolbars in Part 6, Lesson 2, "Using Smart Toolbars."

The Standard toolbar is a *smart* toolbar—its buttons change depending on whether you're looking at a Web page or a folder, so that you have only the buttons that are useful for that view. If you want to see at a glance which buttons are which, you can turn on text labels (see Figure 6.2).

Figure 6.2   Text labels identify the buttons on the Standard toolbar.

To turn text labels on or off, follow these steps:

1. Right-click the toolbar.

2. Click **Text Labels**.

Displaying or Hiding a Toolbar

To display or hide a WebView window toolbar, follow these steps:

1. Right-click the menu bar or any toolbar.
2. Click the name of the toolbar you want to show or hide.

Moving a Toolbar

The WebView window toolbars cannot be moved very far, but they can be moved to separate tiers at the top of the window, or they can be moved to the same tier to create more viewing area in the window. Figure 6.3 shows one toolbar arrangement.

Drag this to move
the toolbar

Figure 6.3 Make the toolbars more convenient by moving them to separate tiers.

To move a toolbar, follow these steps:

1. Point to the vertical bar at the left end of the toolbar until you see a two-headed arrow.
2. Drag the toolbar up or down to a different tier. (When you drag the toolbar, the two-headed arrow becomes a split two-headed arrow.)

Resizing a Toolbar

Sometimes you need to make a toolbar longer or shorter so you can get to the buttons on that toolbar or the toolbar next to it. To resize a toolbar, point to the vertical bar at the left end of the toolbar until you see a two-headed arrow, then drag the end of the toolbar to the size you want.

A WebView Look at Your Computer

A WebView window is the new Internet Explorer 4.0 folder/browser window that enables you to explore the Internet or navigate your hard drive using the same window and the same navigation tools.

The new Web-style settings (shown in Figure 6.4) include underlined, single-click links to your hard drive folders, and a second window pane on the left side that displays information about the link you're pointing at. The second pane also has links to the Microsoft Web site for more information.

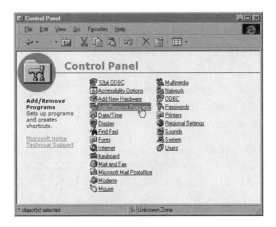

Figure 6.4   The Control Panel folder in a WebView window.

 TIP   **I Don't See the Web Page Stuff**   If you have the Web-style folder view turned on and you don't see the Web page panel on the left side of your folder window, try dragging the lower-right corner of the folder window to make the window larger.

If you want your folder windows to look like the Windows 95 windows that you're used to, follow these steps:

1. Click **Start**, then point to **Settings**.
2. Click **Folders & Icons**.
3. On the **General** tab, click the **Classic Style** option button. This option changes your settings to the default Windows 95 settings: double-click mode and multiple windows.
4. Click **OK**.

If you want an individual folder window to look like the Windows 95 windows you're used to, follow these steps:

1. Open a folder window.

2. Open the **View** menu and select **As Web Page**. A check mark appears next to the As Web Page command, indicating that the new settings are turned on; clicking the command to remove the check mark turns the new settings off.

If you want to pick and choose which new WebView features to keep, follow these steps:

1. Click **Start**, then point to **Settings**.

2. Click **Folders & Icons**.

3. On the **General** tab, click the **Custom, Based on Settings You Choose** option button.

4. Click the **Settings** button.

5. On the Custom Settings dialog box (see Figure 6.5), click option buttons for the settings you want.

6. Click **OK**, and then click **OK** again.

Figure 6.5   Customize your window behavior in the Custom Settings dialog box.

Using Navigation Tools

The Navigation tools in the WebView window include the Address toolbar, the Links toolbar, and the Back, Forward, Up, and Home buttons on the Standard toolbar (see Figure 6.6).

You can learn more about using the Address and Links toolbars in Part 6, Lesson 2.

The Up button appears on the Standard toolbar when you're viewing a folder in the WebView window. It navigates up your hard drive's file tree toward the hard drive.

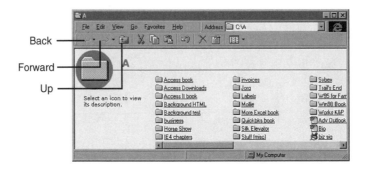

Figure 6.6   The Navigation buttons on the Standard toolbar.

The Home button appears on the Standard toolbar when you're viewing a Web page in the WebView window. It navigates directly to your browser's default home page.

The Back and Forward buttons are always on the Standard toolbar, regardless of what you're viewing. They navigate through pages and folders you've already visited.

To go directly to a folder or Web page you previously visited (instead of click-click-clicking through them one by one), follow these steps:

1. Click the drop-down arrow on the side of the Back or Forward button.
2. Click the name of the folder or Web page you want.

Creating a Custom WebView Window

Only the My Computer and Control Panel windows are configured by Internet Explorer 4.0 to look like Web pages, but you can configure your other folder windows to look and act like Web pages. You also can use a picture as a window background, just as you'd use a picture as a desktop background.

Using a Picture as a Folder Background

You can use any picture on your hard drive as a folder background—a company logo, a graphic you created in Windows Paint, or the picture you're using as desktop wallpaper (see Figure 6.7).

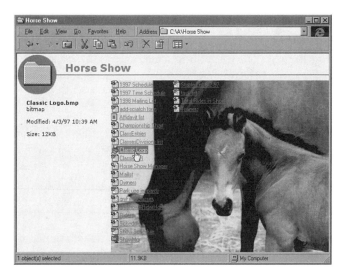

Figure 6.7   A scanned photograph is the background in this folder.

To customize a folder by adding a picture to the folder background, follow these steps:

1. Open the folder you want to customize.
2. Right-click the folder background, and click **Customize This Folder**. The Customize This Folder Wizard starts.
3. Click the **Choose a Background Picture** option button, then click **Next**.
4. Click a picture on the list (these are pictures in the Windows folder), or click **Browse** to find a picture in another folder.

5. Under Icon Caption Colors, click the button next to **Text** and select a color that contrasts with the new background so you'll be able to read the file names against the background picture. Then click **OK**.

6. Click **Next**, then click **Finish**. Your picture is tiled in the background of the folder.

TIP

I Don't Want the Picture Tiled   You cannot center a picture in a folder background, but you can open your picture editor (Windows Paint or another photopaint program) and resize the picture to make it larger so it covers the entire folder background. It is still tiled, but if you make the picture large enough, you'll only see one tile.

Turning Your Folder into an HTML Page

You can turn your folder into a custom HTML page and customize it further by adding more HTML tags.

TIP

HTML?   Internet Explorer 4.0 creates a bare-bones HTML page for you even if you don't have FrontPage Express or another HTML editor installed; but you can do more with the Web page if you install FrontPage Express (included in the Full Installation of Internet Explorer 4.0). To install FrontPage Express, run the **ie4setup.exe** file (in your Internet Explorer 4.0 Setup folder) and select the **Full Installation**.

To customize a folder to look and act like a Web page, follow these steps:

1. Open the folder you want to customize.

2. Right-click the folder background, and click **Customize This Folder**. The Customize This Folder Wizard starts.

3. Verify that the **Create or Edit an HTML Document** option is selected, and click **Next**.

4. Read the next wizard step, and click **Next**. FrontPage Express (Internet Explorer 4.0's HTML editor) starts.

5. If you're familiar with HTML, make any changes you want on this page. If not, you can learn more about it in Part 5.

6. Click **File**, then click **Save**.

7. Click **File**, then click **Close**. The folder Web page is closed, but FrontPage Express is still open.

8. Click **File**, then click **Exit**. FrontPage Express closes, and the Customize This Folder Wizard appears.

9. Click **Finish**. Your finished Web page folder appears.

To edit the HTML page and customize it further, repeat the preceding procedure.

Undo Customization

Tired of looking at your masterpiece? To remove the picture or HTML look from a folder, follow these steps:

1. Right-click the folder background and click **Customize This Folder**.

2. Click the **Remove Customization** option button, then click **Next**.

3. Click **Next** again.

4. Click **Finish**. The folder is restored to its original state.

In this lesson, you learned about using and customizing WebView windows. In the next lesson, you will learn about the features in the new Start menu.

Using the New Start Menu

In this lesson, you learn how to use and customize the new Start menu.

An Overview of the New Start Menu

The new Start menu is a beefed-up, more functional version of the old Start menu. If you're familiar with the old Start menu, you'll find that it still does everything you're familiar with—but it also does a lot more.

The new Start menu has these new features:

- The Programs and Favorites menus can be reorganized simply by dragging files and folders to a new location.
- You can add shortcuts to files and folders by dragging and dropping them on the Start button.
- The Find menu has more options for finding things.
- The User Log-off command is more conveniently placed, at the bottom of the initial Start menu.

To add a shortcut to a file, folder, or Web page to the Start menu, drag the file name, folder name, or link from the folder/browser window and drop it on the Start button. The new shortcut appears at the top of the Start menu.

To remove a shortcut from the Start menu, follow these steps:

1. Click the **Start** button.
2. Point to **Settings**, then click **Taskbar & Start Menu**.
3. On the Start Menu Programs tab, under Customize Start Menu, click the **Remove** button.

4. In the Remove Shortcuts/Folders dialog box (see Figure 7.1), select the shortcut you want to remove, then click **Remove**.

5. Click **Close**, then click **OK**.

Figure 7.1 The Remove Shortcuts/Folders dialog box.

The Programs Menu

You can rearrange program shortcuts by dragging them to different locations, as shown in Figure 7.2.

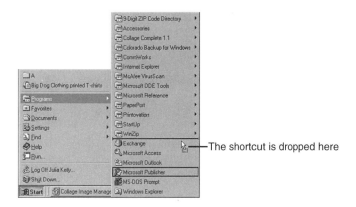

The shortcut is dropped here

Figure 7.2 Drag a program shortcut to a new location on the Programs menu.

421

TIP **A Lot of Nested Menus** If you use a program often, you can start it more conveniently by dragging its shortcut to a menu closer to the Start menu. For example, instead of clicking **Start**, then **Programs**, then **Accessories**, then **Games** to open Minesweeper, you can drag the Minesweeper shortcut to the Programs menu and click only twice to reach it.

The Favorites Menu

The Favorites menu displays a list of all the Web links you've saved in your Favorites folder. To go to a favorite Web page, click **Start**, point to **Favorites**, and click the name of the Web page you want. Your browser launches and goes to the Web page.

The Favorites menu organizes its links in alphabetical order, but if you have a lot of links, it can be annoying to have to scan the menu to find the one you want. You can rearrange the list of links into any order you want, and make your most-used Favorites easier to spot. To reorganize the Favorites list, open the Favorites menu and drag a favorite link to a new location (see Figure 7.3).

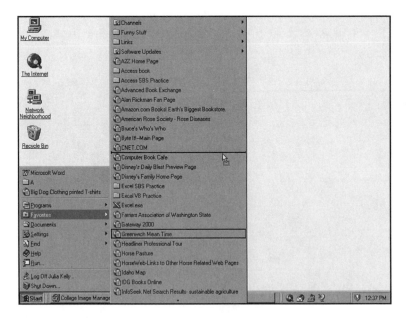

Figure 7.3 Drag links on the Favorites menu to reorganize them.

To remove a link from the Favorites menu, follow these steps:

1. In a folder or browser window, click **Favorites**, then click **Organize Favorites**.

2. Click the link you want to remove, then click the **Delete** button.

3. Click **Close**.

The Documents Menu

The Documents menu keeps a list of files you've opened recently. To reopen a file quickly, click **Start**, point to **Documents**, and click the name of the file you want to open. The file's program is launched, and the file is opened.

Name Changes If you change the name of a file, the old name remains on the Documents menu and Windows can't find it. You must open the file by another means before the new file name appears on the Documents menu.

CAUTION

To clear the Documents menu, follow these steps:

1. Click the **Start** button.

2. Point to **Settings**, then click **Taskbar & Start Menu**.

3. On the Start Menu Programs tab (see Figure 7.4), under Documents Menu, click the **Clear** button.

4. Click **OK**.

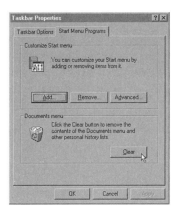

Figure 7.4 The Start Menu Programs tab.

The Settings Menu

The Settings menu gives you quick access to the following items:

- The Control Panel folder, where you can change your system settings, uninstall software programs, and add new features of existing software programs.
- The Taskbar and Start Menu settings dialog box, where you can change Start menu programs, clear the Documents menu, turn Taskbar AutoHide on or off, and hide or display the taskbar's clock.
- The print queue dialog box for any printers, fax programs, or scanners on your network. You can check the progress of documents being printed or faxed, and pause or delete them.
- The Folder Options dialog box, where you can switch between Web style and Classic style folder and icon views or mix and match your own settings.
- Active Desktop settings, where you can turn the Active Desktop on or off, open the Display Properties dialog box to customize your desktop, and update your subscribed Web pages.

The Find Menu

The Find menu still finds files and folders on your hard drive, but it also finds other computers on your network, e-mail addresses, and Web pages.

To look for something with the Find command, click **Start**, then point to **Find**, and click the command for what you want to look for.

You can look for any of the following:

- People, using your Windows Address Book or any of several Internet directory services, including Switchboard, Four11, Infospace, Bigfoot, and WhoWhere.
- Files and folders on your hard drive or company network.
- Another computer on your network.
- Information on the Internet, using a variety of search engines available at the Microsoft Web site.

To learn more about searching, see Part 6, Lesson 10, "Performing Searches."

TIP   **Can I Find Anything Else?**   If you have Microsoft Outlook installed, you can use the Find command to locate a contact, a note, or anything else you've saved in Outlook. Click **Start**, point to **Find**, then click **Using Microsoft Outlook**. The Outlook Find dialog box appears, and you can search for any Outlook item.

The Help Command

The Help command opens Help files for Windows 95 and a few files for Internet Explorer 4.0. To get help with Windows 95 or Internet Explorer 4.0, follow these steps:

1. Click the **Start** button.
2. Click **Help**. The Windows 95 Help window opens.

See Part 6, Lesson 11, "Exploring the New Help System," to learn more about Internet Explorer 4.0's new Help system.

The Run Command

The Run command is a quick method for running a program, and it keeps a list of what you've run previously so you can run those programs again without having to browse for them. When you browse for a program from the Run dialog box, it looks specifically for program files so you don't have to wade through long lists of non-program files to find what you want.

The Run command is a convenient way to perform a computer-maintenance task like running Scandisk or Defrag. To run a program using the Run command, follow these steps:

1. Click the **Start** button.
2. Click **Run**.
3. If you've run the program you want before, click the **Open** drop-down arrow.
4. Click the name of the program you want to run.

   If you haven't run that particular program before, you'll have to browse for it. Click the **Browse** button, and then browse through your file tree to find the program you want. When you find it, click the program's name and click **Open**.

5. In the Run dialog box, click **OK**.

In this lesson, you learned to use and customize the new Start menu. In the next lesson, you will learn about subscriptions to Web sites.

Managing Subscriptions

In this lesson, you learn how to use subscriptions to download current information from your favorite Web sites automatically.

What Are Subscriptions?

Subscriptions are a way to save time getting the Internet information you want. A subscription doesn't replace surfing or searching the Web to locate information, but it automates the process of downloading current information from Web sites that you read frequently, like an online magazine or newspaper. You can use a subscription to download newspaper stories, financial information, or sports scores while you're away from your computer (perhaps at lunch or overnight) and have the information waiting for you to read, offline and at your leisure, when you return.

Internet Explorer 4.0 uses a Web crawling agent to go online at scheduled intervals, visit specific sites, check for changed information at each site, and then either download the new Web pages or notify you that pages have changed so you can choose which ones to download.

 Web Crawling Agents A Web crawling agent, or Web crawler, is a software program that goes online to search out and download Web sites and follow links to more Web sites—all without your guidance or attention. It's like a robot Internet surfer.

Subscribing to a Site

To subscribe to a site, you must add it to your Favorites list, then subscribe to it and set a schedule for the Web crawler to go and check it for changed information. To subscribe to a site, follow these steps:

1. In your browser, open the Web page you want to subscribe to.

2. In the browser window, click **Favorites**, then click **Add To Favorites**.

3. In the Add Favorites dialog box (see Figure 8.1), click one of the following option buttons:

Select **Yes, but Only Tell Me When This Page Is Updated** if you want to be notified of changes but don't want the pages downloaded automatically.

Select **Yes, Notify Me of Updates and Download the Page for Offline Viewing** if you want to have changed pages automatically downloaded.

If you check the latter option, your first wizard step asks if you want to download only this page or all linked pages. Be careful about downloading all linked pages because you could end up downloading many megabytes of information.

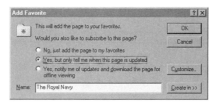

Figure 8.1 Subscribing to a new favorite.

4. Click **Customize**. The Subscription Wizard starts.

5. In the first wizard step, you can choose to be notified of changes via e-mail. This is helpful if you're on the road with your laptop and checking in with your home-base computer; if you select the No option, a small red asterisk appears on the page icon in the Subscriptions dialog box to notify you of changes.

6. In the second wizard step, fill in any user name and password required by your subscribed site (if it's a site you normally have to log into with a password, the Web crawler needs your password to check the site for you). Most Web sites don't need passwords, however. Click **Finish** to complete your subscription.

7. Click **OK** to close the Add Favorites dialog box. The Web page is added to your Favorites list and will be checked on the schedule you set. (See the following section, "Customizing Subscription Settings," for details on setting up a schedule.)

If the site is already on your Favorites list, follow these steps to subscribe:

1. In your browser window, click **Favorites**.

2. Right-click the site you want to subscribe to, then click **Subscribe**.

3. Follow steps 5 through 7 of the preceding list to complete the subscription.

Customizing Subscription Settings

When a subscribed site has changed, your notification appears as a red asterisk on the page icon in your Subscriptions dialog box, like the ones shown in Figure 8.2. You can switch your subscription settings from mere notification to actually downloading the changed information, and you can change the site-checking schedule.

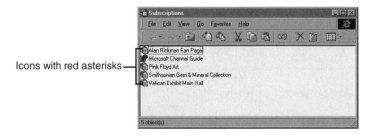

Icons with red asterisks

Figure 8.2   Two of the subscriptions have changed contents, as indicated by the asterisks on their icons.

To switch your notification settings, follow these steps:

1. In your browser window, click **Favorites**, then click **Manage Subscriptions**.

2. In the Subscriptions dialog box, right-click the Web site you want to change, then click **Properties**. The Subscription tab (see Figure 8.3) shows your current subscription settings.

Figure 8.3 The Subscription tab, where you'll find your current settings.

Changing Notification Settings

On the Receiving tab (see Figure 8.4) you can change the settings for notification of site changes.

Figure 8.4 Set notification preferences on the Receiving tab.

429

These are the settings you can select on the Receiving tab:

- You can be notified by e-mail of changes in the Web site. If you want to be notified by e-mail, but at a different address, click the check box under **Notification**, then click the **Change Address** button and type the address to which you want e-mail notification sent.

- To select notification only, in the Subscription Type area, click the **Only Notify Me When Updates Occur** option. This option is much faster than actual automatic downloading and enables you to download the changed site separately from other subscribed sites.

- To direct the Web crawler to download the site automatically whenever it changes, click the **Notify Me When Updates Occur and Download for Offline Viewing** option. Then click the **Advanced** button to select download options from the Advanced Download Options dialog box.

- In the Advanced Download Options dialog box (see Figure 8.5), you can set a maximum size for downloads, and choose which types of page content to download (images, sounds, video, etc.). You can direct the Web crawler to download only the subscribed page, or follow links on that page and download other pages within that Web site (up to five levels deep). You also can have the Web crawler follow links to pages outside the subscribed Web site and download those pages. Be careful with this option, because you can easily fill your hard drive with downloaded Web pages.

Figure 8.5   The Advanced Download Options for a specific site.

TIP **Links Don't Work in Downloaded Pages** After the Web crawler downloads a changed page, it disconnects itself from the Internet. So if you point to a link on a page you've downloaded, you'll see a *not* symbol (a circle with a diagonal slash). To follow the link, click the link, then click the **Connect** button in the dialog box that appears. Your browser connects and follows the link.

Changing Schedule Settings

On the Schedule tab (see Figure 8.6), you can change the Web crawler's update schedule.

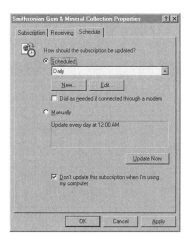

Figure 8.6 Set an update schedule on the Schedule tab.

The following are the settings you can select on the Schedule tab:

- *Scheduled* enables you to set a schedule for the Web crawler to go online and check your subscribed sites for changed information (see Figure 8.7). You can set a daily, weekly, or monthly schedule, and set a time for downloads (overnight is a good choice if your Web crawler will be downloading lots of information). You also can have the Web crawler repeat the check at hourly intervals if you need to catch late-breaking news.

- *Manually* directs the Web crawler to check for changes in a Web site only when you tell it to do so, rather than automatically.

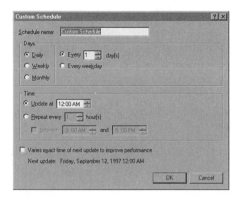

Figure 8.7   Set a custom schedule to check your subscribed sites.

Downloading Subscriptions Now

If you have set your Web crawler to the Manually schedule, you can send it online to download changed information whenever you choose. If you think it will be a long download, send the Web crawler out before you go to lunch, and your new pages will be waiting for you when you return.

Even if you have your subscriptions set to download automatically, you can update them off-schedule whenever you want. This comes in handy if you're on your way out of town and want to check a subscribed site once more before you leave.

Downloading All Your Subscriptions

To download changed pages from all your subscribed sites at your command, follow these steps:

1. In the browser window, click **Favorites**.

2. Click **Update All**. The Web crawler goes online and checks each of your subscribed pages for changes. A Download Progress message box appears while the Web crawler is at work and disappears when the Web crawler is finished.

   While the Web crawler is downloading, you can do any of the following:

   • Click the **Details** button to watch the progress of the downloads (see Figure 8.8).

- To stop the download at any point, click the **Stop** button in the Download Progress message box.
- To skip downloading a specific site, click that site, then click the **Skip** button.

Figure 8.8 A subscription download in progress.

Downloading a Single Site

To download changed pages from a single subscribed site, follow these steps:

1. In your browser window, click **Favorites**, then click **Manage Subscriptions**.
2. Right-click the site you want to check for updated information.
3. Click **Update Now**. The Web crawler goes only to that site to check for changed pages. If there are changes in that site, a red asterisk appears on the icon, and you can open the page by double-clicking it.

Viewing a Changed Site

When changed information has been downloaded, follow these steps to view the downloaded page:

1. In the browser window, click **Favorites**.
2. Point to **Subscriptions**, then click **Manage Subscriptions**.
3. In the Subscriptions dialog box, double-click the page you want to read.

Deleting a Subscription

To unsubscribe to a site, follow these steps:

1. In your browser window, click **Favorites**.

2. Right-click the site you want to unsubscribe, and click **Unsubscribe**.

3. In the Confirm Item Delete message box, click **Yes**. Your subscription is canceled, but the site remains on your Favorites list so you can visit it when you want.

In this lesson, you learned about subscriptions and how you can use them to download current information from the Web automatically. In the next lesson, you will learn about channels.

Managing
Channels

In this lesson, you learn what channels are, how to subscribe to them, and how to update them.

What Are Channels?

Channels are Web sites that come to your computer the way television channels come to your television set. They are a specialized form of subscription to Web sites; you cannot navigate to a channel by typing a URL in your browser, but after you subscribe to a channel, you can view it in your browser window by clicking a channel button on the Channel bar.

If your computer is on a network that has constant Internet access (a constant open line to the Internet, so that channels can *push* information into the network), any channel you subscribe to is automatically updated by the channel's provider and you simply open the channel on your computer to see the latest information. If your computer isn't on a network, channels work like subscriptions—you update them manually or on a Web crawler schedule to get the latest information.

Internet Explorer 4.0 comes with built-in access to many channels, but as time goes by, more channels will no doubt become available on the Internet, and you will be able to add them to your Channel Guide.

It's Subject to Change   What you see in your Channel Guide might differ from what you see in this book due to channel updates by Microsoft.

CAUTION

Using Channels

You can open a channel from the Channel Guide desktop component on your Active Desktop (if you have the Active Desktop turned on), from the Channel bar in your browser window, from the list of channels in the Channels folder on your Favorites menu, or from the Channel Guide in the Channel Viewer.

The Channel Viewer is a full-screen view of your browser window, with toolbars along the top of the screen that AutoHide, and the Channel Guide on the left side of the screen that also slides out of view. The Channel Viewer gives you an unimpeded view of the Web channel (or any other Web site to which you navigate).

To switch between Channel View and a normal browser window view, click **View**, then click **Full Screen**. In this chapter you see channel information demonstrated using the Channel Viewer.

 TIP **See Other Programs Without Switching to the Browser Window**
You can view other open programs on top of the Channel Viewer by pressing **Alt+Tab** (the Alt key and the Tab key simultaneously). A small dialog box appears that contains icons for each open program—hold down the **Alt** key and press the **Tab** key repeatedly to cycle through the icons. When the icon for the program you want has the selection border around it, release the **Alt** and **Tab** keys. The selected program appears on top of the Channel Viewer window.

To use the Channel Viewer, follow these steps:

1. On the Quick Launch toolbar, click the **View Channels** button. The Channel Viewer launches (see Figure 9.1).
2. If the Channel Guide isn't in view on the left side of the screen, move the mouse pointer to the left edge of your screen. The Channel Guide slides into view, and slides out of view when you move the mouse pointer away.
3. If the menu bar and toolbars remain in view at the top of the screen, right-click the menu bar, then click **AutoHide**. The menu bar and toolbars slide out of view until you point at the top of your screen. When all the accessory bars are out of view and a channel is open, the Channel Viewer displays the Web page as the full-screen, as shown in Figure 9.2.

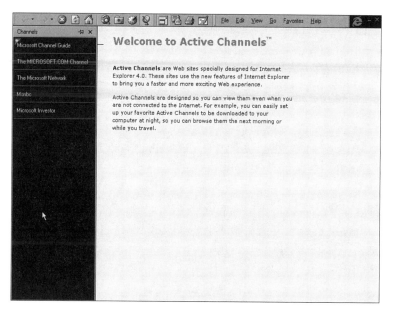

Figure 9.1 The Channel Viewer, a full-screen view of your browser window.

 TIP **Make the Channel Guide Narrower** To make the Channel Guide narrower (or wider), point to the right edge of the Channel Guide until you see a two-headed arrow, and then drag the edge to the width you want.

Figure 9.2 The Channel Viewer displays a page in full, unimpeded glory.

Using the Channel Guide

The Channel Guide is like the remote control for a television set: You click a button to open a channel and see what's on. The Channel Guides (on the Active Desktop and the Channel Viewer) and the Channel bar (in a browser window) work the same way.

The first time you open a channel, you'll get a preview of what the channel offers and the opportunity to subscribe. After you subscribe, you get the latest information on the channel.

To open a channel, click the channel's button on the Channel Guide or Channel bar. If your computer is on a network that's online, the channel opens; if you haven't subscribed to the channel, Internet Explorer 4.0 dials up the Web site so you can see a preview and subscribe.

Subscribing to Channels

When you preview a channel, the channel provider gives you the opportunity to subscribe. The subscription button is a bit different on each channel because it's provided by the individual channel, but each channel uses the Channel Subscription Wizard to guide you through the process of subscribing.

To subscribe to a channel, follow these steps:

1. In the Channel Guide, click the button for the channel you want. Internet Explorer 4.0 dials up the channel.
2. On the preview page, click the button, graphic, or link that indicates subscription (such as an Add Our Channel graphic or button). The Modify Channel Usage dialog box appears (see Figure 9.3).

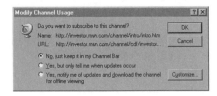

Figure 9.3   The Modify Channel Usage dialog box with default subscription settings.

3. Choose one of the following options from the Modify Channel Usage dialog box:

- **No, Just Keep It in My Channel Bar**   If you select this option, a button for this channel is added to the Channel bar. You can click the button to open the channel, but the channel is not checked for changes automatically.

- **Yes, but Only Tell Me When Updates Occur**   If you select this option, the channel is checked for changed information, and a red asterisk appears on the channel's icon in the Subscription dialog box when the channel has new information (but the changed pages are not downloaded).

- **Yes, Notify Me of Updates and Download the Channel for Offline Viewing**   If you select this option, changed pages are automatically downloaded on the schedule you set so you can open the pages and read them offline.

Which option you choose determines what questions the Subscription Wizard asks in the next few steps.

4. Click **Customize**, and the Subscription Wizard starts. Suppose you selected Yes, Notify Me of Updates and Download the Channel for Offline Viewing. In the first wizard step, select how much new information you want to have downloaded automatically. If you download only the home page, you can go online later to follow the links that interest you. Click **Next**.

5. In the second wizard step, you can choose to be notified via an e-mail message of changes in the channel. If you choose Yes, you can change the e-mail address by clicking the **Change Address** button. After you select an option, click **Next** or **Finish**.

If you chose notification only, you are finished with the wizard; if you chose to have content downloaded, continue to the next step.

6. In the third wizard step, choose a site-checking schedule. You can choose to update Manually or use a Scheduled Update. Click the **New** button to set a schedule.

7. In the Custom Schedule dialog box (see Figure 9.4), set a schedule for your computer to check the channel site. Keep in mind that if you set a schedule for midnight every night (which is convenient because you probably won't be using the computer at that time), the computer must be left on so that Internet Explorer 4.0 can dial into the channel.

8. In the Custom Schedule dialog box, click **OK.** Then click **Finish** in the wizard step. Finally, click **OK** in the Modify Channel Usage dialog box, and your subscription is complete. To update immediately, right-click the channel name in the Channel Guide and click **Update Now**.

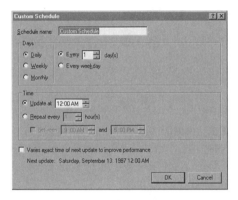

Figure 9.4 Set a custom schedule for channel checking.

Updating Channels

If your computer is on a network, you don't need to update channels because you'll always find the most current information on the channel when you open it. But if you're using a standalone computer and you've set a manual update schedule, you'll need to direct the computer to go online and check your channels for new information. And if you're headed out of the office and want to check a channel for fresh information one last time before you go, you can update manually instead of waiting for the next scheduled update.

To update a specific channel manually, follow these steps:

1. In the browser window, click **Favorites**, then click **Manage Subscriptions**.
2. In the Subscriptions dialog box (see Figure 9.5), right-click the channel you want to update and click **Update Now**. Internet Explorer 4.0 goes online to check the channel for changes and either notifies you of changes or downloads the site, depending on your subscription settings.

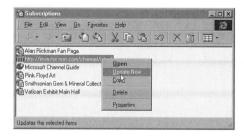

Figure 9.5 In the Subscriptions dialog box, channel icons are different from subscribed-site icons.

To update all channels manually, follow these steps:

1. In the browser window, click **Favorites**.

2. Click **Update All Subscriptions**. Internet Explorer 4.0 goes online to check all subscribed sites and channels for changes and either notifies you of changes or downloads pages, depending on your subscription settings for each subscribed site or channel.

Changing a Channel's Subscription Settings

If you change your mind about what you want downloaded and when, you can change the settings that you originally set in the wizard. To change a channel's subscription settings, follow these steps:

1. In any Channel Guide or Channel bar, right-click the channel or channel folder you want to change.

2. Click **Properties**.

3. On the **Receiving** tab, set options for what you want downloaded.

4. On the **Scheduling** tab, set a schedule for updating and/or downloading.

5. Click **OK** to close the Properties dialog box.

Deleting a Channel

There are bound to be channels you don't want in your channel guide. You can get rid of the visual clutter by deleting channels. To delete a channel, follow these steps:

1. In any Channel Guide or Channel bar, right-click the channel or channel folder you want to delete.

2. Click **Delete**. In the Confirm Folder Delete dialog box, click **Yes**. The folder or channel is moved to the Recycle Bin, so you can get it back if you change your mind.

If the channel was an unsubscribed button in the Channel Guide, you're finished. Close the Subscriptions dialog box.

If the channel was one you had subscribed to, you need to delete the subscription from the Subscriptions dialog box. Continue with step 3.

3. In a browser window, click **Favorites**. Point to **Subscriptions**, then click **Manage Subscriptions**.

4. In the Subscriptions dialog box, right-click the subscription you want to delete, and then click **Delete**.

5. Close the Subscriptions dialog box.

In this lesson, you learned about using and managing specialized subscriptions called Channels. In the next lesson, you'll learn how to search for anything with Internet Explorer 4.0's expanded search capabilities.

Performing Searches

In this lesson, you learn how to search for files and folders, computers on the network, information and specific Web sites on the Internet, and people anywhere.

Searching for a File or Folder

Computers today are capable of storing so much information that it's easy and frustrating to lose a file. Even with Windows 95's long file names, if you can't remember what folder you saved the file in, you can't find the file. Fortunately, Windows has a thorough detective that will find your file for you, even if you only remember part of its name.

To search for a file or folder, follow these steps:

1. Click **Start**.

2. Point to **Find**, then click **Files or Folders**. The Find: All Files dialog box appears.

3. On the **Name & Location** tab (see Figure 10.1) type the file name, and select the part of the hard drive to search. If you want to limit the search to a specific folder to save time, click **Browse** and browse to find the folder. To include subfolders in the search, be sure the **Include Subfolders** check box is checked.

4. Click **Find Now**. The results of the search appear in the lower part of the dialog box.

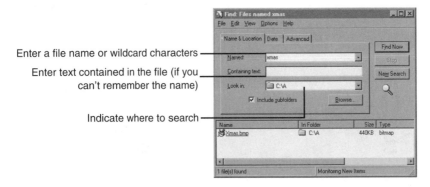

Enter a file name or wildcard characters ⎯

Enter text contained in the file (if you
can't remember the name)

Indicate where to search ⎯

Figure 10.1   A search for a bitmap graphic file that's located somewhere in the A folder of the hard drive.

If you only remember part of a file's name, you can use a *wildcard* character along with the part of the name that you remember, and your search will find all the names that match. Try the wildcard searching techniques in Table 10.1 (they'll each turn up several possibilities, one of which is sure to be your file).

Table 10.1   Wildcard Search Examples

A Search for This :	*Finds This:*
a*	All files that begin with the letter **a**
*a	All files that end with the letter **a**
ab	All files with the text "ab" anywhere in the name
*.doc	All Word documents (files with a .DOC extension)
*.exe	All executable program files (files with a .EXE extension)

TIP   **I Only Remember What the File Was About**   If you remember any text in the file, even a single word, you can search for files that contain the word(s) instead of searching for a file name. Type the word or words in the **Containing Text** box.

You can further narrow your search by limiting it to a specific range of dates. For example, you can search for all files with the name you specify on the Name & Location tab created in the past two months (see Figure 10.2), and you can limit your search to files of a minimum or maximum size by using the Advanced tab.

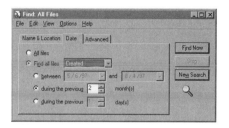

Figure 10.2 Limit your search to a specific date range.

 TIP **Save Your Search** To save your search results, click **Options**, then click **Save Results**; then click **File**, and click **Save Search**. An icon for the criteria and results appears on your desktop. When you click the icon, the Find Files dialog box with your search criteria and results appears on your desktop.

Once you find the file, you can open it directly from the Find: Files dialog box by clicking it.

Searching for a Computer

To search your network for a specific computer (to see if it's online, for example), follow these steps:

1. Click **Start**, then point to **Find**, and click **Computer**.
2. Click the **Named** drop-down arrow and look for the name of the computer, or type the network name of the computer in the **Named** box.
3. Click **Find Now**. If the computer is online, it appears in the lower half of the Find: Computer dialog box, along with its location.

Alternatively, in My Computer or Windows Explorer, you can double-click **Network Neighborhood** to see a list of the computers on the network.

Searching on the Internet

The Internet is a huge repository of information. Where do you begin to look for things? To find the specific information you want, you need to search the Internet with one of several *search engines*, like Lycos or Yahoo (and others). Internet Explorer 4.0 provides several ways to access search engines to conduct your hunt. You can begin a search from the Start menu, or from the folder or browser window by using the Search bar.

Searching from the Start Menu

To search the Internet from the Start menu, follow these steps:

1. Point to **Find**, then click **On the Internet**. Your browser launches and opens the search page at Microsoft's Web site. The Microsoft search page gives you a wide assortment of search engines like the ones shown in Figure 10.3.

2. Enter search keyword(s) in the **Search** box, then click the button that reads **Go Get It** or **Submit** or **Search** (or something similar). The search engine goes out and finds you lots of potentially useful links—just click a link that looks interesting. If it's not what you had in mind, click the **Back** button on your browser toolbar to return to the search results page, and click a different link.

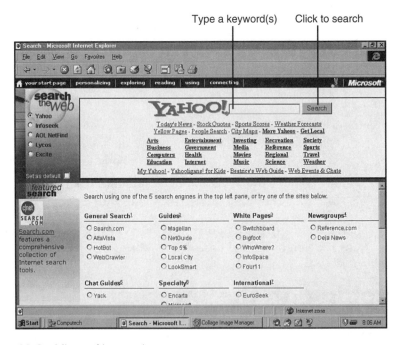

Figure 10.3   Microsoft's search page.

Searching with the Search Bar

In the Internet Explorer 4.0 browser window, you can use an Explorer bar called the Search bar (see Figure 10.4) to search the Internet. To display the Search bar, click the **Search** button on the Standard toolbar.

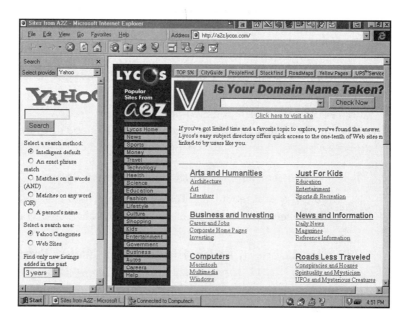

Figure 10.4   The Search bar.

The big advantage to using the Search bar is that your search engine remains available in your browser's left pane, while you click through links to different pages on the right pane. When you're ready to run another search, you don't have to click-click-click your way back to the search engine page, because it's already there and waiting.

TIP   **Will It Stay or Will It Go?**   In Full Screen view, the Search bar automatically slides out of view. You can make it stay in view by clicking the small pushpin icon in the upper-right corner of the bar. To return the Search bar to AutoHide mode, click the pushpin again.

The Search bar opens with a randomly selected search engine from the Microsoft Web site. To select a different search engine, click the **Select Provider** drop-down arrow at the top of the Search bar, then click the search engine you want.

447

Every search engine offers several category links to help you begin a general search; just click a link in the Search bar to take a peek at the offerings in that category.

To search for a specific topic, click in the keyword box at the top of the Search bar, type your keyword(s), and then click the **Search** button (it might be called a Go Get It button or a Seek button, but you get the idea).

Cleaning Out Your Web Page Folders

Whenever you search the Internet, every page you view is downloaded into your Temporary Internet Files folder and History folder. Those folders can get pretty full. To relieve your hard drive of its Web page burden, follow these steps:

1. In the browser window, click **View, Internet Options**.
2. On the **General** tab, under Temporary Internet Files, click **Delete Files**. In the Delete Files dialog box that appears, click **OK**. The folder is cleaned out.
3. Under History, click **Clear History**. In the Internet Properties dialog box, click **Yes**. The History folder (and your History Explorer bar) are cleaned out.
4. Click **OK**.

 TIP   **Use the Address Toolbar**   You can launch your browser, fire up a search engine, and conduct a search with a single entry in the Address toolbar. Display the Address toolbar (either in a folder or browser window or on the taskbar), and type **?** or **go** or **find**, followed by your search keyword(s).

Searching for a Person

Did you ever want to find someone you knew ten years ago but lost track of? Or maybe you're looking for a professional you'd like to hire, but you don't know where he or she is located? There are a number of directory services that look up names and return e-mail and postal addresses.

Different directory services have different databases of information, so if you don't find someone with one directory service, try each of the others. To find a person, follow these steps:

1. Click **Start**, then point to **Find**, and click **People**. The Find People dialog box appears.

2. Click the **Look In** drop-down arrow and select a directory service from the list that appears.

3. Type the person's name in the **Name** box and type his or her e-mail address in the **E-Mail** box (if you know it).

4. Click **Find Now**. Internet Explorer 4.0 connects to the directory service and looks for the name. If you find the name you want, check the address information by clicking the name and then **Properties**. If it is indeed the person you were looking for, you can add it to your Windows Address Book by clicking **Add to Address Book**.

5. If you don't find the person you're searching for, repeat steps 2 through 4, but select a different directory service in step 2.

TIP **Are There Any Other Directories?** There are other directories you can try. One is the Yahoo People Search at **http://www.yahoo.com/search/people**, and another is the Interactive Yellow Pages at **http://yp.gte.net**.

In this lesson, you learned how to search for just about anything except your car keys. In the next lesson, you'll learn about Internet Explorer 4.0's new Help system.

Exploring the New Help System

In this lesson, you learn how to use the new Help system for Internet Explorer 4.0.

About the New Help Window

If you've ever tried to find information that's buried deeply in a program's Help system, you know how annoying it is to click back and forth between the list of Help topics and the actual Help files. It's easier to open a book! Well, the new Help window in Internet Explorer 4.0 attempts to make it much easier to find the help you want.

The new Help window (see Figure 11.1) is a two-pane window. The left pane shows the list of Help topics and the Help file index, and the right pane shows the actual Help file. In the new Help system, you never lose contact with the list of topics, so you can go from one topic to another much more quickly.

To open the Internet Explorer 4.0 Help window, follow these steps:

1. Open a browser window. Only the Internet Explorer 4.0 browser window has the new Internet Explorer 4.0 Help window; a folder window's Help menu displays the standard Windows Help window.

2. Open the **Help** menu and select **Contents And Index**.

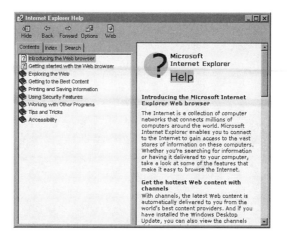

Figure 11.1 The new Help window is much more efficient.

Using the Contents Window

The Contents window displays a list of Help topics organized by topic area on the left side of the window. The main topic areas are identified by closed-book icons, and individual help files are identified by icons that look like a page with a question mark. To find help using the Contents window, follow these steps:

1. Double-click a main topic area. A list of individual Help topics appears below the main topic title (see Figure 11.2).

2. Click the Help title that seems to cover the information you want. The selected Help file appears in the right pane. Each Help file includes links to related Help files.

3. To close the list of individual Help topics (in the left pane), double-click the main topic title.

TIP **I Can't Read the Help Title** To read a truncated Help title, use the scroll bar at the bottom of the Contents window to scroll the title into view.

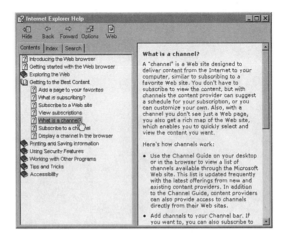

Figure 11.2   Click a Help title on the left, and then read the Help file on the right.

Using the Index Window

Behind the Contents window is the Index window (see Figure 11.3). In the Index window, you can look up a Help topic by looking for a specific word. To find help using the Index window, follow these steps:

1. Click the **Index** tab.

2. Type all or part of a word in the text box at the top of the Index tab. The Index list automatically scrolls to display alphabetical entries that match the letters you type.

3. Find an Index entry that looks likely and double-click the entry. The corresponding Help file appears in the right pane.

4. To check the information in a similar Index entry, double-click another entry. The Index list remains in view, but the Help file in the right pane changes.

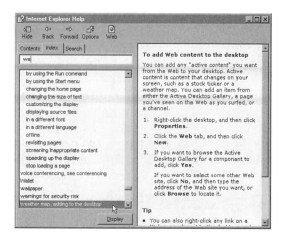

Figure 11.3 The Index tab looks up specific words in the Help files.

Using the Search Window

Behind the Index window is the Search window, where you can look up a Help topic by typing one or more keywords. The Search window provides an intelligent search: It looks up all topics that might relate to the keyword(s) you type. To find help in the Search window, follow these steps:

1. Click the **Search** tab.

2. Type a keyword or keywords in the text box at the top of the Search tab, and then click **List Topics**. The Topic window displays entries that relate to your keyword(s).

3. Find an entry that looks likely and double-click it. The corresponding Help file appears in the right pane.

4. To check the information in another topic, double-click another entry. The Search list remains in view, but the Help file in the right pane changes.

Using Toolbar Buttons

Another new feature is the new toolbar in the Help window. The buttons on the Help toolbar make finding the help you want easier. The following sections discuss each of the toolbar buttons in detail.

The Hide/Show Button

The Hide/Show button hides and displays the left pane of the Help window. If you're using Help to perform a new procedure, you may find the Help window too wide with the left pane showing. To hide the left pane and make the window narrower, click the **Hide** button. The Contents/Index/Search pane disappears.

To display the Contents/Index pane again when you want to look for another Help file, click the **Show** button. The Contents/Index/Search pane reappears.

The Back and Forward Buttons

Have you ever gone searching for the Help file you needed, gotten lost in the maze of Help-file links, and then wanted to quickly return to a Help file you opened previously? That's easy to do now with the new Back button.

To return to a Help file you opened previously, click the **Back** button. Clicking the Back button repeatedly moves you back page-by-page through the Help files you've opened.

After you move back with the Back button, a Forward button becomes available. The Forward button moves you forward page-by-page after you've paged backward through Help topics.

The Options Button

The Options button gives you helpful options for using the Help files you find, including ways to print Help files. Click the **Options** button, and then select an option.

The Web Button

The Web button opens a Help file that contains links to more Help files at the Microsoft Web site.

In this lesson, you learned how to get the most help from Internet Explorer 4.0's new Help system.

Congratulations! You are now an experienced Internet Explorer 4.0 user. But don't put this book on the shelf; keep it near your desk and use it as a quick reference whenever you have a question about using any of the Internet Explorer 4.0 features covered in these lessons.

Index

Complete and Return this Card
for a *FREE* Computer Book Catalog

Thank you for purchasing this book! You have purchased a superior computer book written expressly for your needs. To continue to provide the kind of up-to-date, pertinent coverage you've come to expect from us, we need to hear from you. Please take a minute to complete and return this self-addressed, postage-paid form. In return, we'll send you a free catalog of all our computer books on topics ranging from word processing to programming and the internet.

Mr. ☐   Mrs. ☐   Ms. ☐   Dr. ☐

Name (first) ☐☐☐☐☐☐☐☐☐☐☐☐ (M.I.) ☐   (last) ☐☐☐☐☐☐☐☐☐☐☐☐☐☐☐☐☐

Address ☐☐☐☐☐☐☐☐☐☐☐☐☐☐☐☐☐☐☐☐☐☐☐☐☐☐☐☐☐☐☐

☐☐☐☐☐☐☐☐☐☐☐☐☐☐☐☐☐☐☐☐☐☐☐☐☐☐☐☐☐☐☐

City ☐☐☐☐☐☐☐☐☐☐☐☐☐ State ☐☐   Zip ☐☐☐☐☐ ☐☐☐☐

Phone ☐☐☐ ☐☐☐ ☐☐☐☐   Fax ☐☐☐ ☐☐☐ ☐☐☐☐

Company Name ☐☐☐☐☐☐☐☐☐☐☐☐☐☐☐☐☐☐☐☐☐☐☐☐☐☐☐

E-mail address ☐☐☐☐☐☐☐☐☐☐☐☐☐☐☐☐☐☐☐☐☐☐☐☐☐☐☐☐

Please check at least (3) influencing factors for purchasing this book.

Front or back cover information on book ☐
Special approach to the content ☐
Completeness of content ☐
Author's reputation ☐
Publisher's reputation ☐
Book cover design or layout ☐
Index or table of contents of book ☐
Price of book ☐
Special effects, graphics, illustrations ☐
Other (Please specify): _____ ☐

How did you first learn about this book?

Saw in Macmillan Computer Publishing catalog ☐
Recommended by store personnel ☐
Saw the book on bookshelf at store ☐
Recommended by a friend ☐
Received advertisement in the mail ☐
Saw an advertisement in: _____ ☐
Read book review in: _____ ☐
Other (Please specify): _____ ☐

How many computer books have you purchased in the last six months?

This book only ☐   3 to 5 books ☐
books ☐   More than 5 ☐

4. Where did you purchase this book?

Bookstore ☐
Computer Store ☐
Consumer Electronics Store ☐
Department Store ☐
Office Club ☐
Warehouse Club ☐
Mail Order ☐
Direct from Publisher ☐
Internet site ☐
Other (Please specify): _____ ☐

5. How long have you been using a computer?

☐ Less than 6 months   ☐ 6 months to a year
☐ 1 to 3 years   ☐ More than 3 years

6. What is your level of experience with personal computers and with the subject of this book?

	With PCs	With subject of book
New	☐	☐
Casual	☐	☐
Accomplished	☐	☐
Expert	☐	☐

Source Code ISBN: 0-7897-1109-5

7. Which of the following best describes your job title?

Administrative Assistant .... ☐
Coordinator .... ☐
Manager/Supervisor .... ☐
Director .... ☐
Vice President .... ☐
President/CEO/COO .... ☐
Lawyer/Doctor/Medical Professional .... ☐
Teacher/Educator/Trainer .... ☐
Engineer/Technician .... ☐
Consultant .... ☐
Not employed/Student/Retired .... ☐
Other (Please specify): _____ ☐

8. Which of the following best describes the area of the company your job title falls under?

Accounting .... ☐
Engineering .... ☐
Manufacturing .... ☐
Operations .... ☐
Marketing .... ☐
Sales .... ☐
Other (Please specify): _____ ☐

9. What is your age?

Under 20 .... ☐
21-29 .... ☐
30-39 .... ☐
40-49 .... ☐
50-59 .... ☐
60-over .... ☐

10. Are you:

Male .... ☐
Female .... ☐

11. Which computer publications do you read regularly? (Please list)

_____
_____
_____
_____
_____
_____
_____
_____
_____
_____

Comments: _____

Fold here and scotch-tape to ma

Check out Que® Books on the World Wide Web
http://www.quecorp.com

As the biggest software release in computer history, Windows 95 continues to redefine the computer industry. Click here for the latest info on our Windows 95 books

Examine the latest releases in word processing, spreadsheets, operating systems, and suites

Find out about new additions to our site, new bestsellers and hot topics

Make computing quick and easy with these products designed exclusively for new and casual users

The Internet, The World Wide Web, CompuServe®, America Online®, Prodigy® —it's a world of ever-changing information. Don't get left behind!

In-depth information on high-end topics: find the best reference books for databases, programming, networking, and client/server technologies

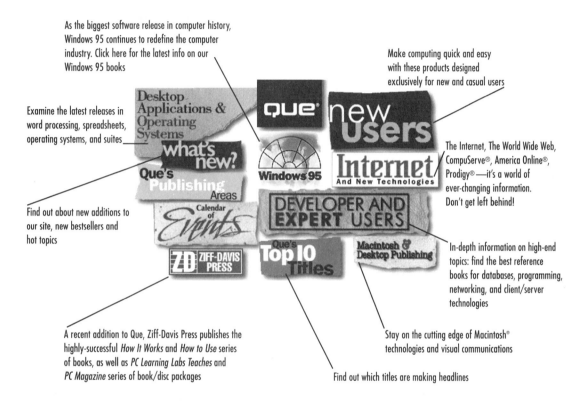

A recent addition to Que, Ziff-Davis Press publishes the highly-successful *How It Works* and *How to Use* series of books, as well as *PC Learning Labs Teaches* and *PC Magazine* series of book/disc packages

Stay on the cutting edge of Macintosh® technologies and visual communications

Find out which titles are making headlines

With 6 separate publishing groups, Que develops products for many specific market segments and areas of computer technology. Explore our Web Site and you'll find information on best-selling titles, newly published titles, upcoming products, authors, and much more.

- Stay informed on the latest industry trends and products available
- Visit our online bookstore for the latest information and editions
- Download software from Que's library of the best shareware and freeware

MACMILLAN COMPUTER PUBLISHING USA

A VIACOM COMPANY

Technical
Support:

If you need assistance with the information in this book or with a CD/Disk accompanying the book, please access the Knowledge Base on our Web site at http://www.superlibrary.com/general/support Our most Frequently Asked Questions are answered there. If you do not find the answer to your questions on our Web site, you may contact Macmillan Technical Support (317) 581-3833 or e-mail us at support@mcp.com.